“Youth ministry is a valuable investment, yet the strategies fail to reflect the values we seek to champion. *Youth Ministry Deconstructed* challenges leaders to critically examine this disconnect. We must reimagine our strategies to align with our biblical mission, values, and purpose, leading to a more impactful ministry for teenagers.”

—**Brent Baskin**, PhD, professor and department chair of Christian Studies, Shorter University

“Does your ministry need change? How would you know? David Odom provides a clear and concise approach to evaluating your youth ministry and rebuilding it for effective disciple-making. Fair warning! Engaging in this process may lead to a complete demolition and renovation of your ministry, requiring a change in philosophy that leads to a change in strategy. Radical change is never easy, but faithful youth ministers will embrace this challenge to carefully examine the goals and outcomes of their ministry.”

—**Mark Cannister**, EdD, professor of Christian Ministries, Gordon College

“All of us, as leaders of student ministry, come to a place at some point where we know something is wrong and something needs to be fixed. However, we often don’t get past this feeling because of a lack of time (the grind of ministry just keeps going!) and a lack of tools. The gift Dr. Odom has given us is a fantastic, comprehensive, biblically based, and intensely practical tool for evaluating our assumptions and ministry models so that we can see where we are falling short biblically and practically. I would challenge you now to make time with some key leaders in your ministry or fellow leaders of student ministries to read through and work through the reading and assessments. I am so excited to see the changes that can take place in student ministries across the globe as we launch into the future with tools like *Youth Ministry Deconstructed*!”

—**Jonathan Denton**, PhD, associate professor of Christian Studies/Student Ministry, Charleston Southern University

"With the right tools, you can build almost anything—including a youth ministry shaped by Scripture and Christ-centered mentoring. David Odom provides the tools, blueprint, and insights needed to deconstruct what is not working and reconstruct youth ministry in a way that builds lasting faith in the emerging generation."

—**Ron Hunter Jr**, PhD, CEO, D6 Family Ministry

"'Deconstruction' suggests urgency, immediacy, and deep analysis. Author David Odom recommends such a mindset for leaders involved in twenty-first-century youth ministry. Superbly qualified to speak to this task, Odom sounds the alarm for rethinking youth ministry based on years of experience and meticulous research. Youth leaders will find this text readable and practical. Much-needed tools for analysis and rebuilding are included."

—**Karen Jones**, PhD, chair of the Institute for Christian Thought and Practice, Huntington University

"As a youth pastor of twent-nine years and now a professor teaching youth ministry to the next generation of leaders, I fully agree with David Odom's call to rethink the youth ministry models that were 'built for a culture that no longer exists.' David provides very practical tools and steps to critically examine and question the assumptions and practices of youth ministry to improve the effectiveness of discipleship for both teenagers and parents. This is a book I will use in my classes and ministry coaching sessions to help youth pastors evaluate and innovate ministry practices for greater effectiveness for the gospel of Jesus Christ!"

—**Dave Keehn**, PhD, professor/department chair of Christian Ministries, Biola University, and leadership coach and president, Adam Keehn Foundation

"David Odom points out the big problem we face in youth ministry today: Largely, we are not producing young people with a lifelong commitment to follow Jesus. We tend to lean on old ministry models that have not proven effective in today's culture, and we measure our ministries by the wrong metrics: thinking attendance equals faithfulness. Odom challenges our assumptions and suggests the hard work of tearing up what doesn't work and rebuilding youth ministry with new metrics. Odom gives us an approach that is challenging but essential for the future of youth ministry . . . and the church."

—**Paul Kelly**, PhD, chair and professor of Educational Leadership, Gateway Seminary

"This book is a much-needed wake-up call. David Odom doesn't just suggest surface-level tweaks—he calls us to rebuild youth ministry on what truly matters: Jesus, discipleship, the local church, and the family. If you're tired of students walking away from their faith after graduation, this book is for you. It's biblical, practical, and urgent. Read it and be challenged to lead a ministry that lasts."

—**Shane Pruitt**, PhD, national Next Gen director, North American Mission Board, and author of *Calling Out the Called*

"For too long, youth ministry thought leaders have aimed resources at improving practices through pruning. We've assumed occasional maintenance trims are all we need. But too many of us are concluding, as David does, that the fruit we're seeing from youth ministry is an unacceptable offering to the Lord. Our modest change tactics must give way to meta-changes that clear the land to plant new orchards. This book calls for the deconstruction of youth ministry as it's widely practiced and offers us a way to do so. Sign me up for this faithfulness endeavor with Jesus."

—**Dave Rahn**, PhD, retired director of the Graduate Youth Ministry Leadership Program, Huntington University; senior research consultant, TENx10 Collaboration; and senior consultant, Arbor Research Group

"At Southwestern Seminary, Shane Pruitt and I don't believe in wasting our students' time. We only ask them to absorb the most substantial books about student ministry. What is the finest recommendation I can give to Dr. David Odom's new book, *Youth Ministry Deconstructed*? From now on, that will be one of our valued textbooks. Student ministry does not need some tweaks here and there. We need to completely erase the whiteboard and then build student ministry from the ground up. David's book provides the clearest guidance for doing just that."

—**Richard Ross**, PhD, senior professor of Student Ministry, Southwestern Baptist Theological Seminary

YOUTH MINISTRY DECON-STRUCTURED

David Odom

YOUTH MINISTRY DECON-STRUCTED

Rethinking Your Ministry to Build Lasting Faith in Students

ACADEMIC®
BRENTWOOD, TENNESSEE

Youth Ministry Deconstructed: Rethinking Your Ministry to Build Lasting Faith in Students

Published by B&H Academic®
Brentwood, Tennessee

ISBN: 979-8-3845-0304-0

Dewey Decimal Classification: 259.23
Subject Heading: YOUTH MINISTRY \ CHURCH WORK WITH YOUTH \ YOUTH

Cover design by Brian Bobel. Cover illustration adapted from image by Alla/AdobeStock, generated using AI.

Printed in the United States of America

31 30 29 28 27 26 VP 1 2 3 4 5 6 7 8 9 10

To my beloved wife, Natalie

CONTENTS

INTRODUCTION

Demolition

The Need for Deconstruction

In the 1970s, I lived in a house with dark wood paneling and red shag carpeting in the den mixed with lemon-colored wallpaper in the kitchen. The house had a small formal living room and a separate dining room. The kitchen and living room were also separated, and all the bedrooms were small. If I bought that house today, I'd make significant changes—not just to the carpet and wallpaper. I'd start with an inspection of the roof and foundation. A house built in the sixties would likely now have significant issues. Leaky pipes and soil erosion may have critically damaged the concrete slab. Years of wear and tear also take a toll on roof shingles and support beams. Even if the foundation and roof were in decent shape, I'd want to change the overall floor plan. Many of today's modern homes utilize an open concept for the main living areas and kitchen—so I'd like to expand the footprint of these areas and tear down walls. In addition to a new foundation, new beams would need to be added to support the roof's weight. I'd also remove the wood paneling and replace all the light fixtures and switches. A cost evaluation of these changes may mean starting from scratch would be more economical. Basically, it would mean a total demolition of the existing structure.

Why do I tell you this story? Because youth ministry as we know it is over sixty years old and built for a culture that no longer exists. Like an old house, its age is showing. A renovation is needed that reaches not only teenagers but also parents and helps connect young people to the congregation. It may be time to deconstruct your youth ministry and build a more effective one. I've written this book for that purpose.

We are not building lifelong faith in students. In fact, the faith of many students doesn't even last through high school. You've heard the statistics before about the number of teenagers leaving the church after high school. The hard truth is that about half of the active teens in the youth group drift from God and leave the church after high school.[1] But the situation is actually much worse. About 40 percent of youth group members will become "lethargic church adults, showing little transformation and making little Kingdom impact."[2] Richard Ross says that only 10 percent of church teenagers "can express their core beliefs, can lead someone else to saving faith, and choose to embrace Christ's mission for their lives."[3]

How can this be? Who is to blame? We can attempt to blame our godless culture or college campuses, but the real problem is with the way we approach youth ministry. David Kinnaman points out that the high levels of disengagement among young adults "suggest that youth ministry fails too often at discipleship and faith formation."[4] A college cam-

---

[1] See Kara Powell, Jake Mulder, and Brad Griffin, *Growing Young: 6 Essential Strategies to Help Young People Discover and Love Your Church* (Baker, 2016), 17.

[2] Richard Ross, *Youth Ministry That Lasts a Lifetime* (Seminary Hill, 2017), 9.

[3] Ross, 9; Barna, "Research Shows Parenting Approach Determines Whether Children Become Devoted Christians," April 9, 2007, https://www.barna.com/research/research-shows-parenting-approach-determines-whether-children-become-devoted-christians/.

[4] David Kinnaman, "Most Twentysomethings Put Christianity on the Shelf Following Spiritually Active Teen Years," September 11, 2006, https://www.barna

pus does not cause the problem; it "exposes the shallow-faith problem of many young disciples."[5]

The current youth ministry model is an old approach patterned after a parachurch model with high-energy activities and programs specifically for teenagers. "A parachurch model that was effective in evangelizing segments of lost teenagers was not effective in giving Christian teenagers a lifetime faith, lifetime Kingdom impact, and lifetime love for the church."[6] Walt Mueller laments the everyday practices of youth ministry. "We cloister [teenagers] together with their peers in a trendy room designed to draw and keep them, which might actually promote the irrelevance of anything in the church that exists outside of that room. This is tragic."[7] Indeed, it is tragic and unnecessary. Real change is needed in youth ministry.

Deconstruction vs. Makeover

Have you ever had a makeover? Maybe you've seen one of the dozens of makeover shows on television. You know the basic premise: a drastic change in a person's appearance. Someone changes the hairstyle, another does the makeup, and another improves the wardrobe. The changes can be striking! The problem with a makeover is that it does little to impact what's deep inside. The same is true in youth ministry. We can remodel youth rooms—paint walls, build stages, put up lights and screens—but

.com/research/most-twentysomethings-put-christianity-on-the-shelf-following-spiritually-active-teen-years/.

[5] Barna Group, "Five Myths about Young Adult Church Dropouts," November 16, 2011, https://www.barna.com/research/five-myths-about-young-adult-church-dropouts/.

[6] Ross, *Youth Ministry That Lasts a Lifetime*, 15.

[7] Walt Mueller, "Why Youth Ministry Shouldn't Be the Greatest Show on Earth," June 1, 2017, https://cpyu.org/2017/06/01/why-youth-ministry-shouldnt-be-the-greatest-show-on-earth/.

these changes are pointless unless we address ministry foundations. What is needed is a total renovation—top to bottom—including the foundation. This requires deconstruction.

Deconstruction has been a popular and controversial topic in religious circles in recent years. Deconstructing faith refers to the process of critically examining and questioning the foundations and assumptions of Christian belief.[8] Proponents say that deconstructing faith can help individuals develop a deeper understanding of their own beliefs.[9] By questioning and examining the underlying assumptions, a person can come to a clearer and more nuanced understanding of faith. They also argue that this process can foster critical thinking and help individuals identify conflicts or inconsistencies within a belief system and address them thoughtfully and reflectively.

On the other hand, critics argue that deconstruction can lead to skepticism and disbelief. By questioning and examining the foundations of the Christian faith, many have come to doubt the Bible's validity or truth and

---

[8] See David Hayward, http://nakedpastor.com. Hayward was among the first to use the term *deconstruction* in reference to a questioning of orthodox faith and Christian practices. Alisa Childers, *Another Gospel? A Lifelong Christian Seeks Truth in Response to Progressive Christianity* (Tyndale, 2020), 24. Childers defines deconstruction as "the process of systematically dissecting and often rejecting the beliefs you grew up with." Preston Ulmer, *Deconstruct Faith, Discover Jesus: How Questioning Your Religion Can Lead You to a Healthy and Holy God* (NavPress, 2023), 6. Ulmer prefers Melanie Mudge's definition of deconstruction: "the taking apart of an idea, practice, tradition, belief, or system into smaller components in order to examine their foundation, truthfulness, usefulness, and impact." Melanie Mudge, "What Is Faith Deconstruction?" *Sophia Society* (blog), March 7, 2022, https://www.sophiasociety.org/blog/what-is-faith-deconstruction.

[9] See Ulmer, *Deconstruct Faith, Discover Jesus*, 92. Ulmer offers his Deconstruction Wheel to help people "break down specific problems they have with the faith." He views deconstruction as "deweeding a flower bed" that can lead to a stronger personal faith.

Christ's saving work.[10] Rather than critically examining church leaders and practices, some eventually lose their faith altogether.[11]

I am not an advocate of faith deconstruction. I'm not a progressive Christian or liberal theologian. I am a Southern Baptist minister and seminary professor. But I do believe there is nothing wrong with a critical examination of faith; in fact, I encourage it. I also think our churches and youth groups should be safe places for expressions of doubt and questions about faith. We should see questioning and doubts as "faith-forming opportunities rather than freak-out moments of failure."[12]

This book is not about faith deconstruction; it is about deconstructing youth ministry. I seek to apply the concept of deconstruction to youth ministry practices. Deconstructing youth ministry refers to the process of critically examining and questioning the assumptions and practices of youth ministry to improve the effectiveness of ministry to teenagers and parents. It is the process of systematically dissecting and rejecting the old ways of doing youth ministry. Deconstructing youth ministry encourages you to rethink your ministry mindset and jettison previously held beliefs about reaching and leading young people.

Deconstructing youth ministry is not a new idea. Church leaders haven't used the term *deconstruction*, but they've been calling for change

---

[10] Deconstruction leads some to totally reject Christian faith, known as *deconversion*. Others reconstruct their faith into a more mature belief system. See Tyler Huckabee, "Deconstruction Isn't the Endpoint—It's Part of a Process," https://relevantmagazine.com/life5/new-you/deconstruction-isnt-the-endpoint-its-part-of-a-process/. Huckabee notes that some people confuse the "process of deconstruction" with the possible end result—deconversion.

[11] See Trevin Wax, "Doubt Your Way Back to Truth" in *Before You Lose Your Faith: Deconstructing Doubt in the Church*, ed. Ivan Mesa (The Gospel Coalition, 2021), 8. I recommend this book for anyone currently deconstructing faith. I also recommend Halee Gray Scott's book, *Not a Hopeless Case: 6 Vital Questions from Young Adults for a Church in Crisis* (Zondervan, 2023) for anyone working with young adults and those who are deconstructing.

[12] Powell, Mulder, and Griffin, *Growing Young*, 157.

for over thirty years. Back in 1994, Mark DeVries offered a severe critique of youth ministry and advocated for greater parent engagement in *Family-Based Youth Ministry*. In 2000, Merton P. Strommen and Richard A. Hardel called for a change in *Passing On the Faith: A Radical New Model for Youth and Family Ministry,* as they revealed that only 10 percent of church families discuss faith regularly. Christian Smith and Melinda Lundquist Denton showed us the need for deconstruction in 2001 with the release of the groundbreaking results of the National Study of Youth and Religion. In their book, *Soul Searching: The Religious and Spiritual Lives of American Teenagers*, one of the research findings was that most students' faith mirrors their parents' faith. Reggie Joiner released *Think Orange* in 2009. In it, he argued for an integrated strategy that combined church and home influences. That same year, Timothy Paul Jones wrote *Perspectives on Family Ministry: 3 Views,* which outlined the history of family ministry and gave names to each of the three approaches.[13] Also, in 2009, Eric Geiger and Jeff Borton revealed the need for a clear youth discipleship strategy in *Simple Student Ministry*. Mark Senter noted four distinct cycles of youth ministry in America in *When God Shows Up: A History of Protestant Youth Ministry in America* (2010). According to Senter, a fourth cycle began in the 1990s. The family-integrated movement or intergenerational youth ministry is the current theme of the fourth cycle of youth ministry. In 2011, Voddie Baucham advocated deconstructing youth ministry (without reconstruction) in his polarizing book, *Family Driven Faith.*

While many others have encouraged the integration of youth and family ministry, three voices have significantly influenced current youth ministry trends and calls for an expanded view of youth ministry: Kara Powell, Chap Clark, and Richard Ross. Kara Powell, executive director of

---

[13] See Jared Kennedy, "Where Did Youth Ministry Go Wrong? Identifying a Way Forward," https://www.crossway.org/articles/where-did-youth-ministry-go-wrong-identifying-a-way-forward/.

Fuller Youth Institute and coauthor of several *Sticky Faith* (2011) resources, advocates for intergenerational relationships and partnerships with parents in youth ministry. In his book *Adoptive Youth Ministry* (2016), Chap Clark challenges youth leaders to integrate youth into the congregation by spiritually "adopting" students. Richard Ross championed "ministry in thirds" in his book *Youth Ministry That Lasts a Lifetime* (2017). Ross envisions a youth ministry with a balanced emphasis on teenagers, parents, and the congregation.

More recently, books such as Kara Powell and Jake Mulder's *Growing Young* (2016), Preston Cave's *Family Ministry That Counts* (2018), Christopher Talbot's *Remodeling Youth Ministry* (2017), and Tim McNight's *Navigating Student Ministry* (2022), have called for significant changes in youth ministry. For instance, Christopher Talbot describes deconstruction when he says we must "eliminate any methodologies, structures, and practices that hinder the maturation process."[14]

The problem is that with all these leaders calling for change for over three decades, we have seen little movement in how many leaders practice youth ministry. Many youth ministry leaders are still doing what youth leaders have done since the 1960s. I know this is true from my research and interviews of youth leaders nationwide. For example, 61 percent do not help families and teenagers talk about faith together.[15] Forty percent of youth leaders don't help connect teenagers with older and younger church members.[16] Only 46 percent of leaders provide parenting and discipleship resources.[17] Only 35 percent of youth leaders believe their church has a straightforward discipleship process.[18] Eighty-one percent do not provide

---

[14] Christopher Talbot, *Remodeling Youth Ministry: A Blueprint for Ministering to Students* (Welch College, 2017), 30.

[15] See Youth Ministry Arenas Research, https://www.nobts.edu/ymarenas/.

[16] Youth Ministry Arenas Research.

[17] Youth Ministry Arenas Research.

[18] Youth Ministry Arenas Research.

opportunities for older adults to disciple or mentor parents of teenagers.[19] Eighty-one percent do not provide opportunities for parents of teenagers to meet together for prayer and support.[20]

It's Time to Break Things

Deconstruction is a controversial term to use in reference to a critical evaluation of youth ministry. It's harsh language, and I don't use the term *deconstruction* lightly. I'm naturally optimistic, but I'm not optimistic about the current trajectory of youth ministry. Significant change is needed. We must focus on developing lasting faith in teenagers that carries them beyond the comfortable confines of the youth group into adult faith for the real world. If we don't change course, I'm afraid we will continue to see declines in decisions for Christ and church attendance. It's time for a radical shake-up and disruption of the status quo. Facebook founder Mark Zuckerberg famously said, "Move fast and break things." Zuckerberg meant this to be a mantra for internal design and management processes, but it also became a refrain for entrepreneurs regarding disruption.[21] Youth ministry needs disruption, and I recommend deconstructing youth ministry for three primary reasons.

To begin with, deconstructing youth ministry will assist you in identifying and resolving core issues within your youth ministry. For example, by questioning basic assumptions, you may find areas that do not support your youth ministry's biblical mission and goals. John Maxwell reminds us that

---

[19] Youth Ministry Arenas Research.

[20] Youth Ministry Arenas Research.

[21] See Hemant Taneja, "The Era of 'Move Fast and Break Things' Is Over," *Harvard Business Review*, January 22, 2019, https://hbr.org/2019/01/the-era-of-move-fast-and-break-things-is-over.

"you only get answers to the questions you ask."[22] So, by going through this process, you can address problems that hinder your ministry's efficacy and create a plan for effectively reaching teenagers and parents.

Second, deconstructing youth ministry can help you better understand and serve the spiritual needs of youth. Moving through this process can give you a clearer picture of your students' spiritual maturity and the state of discipleship in your church. This, in turn, can lead you to develop more relevant and transformative ministry environments.

Finally, deconstructing youth ministry can free you to explore and innovate your youth ministry. You will be challenged to jettison outdated approaches and think outside the box by questioning why you practice ministry the way you do. This can help you produce a ministry that encourages spiritual maturity and more effectively develops teenagers and parents into disciple-makers. I believe deconstructing youth ministry can be a valuable and enriching process that helps you identify and address problems or challenges in your current ministry to teenagers. While this process may involve questioning and challenging traditional youth ministry, it can ultimately lead to more effective and transformative ministry to teenagers and parents.

Challenging assumptions is a foundational aspect of deconstruction. Assumptions can lead to the reinforcement of confirmation bias, something all youth leaders are susceptible to. It's the tendency to seek and interpret information that supports our preexisting beliefs while disregarding contradictory evidence. For example, we succumb to confirmation bias when we imagine that the spiritual maturity of a few students is representative of the whole youth group. This bias can hinder critical thinking and prevent you from objectively evaluating situations. By recognizing your assumptions and actively seeking other perspectives and evidence,

[22] John Maxwell, *Good Leaders Ask Great Questions: Your Foundation for Effective Leadership* (Center Street, 2014), 4.

you can overcome confirmation bias and develop a clear understanding of your ministry.

Evaluating Youth Ministry

Jesus never administered a formal examination, but he did evaluate his disciples.[23] For example, he assessed the extent of their faith when they were caught in a storm on the Sea of Galilee (Matt 8:26; Mark 4:40). He examined their comprehension of his mission when he asked, "Who do you say that I am?" (Matt 16:15; Mark 8:29). He assessed Peter's devotion by asking "Do you love me?" three times (John 21:15–17). Jesus routinely "asked questions and posed problems to reveal what His listeners understood and believed."[24] Evaluation refers to making a judgment about the value of something,[25] and it is essential for improvement. Evaluation helps us sharpen skills and clarify goals. It helps us determine whether or not we are accomplishing our mission and reaching our goal. Without evaluation, we can't know if we are accomplishing what we set out to do.

Deconstructing youth ministry is all about transparent and honest assessment. Evaluating is vital because you do not have a clear picture of your youth ministry's effectiveness without it. Rather than fearing evaluation, you must embrace it. Let's look at four reasons why evaluation is essential in youth ministry:

1. Evaluation allows you to assess the effectiveness of your youth ministry in achieving its stated outcomes. I'll address goals and outcomes later in chapter 2. As you evaluate, you can determine whether your ministry is leading youth toward spiritual transformation by

---

[23] See William Yount, *Created to Learn: A Christian Teacher's Introduction to Educational Psychology*, 2nd ed. (B&H, 2010), 480.

[24] Yount, 480.

[25] See *Merriam-Webster Dictionary*, "evaluation," accessed July 10, 2025, https://www.merriam-webster.com/dictionary/evaluation.

measuring outcomes such as spiritual growth, relational engagement, and retention.

2. Evaluation can help you identify areas for improvement in your youth ministry. By analyzing the ministry's strengths and weaknesses, you can make informed decisions about where to focus your efforts and resources to increase its effectiveness and impact. Evaluation gives you insights into making informed decisions about your youth ministry. You can make effective choices by using this data to guide your decision-making. From budgets to volunteers, curriculum choices to preaching topics—all of these can be informed by results from the evaluation.
3. Evaluation provides you with data and information to communicate with parents and church leaders. By sharing information about the impact and effectiveness of your youth ministry, you can build support for your ministry and demonstrate its value and importance. And not just the positive results—discouraging findings can also provide the necessary fuel to spark greater support for your youth ministry.
4. Finally, evaluation promotes accountability among leaders and volunteers. Establishing clear goals and objectives and measuring progress toward those outcomes is crucial. This ensures that everyone involved is working toward the same objectives and is accountable for their role in achieving them. By evaluating your ministry regularly, you can ensure that it positively impacts the young people it serves and achieves its goals and objectives.

Youth leaders know they want to make disciples who make disciples, but rarely do they take steps to figure out whether or not they are doing it. Perhaps you are concerned that you don't know whether the programs and activities of your youth ministry are making a difference in the spiritual lives of teenagers. Maybe you realize that to build a faith that lasts a lifetime, you also need to invest in parents, but you don't know how to start. Or perhaps you are reaching some teenagers and parents but feel that something is holding you back from the potential you know you could have.

Tony Morgan draws upon his experiences in both the corporate world and church ministry to compare the bottom line of business—money—and the bottom line of ministry—fulfilling the Great Commission in Matt 28:19–20.[26] "Go therefore and make disciples of all nations, baptizing them in the name of the Father and of the Son and of the Holy Spirit, teaching them to observe all that I have commanded you. And behold, I am with you always, to the end of the age." Morgan laments that churches are not as committed to their bottom line as businesses are to theirs. Instead, he finds the following characteristics are true too often for many churches:

- They don't track their bottom line. Most people on the team don't know whether or not the church is meeting its discipleship objectives.
- If they aren't growing (making disciples and baptizing new believers), then many churches don't have a sense of urgency that change needs to happen.
- If there's a sense that what they're doing isn't working, churches tend to settle. They build ministries and programming around the people who are already at the church rather than consider how they can reach more people and grow the kingdom.
- They are rarely focused. If something isn't adding to the bottom line, it doesn't matter. They keep doing it.[27]

Are you tracking "the bottom line" in your youth ministry? Are you communicating the urgency of reaching today's teenagers? Are you discipling students to be disciple-makers? If you are like most leaders, you will benefit from introspection and reflection. That's the purpose of

---

[26] See Tony Morgan, *The Unstuck Church: Equipping Churches to Experience Sustained Health* (Thomas Nelson, 2017), 5.

[27] Morgan, 5.

deconstructing youth ministry—to critically evaluate your ministry to teenagers and parents to be more effective. It is a progress check—a performance indicator—an assessment. Formal testing is rarely, if ever, done in non-academic settings. In my experience, evaluation and assessment are generally not part of youth ministry.

Barna's research reveals a lack of awareness between most church leaders' assessment of discipleship effectiveness and their churches' rates of participation in discipleship activities.[28] Clint Grider calls this lack of assessment the "awareness gap." The awareness gap is between "what we think is happening in people as a result of our efforts and what is actually happening."[29] He also warns against the "closeness bias"—you may be close to a few students and make assumptions about the rest of the group. We think we know them and their spiritual progress—but we may not. You need to use deconstruction metrics to get a clear picture of what is happening in your youth ministry.

Deconstruction Metrics

To measure ministry progress, we use metrics. Metrics are crucial for evaluating key performance indicators (KPIs) and assessing progress. They provide a clear and objective way to measure whether or not we are achieving a goal. Metrics also provide a benchmark against which we can measure progress. The use of metrics also provides transparency and accountability of results. They can also help churches identify areas of improvement. The most common metric is attendance. Youth attendance at events or Bible study is most churches' primary form of evaluation.[30] We use attendance as a metric because it is easy to track. Yet attendance alone is not a clear indicator

---

[28] See Barna, *State of Discipleship: A Barna Report Produced in Partnership with The Navigators* (The Navigators, 2015), 69.

[29] Clint Grider, *Mind the Gap: Leading Your Church to Agility and Effectiveness in Any Environment* (B&H, 2023), 6.

[30] Barna, *State of Discipleship*, 70. Barna found that participation was the most common objective indicator. For example, they found most churches track service

of whether or not a student or parent is growing as a disciple. Chapters 1–5 are all about metrics—biblical metrics, discipleship metrics, ministry metrics, process metrics, and environmental metrics—to evaluate your ministry.

Evaluation is a part of my life as a seminary professor. I administer exams, assign research papers, and require class presentations. In return, I'm evaluated on my teaching and administration. I'm also part of groups of professors who evaluate courses and educational outcomes. But before I began teaching, I also evaluated my youth ministry regularly. I formally and informally evaluated events, programs, interns, and volunteers. So, it's not surprising that I would write a book on youth ministry evaluation.

My friend and mentor, Richard Ross, inspired the research that led to this book. Dr. Ross is senior professor of student ministry at Southwestern Baptist Theological Seminary. He has championed what he refers to as "ministry in thirds."[31] Ross envisions a youth ministry with a balanced emphasis on teenagers, parents, and the congregation. Additionally, Ross believes seminaries should revise their youth ministry training to reflect this threefold emphasis. Conversations with Ross and the content of his book *Youth Ministry That Lasts a Lifetime* served as the catalyst for my own research project and this book.

I rely on my twenty-five years in local youth ministry and ten years of teaching and consulting experience to write this book. In addition, when I refer to *my research* I'm referring not only to an exhaustive review of published literature on youth ministry, but also to my own research studies. The two projects I've conducted in recent years have been developing Spiritual Growth surveys for youth and parents (appendix) and my research study on the Youth Ministry Arenas. In addition, as part of my research for this book, I conducted qualitative research with youth ministry leaders. This involved initial interviews with over 100 youth pastors across the country

---

attendance, participation in classes (including discipleship classes, Bible studies, Sunday school and small groups), and overall numbers of members and baptisms.

[31] Ross, *Youth Ministry That Lasts a Lifetime*, 6.

from churches of all sizes and culminated in in-depth follow-up interviews with a select few for inclusion in chapter 10.

This book is about radical change. A change in youth ministry philosophy that results in a change in strategy. This book is both philosophical and practical. The philosophy side seeks to broaden your view of youth ministry to include parents and the whole church congregation. On the practical side, this book seeks to provide real-life examples from ministry leaders to inspire you toward change. However, this book does not seek to explain every aspect of youth ministry. Additionally, there are no silver bullets—no one youth ministry formula or strategy that works in all contexts. Instead, this book focuses on critically evaluating your youth ministry and leading you to make significant changes as you see fit. Although there are no guarantees, I truly believe that if you follow the steps outlined here, it will result in a youth ministry better equipped to effectively minister to teenagers and parents.

To that end, I've organized the book into two sections: deconstructing and reconstructing. The book's first section will deconstruct the underlying assumptions of youth ministry. We can assume a lot in youth ministry. Leaders often come into the role with certain assumptions or beliefs about teenagers and their needs. These assumptions can impact how you interact with young people, the types of programs you offer, and the overall success of your ministry. So I'm going to address several crucial assumptions. Chapter 1 presents the biblical metrics by which leaders should measure youth ministry effectiveness. According to Duffy Robbins, "youth ministry is primarily a theological enterprise."[32] Therefore we need a biblical and theological framework from which to operate. As said by Eric Geiger and Jeff Borton, "We need a renewed commitment to the essence of the gospel, to the essence of the movement of the church. And we need a renewed commitment to the essence of student ministry."[33] As such,

---

[32] Duffy Robbins, *This Way to Youth Ministry: An Introduction to the Adventure* (Zondervan, 2004), 18.

[33] Eric Geiger and Jeff Borton, *Simple Student Ministry: A Clear Process for Strategic Youth Discipleship* (B&H, 2009), chapter 1.

I will address several underlying assumptions: (1) *My church clearly understands the biblical rationale for youth ministry*, (2) *the way I operate my youth ministry is biblical*, and (3) *I build my ministry on the biblical purposes of youth ministry.*

In chapter 2, I present discipleship metrics by which you can measure the spiritual growth of teenagers and parents. I will address assumptions and practices associated with the target of youth ministry—students.[34] The assumptions addressed in this chapter include: (1) *My youth ministry has clear goals and outcomes for students*, and (2) *students in my youth ministry are growing toward spiritual maturity.* I will introduce discipleship metrics to assess student spiritual growth. The second focus of chapter 2 is on parents. Why? Parents are the single most significant influence on the spiritual lives of students.[35] If you are serious about reaching teenagers, you must be serious about reaching parents. Therefore, you must assess how effectively you partner with parents to help them disciple their teens. Are parents of teenagers coming to faith in Jesus at your church? Are parents becoming disciples who make disciples? This chapter will introduce you to a research study I participated in called the Student Assessment of Effective Faith Factors (SAEFF). Some of the assessment questions in the surveys in the appendix are based on the SAEFF. I will show you how you can use this assessment to get real answers about the faith journeys of young people and parents in your church.

Chapter 3 will follow up with a deconstruction of the systems and structures of your youth ministry. This chapter focuses on ministry metrics you can use to evaluate the overall effectiveness of your youth ministry, and I address three assumptions: (1) *The current structures and programs of my youth ministry produce disciple-makers*, (2) *parents are prepared to lead at home spiritually*, and (3) *teenagers will naturally come to value the church on their own.* I will

---

[34] See Morgan, *The Unstuck Church*, 20. Morgan reminds church leaders of the need to identify who you are trying to reach. Leaders need to identify their target audience.

[35] See Vern Bengtson, Norella Putney, and Susan Harris, *Families and Faith: How Religion Is Passed Down Across Generations* (Oxford University Press, 2017), 195.

introduce you to the Youth Ministry Arenas to evaluate these assumptions and practices. Although there is broad consensus on the purpose and goal of youth ministry, there is varied disagreement on how to accomplish it. This chapter focuses on how you organize your ministry to students and parents. The chapter provides an overview of the Youth Ministry Arenas Assessment and how to use it to evaluate your ministry effectively. This assessment of youth ministry was birthed from a research project I led as director of the Youth Ministry Institute at New Orleans Baptist Theological Seminary.

Chapter 4 is about deconstructing your discipleship process for teenagers and parents. I address four assumptions in this chapter: (1) *My church recognizes the need for discipleship*, (2) *my church understands the roles of a disciple and disciple-maker*, (3) *my church has a clearly defined discipleship process*, and (4) *my church communicates our discipleship process.* The three discipleship processes discussed are moving youth from spiritually lifeless to spiritually fruitful, parents from spiritual wanderers to spiritual leaders, and youth from consumers to contributors.

Chapter 5 focuses on assessing discipleship environments for youth and parents. Discipleship environments are the avenues by which spiritual growth occurs. The five environments discussed in this chapter are the church group, youth group, small groups, micro-groups, and mentoring relationships. The assumptions questioned in this chapter are: (1) *My volunteers understand the need to build godly relationships with teenagers and parents*, (2) *my ministry provides the best discipleship environments for optimal spiritual growth*, and (3) *the entry points of my ministry effectively connect people to our discipleship environments.*

In chapter 6, I will help you do some "survey work" to put chapters 1–5 into practice and assess your youth ministry. I've provided assessment tools you can access in a variety of ways. The easiest way is to assess by going online to our website (deconstructingym.com) and taking the assessments there. As a ministry leader, you can take the assessment online. You can also copy links to the assessments or download PDF versions to copy and distribute to others. You can also use the text version of the assessments found in the appendix. Perhaps you'd like to customize the assessment for your context—we can help with that. The Youth Ministry Institute at New Orleans Baptist Theological Seminary will help you tailor an assessment to meet your specific needs. Finally, you may choose to focus on an informal assessment by talking with leaders, parents, and students. This type of evaluation can give you good but limited feedback, and you must carefully avoid confirmation bias.

The book's second section focuses on establishing an action plan for reconstructing your youth ministry. While the first section focuses on testing the assumptions of youth ministry, this section emphasizes reconstructing ministry practices.

Chapter 7 is all about leading change in your church. This chapter will help youth leaders understand how to effectively lead the changes discussed in this book. Ministry practices addressed in this book are being a change leader in youth ministry and leading change in four phases.

Chapter 8 focuses on leadership development in youth ministry. You shouldn't do youth ministry alone. This chapter will help you recruit and train adult volunteers, as well as assist with the development of student leaders. I'll cover topics such as what to look for in volunteers, recruiting adult leaders, and training volunteers.

In chapter 9, I'll lead you through the Reconstruction Framework to help you rebuild your youth ministry. This chapter will help leaders reconstruct youth ministry through the practical application of the discipleship process and environments in chapters 4 and 5. The ministry practices in this chapter are building a reconstruction team, leading teenagers in the youth group, leading teenagers in families, and leading teenagers in the congregation.

In chapter 10, you will find examples from churches of different sizes—normal to mega-churches. These are real-life examples from youth ministry leaders around the country who serve in churches like yours. You'll benefit from their insights and be challenged to implement changes in your own ministry.

Proceed at Your Own Risk

Deconstructing youth ministry is not for the faint of heart. This endeavor is not without risk. For starters, you risk bruising your pride or ego. When you critically examine the youth ministry you lead at your church, you have to go into it knowing that it will not be easy. If you conduct an honest assessment, you will inevitably find issues that must be addressed. Beginning this process shows that you are a person with a thick skin and are not easily shaken.

You also risk your time. Deconstructing youth ministry takes time. You may think of evaluation as a waste of time. However, this process will help you identify areas where you are less effective with your time management. Therefore, your time on deconstruction and reconstruction will save you time in the long run. According to Clint Grider, "The cost of evaluation isn't a tax; it's an investment, and the return on that investment is extremely high."[36]

You risk social capital. The low-risk approach to deconstruction would be not to share your findings with anyone. But this will result in little to no change within your ministry. Don't read this book alone. Gather your volunteers and leaders to read the book and discuss the questions raised. But as you do, remember that this process may cost you social capital. Social capital refers to your reputation and standing among peers. A transparent assessment may cause some to view you negatively. The reality is that your willingness to initiate and engage in this process demonstrates a high level of leadership. Weak leaders run from evaluation. Strong leaders welcome it because they realize that the only way to improve is to critique how things are going. You risk the wrath of pastors, volunteers, and students who are accustomed to and like the way things are and don't want things to change. But this process will clearly reveal the changes needed for effective ministry to students and parents.

---

[36] Grider, *Mind the Gap*, 38.

Consider reading this book along with another youth pastor in your area. You could meet for coffee each week and discuss ways to implement various aspects of the book. If you can't read this book with others, consider journaling as you read. You can jot down ideas and questions for consideration.

I write this book from my perspective as a Southern Baptist minister. Still, I believe you will find ideas in this book applicable to various denominations and ministry settings. I draw from my twenty-five years of experience in local church youth ministry and ten years teaching youth ministry at the undergraduate, graduate, and doctoral levels. This book was years in the making. It is based on the research and writing of countless others and my own ministry experiences and research. I pray that this book will challenge and encourage you to make significant changes to the way you do youth ministry. I've written this book to add my voice to others who have called for radical changes in youth ministry practices. I hope you will read these pages with an open mind, take an honest look at your ministry practices, and embrace the changes so desperately needed in youth ministry.

PART 1

Deconstruct Your Youth Ministry

CHAPTER 1

BIBLICAL METRICS

EVALUATING THE MISSION AND PURPOSE OF YOUTH MINISTRY

Throughout my time in youth ministry, I frequently used illustrations in my youth talks. I think stories and illustrations are essential in helping people understand biblical truth. One of my favorite illustrations is *The Life-Saving Station.*

> There once was a life-saving station on a dangerous seacoast where shipwrecks often occurred. The building was small, and there was just one boat, but the members of the life-saving station were committed and kept a constant watch over the sea. Whenever a ship wrecked on the rocky shore, members unselfishly did whatever it took to save lives. In fact, so many lives were saved at this station that it became famous.
>
> As a result, many people wanted to be associated with the station to give their time, talent, and money to support its important

work. New boats were bought, new crews were recruited, and a formal training session was offered. As the membership of the life-saving station grew, some became unhappy that the building was so primitive and that the equipment was so outdated. They wanted a better place to welcome the survivors pulled from the sea. So they raised money to replace the emergency cots with beds and put better furniture in the enlarged and newly decorated building.

Soon the life-saving station became a popular gathering place for its members. They met regularly, and when they did, it was apparent how they loved one another. They greeted, hugged, laughed, and cried together as they shared the events that had been going on in their lives. But after a while, fewer members were interested in going out to sea on life-saving missions, so they hired lifeboat crews to do this for them.

About this time, a large ship wrecked off the coast, and the hired crews brought boatloads of cold, wet, dirty, sick, and half-drowned people into the life-saving station. Soon the beautiful meeting space became a place of chaos. The fancy carpets got dirty, and some of the furniture got scratched. As a result, the property committee immediately had a shower built outside the station where victims of shipwrecks could be cleaned up before coming inside.

The next meeting of the life-saving station members was contentious. Most of the members wanted to stop the club's life-saving activities, for they were unpleasant and a hindrance to the normal fellowship of the members. Others insisted that life-saving was their primary purpose and pointed out that they were, in fact, called a "life-saving station." But they were finally voted down and told that if they wanted to save the lives of the shipwrecked, they could begin

> their own life-saving station down the coast. And do you know what? That's what they did.
>
> As the years passed, the new station experienced the same changes that had occurred in the old. It evolved into a place to meet regularly for fellowship, meetings, and for special training sessions about their mission, but few went out to the drowning people. The shipwrecked people were no longer welcomed in that new life-saving station. So another life-saving station was founded further down the coast. History continued to repeat itself. And if you visit that seacoast today, you will find a number of beautiful meeting places with ample parking and plush carpeting. Shipwrecks are frequent in those waters, but most of the people drown.[1]

The moral of the story is clear. The church is a life-saving station. If we are not careful, our focus can drift, and we can forget our true purpose. Churches can get side-tracked and begin doing things that distract from why they were established. You can lose your focus in youth ministry as well. This can happen when leaders, parents, and students begin to focus inward instead of outward. Two ways youth ministry typically gets side-tracked are fun and safety. Youth ministry is known for fun—gaga ball, lock-ins, camps, and retreats. When youth ministry focuses on fun, success becomes defined as "high-energy events that students experience in isolation from other generations."[2] In addition to fun, youth ministry can also drift toward emphasizing safety.[3] Christian parents are concerned that their

---

[1] Wayne Rice, *Hot Illustrations for Youth Talks* (Youth Specialties, 1993), 104.

[2] Timothy Paul Jones, "Family Ministry: Leaving Behind the One-Eared Mickey Mouse Model of Youth Ministry," January 28, 2020, https://www.timothypauljones.com/family-ministry-the-mickey-mouse-model-of-youth-ministry/.

[3] See Mark Cannister, *Teenagers Matter: Making Student Ministry a Priority in the Church* (Baker, 2013), 2.

children should be protected and kept safe from what they view as a disturbing and dangerous world. According to Pete Ward, "In this context, youthwork becomes the means by which Christian parents seek to extend their influence on teenagers who are seeking more independence and freedom from the home."[4] We have lost sight of our biblical purposes and goals when youth ministry is primarily about safety and fun.

Deconstructing youth ministry begins by testing the assumptions concerning the mission and purposes of youth ministry. This chapter will examine three assumptions: (1) *My church and I clearly understand the biblical rationale for youth ministry*, (2) *the way I operate my youth ministry is biblical*, and (3) *I build my ministry on the biblical purposes of youth ministry.* To evaluate these assumptions and practices, we need to first rediscover why we do youth ministry. To accomplish this, we must look to our ultimate source of authority—God's Word. The first assumption I want to question relates to the biblical basis of youth ministry. I critique these assumptions not because I don't believe the truth of Scripture but because I desire us to be faithful to the task to which God has called us. With this in mind, let's look at the first assumption.

Assumption: My Church and I Clearly Understand the Biblical Rationale for Youth Ministry

As a youth leader, you undoubtedly understand the biblical rationale of youth ministry. But, chances are, many of your volunteers, parents, and students do not. So, the first step in deconstructing youth ministry is solidifying your understanding of the biblical rationale and communicating it to your people.

---

[4] Pete Ward, *Growing Up Evangelical: Youthwork and the Making of a Subculture* (Wipf and Stock, 2013), 166.

Four Biblical Rationales for Youth Ministry

To begin with, I'll state the obvious—the Bible does not mention youth ministry. Although some scholars believe that many of the first disciples were teenagers, Jesus was *not* the first youth minister. Referring to Jesus as the first youth leader is anachronistic because our modern definition of adolescence is quite different from young people in the Bible.[5] By age thirteen, many young people in Jesus's day had adult responsibilities. In addition, our concept of adolescence as a period between childhood and adulthood is a relatively new one.[6] However, Scripture's lack of explicit reference to youth ministry does not negate its importance. For instance, many elements of modern churches are not mentioned in Scripture: preschool, children's, youth, and college ministry, as well as administrators.

Voddie Baucham is outspoken in his criticism of youth ministry. He asserts that youth ministry is not biblical. As a result, he advocates for his version of deconstruction that brings about a total dismantling of youth ministry in the local church. To Baucham, the answer is to focus solely on a version of family ministry that eliminates any age-graded programs.[7] I disagree with Baucham. I believe there is a biblical rationale for youth ministry and other age-graded ministries.[8]

---

[5] See Brian Crosby, "Responses to the Gospel Advancing View" in *Youth Ministry in the 21st Century: Five Views*, ed. Chap Clark (Baker Academic, 2015), 18.

[6] G. Stanley Hall is credited as the first person to use the term *adolescence* to refer to the period between childhood and adulthood. He called adolescence a "period of storm and stress." See G. Stanley Hall, *Adolescence: its psychology and its relations to physiology, anthropology, sociology, sex, crime, religion and education* (D. Appleton, 1904).

[7] See Voddie Baucham, *Family Driven Faith: Doing What It Takes to Raise Sons and Daughters Who Walk with God* (Crossway, 2007).

[8] See Jay Sedwick, "In Between: Adolescents," in *Invitation to Educational Ministry: Foundations of Transformative Christian Education*, ed. George M. Hillman, Jr. and Sue G. Edwards (Kregel, 2018), 163.

The Call to Make Disciples of All Nations

Jesus commissioned his disciples in Matt 28:19–20, Mark 16:15, Luke 24:46–48, John 20:21, and Acts 1:8.[9] The most familiar passage is in Matt 28:19–20:

> "Go therefore and make disciples of all nations, baptizing them in the name of the Father and of the Son and of the Holy Spirit, teaching them to observe all that I have commanded you. And remember, I am with you always, to the end of the age."

Jesus gave us the task of fulfilling the Great Commission. This command applies to all people, including young people. The purpose of youth ministry is the same purpose of the church—to make disciples who make disciples.[10] Mark Cannister writes, "A biblical theology of discipleship recognizes that in the Gospels and Acts, the term *disciple* most commonly describes a true follower of Christ and that the imperative in Jesus' commission to *make disciples* is understood to mean making disciples out of nonbelievers."[11] Youth ministry provides opportunities for young people to hear the truth of the gospel and to grow in their faith, which can ultimately lead to them becoming disciples who make disciples. You must ask yourself: *Am I helping accomplish the Great Commission within the context of youth ministry in my church?* At the most basic level, youth ministry is about reaching teenagers with the gospel of Jesus and nurturing them to grow in their faith. According to Cannister, "Call it what you will—evangelism, discipleship, spiritual formation, or Christian education: the bottom line is transforming lives with the message of God's grace."[12]

---

[9] See Preston Nix, "Motivations for Fulfilling the Great Commission" in *Engage: Tools for Contemporary Evangelism*, ed. Wm. Craig Price (Iron Stream Media, 2019), 3.

[10] See Darren DePaul, "Making Disciples Who Make Disciples," *Gospel-Centered Youth Ministry*, ed. Cameron Cole and Jon Nielson (Crossway, 2016), 40.

[11] Mark Cannister, *Teenagers Matter: Making Student Ministry a Priority in the Church* (Baker, 2013), 28.

[12] Cannister, xxiii.

Veteran youth leader Duffy Robbins says, "The primary task of youth ministry is to focus on God and the glorification of God."[13] How do we glorify God? We fulfill his mission.

Making disciples is not merely making converts. Mark Cannister says, "We cannot assume our work is done following the recitation of a prayer accepting Jesus as Lord and Savior. On the contrary, the work has just begun."[14] Tracking conversions (baptisms or decisions for Christ) is essential and necessary, but it is only part of the task of the Great Commission. The ultimate goal is to lead students to continue the process of disciple-making. Healthy disciples should naturally produce more disciples.[15]

Passing on Faith to the Next Generation

The Bible emphasizes the importance of parents and older generations taking on this responsibility of passing on faith to the next generation. In Deut 6:4–9, God commands the Israelites to teach their children about God's commandments and to talk about them "when you sit at home and when you walk along the road, when you lie down and when you get up." This instruction is not confined to one place, like worship on Sunday, but involves every aspect of life.[16] Parents are to impress God's commandments throughout the everyday rhythms of life. The psalmist echoes this command in Ps 78:4–7, emphasizing the need for the previous generation to "tell a future generation the praiseworthy deeds of the Lord, his might, and the wondrous works he has performed." This involves leading youth to experience the transforming work of God's Word in every area of their lives.

---

[13] Duffy Robbins, *This Way to Youth Ministry: An Introduction to the Adventure* (Zondervan, 2004), 18.

[14] Cannister, *Teenagers Matter*, xxiii.

[15] See Barna, *State of Discipleship: A Barna Report Produced in Partnership with The Navigators* (The Navigators, 2015), 69.

[16] See Michael McGarry, *A Biblical Theology of Youth Ministry* (Randall House, 2019), 24.

Yet the National Study of Youth and Religion revealed that most teens could not articulate their beliefs.

> They had extreme difficulty in explaining how it [faith] affected their lives, other than to say it makes them happy, helps them have a better day, and helps them make some good moral decisions. It seems like religion operates in the background—it's just part of the wallpaper; part of the furniture.[17]

It is clear that God values the spiritual development of young people and entrusts older generations with the task of nurturing their faith. Therefore, a biblical rationale for youth ministry is to provide a vehicle to impress God's commands upon the next generation.

The Church's Role as a Community of Believers

The church is called to be a community of believers that supports and encourages one another in their faith. In 1 Cor 12:12–27, Paul compares the church to a body with many parts and emphasizes the importance of each part working together for the good of the whole. This includes young people who are vital to the church community.

> Youth ministry is a disciple-making ministry where the gospel is proclaimed and applied to the real-life situations teenagers find themselves facing while they discover their identity as a member of Christ's Church; not simply a church-based club for teenagers to build healthy friendships and stay out of trouble.[18]

Youth ministry helps teens build a community of faith. It is where students learn their place in God's family and find love, support, and a sense

---

[17] Christian Smith and Melinda Lundquist Denton, *Soul Searching: The Religious and Spiritual Lives of American Teenagers* (Oxford University Press, 2009), 82.

[18] McGarry, *A Biblical Theology of Youth Ministry*, 95.

of belonging. Students are encouraged, challenged, and corrected by adults who come alongside them on life's journey.

The Pastoral Role of a Youth Minister

I believe the role of the youth minister is an extension of the pastor's role in the lives of teenagers and families. From this perspective, we can examine Scripture passages on pastors and elders. A pastor or elder is the servant-leader of a local church. The Bible teaches that God gave the church pastors and teachers to equip believers to do the work of the ministry (Eph 4:11). The term pastor comes from the Latin word for shepherd. The apostle Peter describes the shepherding role of pastors in 1 Pet 5:1–4. The youth minister shepherds the church's students, volunteers, and parents. Youth ministers preach, teach, pray, disciple, lead, and serve the congregation's members.

By providing opportunities for young people to learn about God, grow in their faith, and be part of a supportive community of believers, you can help to pass on faith to the next generation and make disciples of all nations. You can summarize each biblical rationale in the following phrases: *make disciples who make disciples*, *impress God's commands to the next generation*, *connect students to a community of believers*, and *shepherd teenagers and families.*

Testing the assumption that your church understands the biblical rationale is the first task of deconstructing youth ministry. I include several reflection questions at the end of the chapter to help you assess your ministry. You can start with this question: To what extent do people in my church understand that we are to make disciples who make disciples?

Assumption: The Way I Operate My Youth Ministry Is Biblical

Just because you understand the biblical rationale of youth ministry doesn't mean the way in which you conduct your ministry is biblical. Christopher Talbot rightly asserts that the way most youth ministries operate is *not* biblical:

"Many models of youth ministry completely separate the youth from contact with both the older members and younger children of the church. When worship, ministry, and fellowship are segregated, it can send the message that the Christian life is highly customized and individualized, especially for teenagers."[19] This segregated approach is a common youth ministry practice.

Authors and researchers have heralded the problems associated with segregating youth from the rest of the church for years. Stuart Cummings-Bond famously illustrated this by describing this approach as the "one-eared Mickey Mouse."[20] Imagine a rudimentary drawing of Mickey Mouse using two circles. A large circle is the head of the mouse, and a smaller circle represents a single ear. In this illustration, the church is the head, and youth ministry is the lone ear "outside the larger church community as a separate entity, operating essentially as its own mini-church."[21]

Suppose you gather students for worship and preaching apart from the rest of the congregation and don't encourage active participation with the larger body of believers. In that case, you are dangerously close to having a church within a church. If all your youth events are designed exclusively for students, you operate a church within a church. If young people can come to your campus and participate in your ministries without interacting with your congregation's older or younger members, then you have a church within a church. And a church within a church is not biblical. Youth ministry veteran Walt Mueller laments this popular approach:

> It's ironic that one of the marks of today's emerging generations is a deep need for community and connectedness, and yet we plan and program in ways that cut them off from experiencing community and connectedness with people who aren't their own age. It's also ironic that while we say we want to see our kids embrace Jesus and

---

[19] Christopher Talbot, *Remodeling Youth Ministry* (Welch College, 2017), 13.

[20] Stuart Cummings-Bond, "The One-Eared Mickey Mouse," *Youthworker Journal* (Fall 1989): 76–78.

[21] Sedwick, "In Between: Adolescents," in *Invitation to Educational Ministry*, 162.

> mature into a deep faith that's integrated into all of life, we separate them from the wisest and most seasoned members of the body. Not only that but we cloister them together with their peers in a trendy room designed to draw and keep them, which might actually promote the irrelevance of anything in the church that exists outside of that room.[22]

Over the last sixty years, this approach has become the dominant model for student ministry. According to Timothy Paul Jones, "The model has become so popular that, in many instances, it has turned into the predominant paradigm not only for youth ministry but also for preschool, children's, and singles ministries."[23] This leads to students being disconnected from the church and parents abdicating responsibility for discipling their teenagers, resulting in youth leaders increasingly embracing the responsibility of discipling young people. We now have decades of youth and family ministry research, books, seminars, and conferences declaring the evils of this approach. The problem is we haven't done what's necessary to do things differently—because it's hard. The easy route is to keep doing the same things you've always done. We do this because this approach is now what is expected of us.

Perhaps this approach is so popular because many leaders view youth ministry as a stepping stone to future ministry. For instance, some leaders feel called to pastor churches, but until they have a church of their own, they can pastor a youth group. They don't yet have a big flock to lead, but a little flock will do. Practically speaking, this is common for many leaders. Leaders need training ground opportunities to serve the church, even if it is not in their specific area of calling. If you feel an ultimate call to another ministry responsibility, I implore you not to separate youth from the rest of the church.

---

[22] Walt Mueller, "Why Youth Ministry Shouldn't Be the Greatest Show on Earth . . ." *Center for Youth/Parent Understanding*, https://cpyu.org/2017/06/01/why-youth-ministry-shouldnt-be-the-greatest-show-on-earth/.

[23] Timothy Paul Jones, *Perspectives on Family Ministry: Three Views* (B&H, 2009), 11.

I am not saying that every youth ministry has unbiblical motives. As a youth minister, associate pastor, interim pastor, and now seminary professor, I've worked with ministry leaders around the country who genuinely love God and want to lead biblical youth ministries. But, like Timothy Paul Jones notes, "The ministry models that many ministers have inherited in local churches are fundamentally flawed. As a result, well-intended ministers have attempted to pursue tasks in the sole context of the church that God designed to occur in partnership with another context. That other context is the family."[24]

Biblical Youth Ministry

So if the "one-eared Mickey" approach is not biblical, then what type of approach is? Youth ministry that supports parents as primary spiritual leaders and connects teenagers to the entire church is biblical.[25] A biblical youth ministry understands that parents are the primary influencers of faith. A biblical youth ministry will undoubtedly provide opportunities for teens to be discipled by leaders, but not to the exclusion of parents. A biblical youth ministry seeks to provide training and resources to help parents disciple their students. Organizations such as Lifeway, Orange, and D6 Family have championed ministry to parents and families within the context of youth ministry.[26]

Testing the assumption that you operate a biblical youth ministry is a crucial next step in deconstruction. Review the questions at the end of the chapter. You can start by reflecting on this question: To what extent do parents understand their role as the most significant spiritual influence on

---

[24] Jones, 13.

[25] See Richard Ross, *Youth Ministry That Lasts a Lifetime* (Seminary Hill, 2017), 50; Cameron Cole, "The Flawed History of Youth Ministry in Less than 400 Words," https://rootedministry.com/flawed-history-youth-ministry-less-400-words/.

[26] You can find Lifeway resources at https://lifeway.com, Orange resources at https://thinkorange.com, and D6 Family content at https://d6family.com.

their teenager? In chapter 3, I'll share more about operating a biblical youth ministry for teenagers in families and teenagers in the congregation.

Assumption: I Build My Ministry on the Biblical Purposes of Youth Ministry

Perhaps you rely on your gut feelings for much of what you do in youth ministry. The problem is that sometimes your gut is wrong.[27] Your assumptions about youth ministry's purpose can lead to poor decisions. Therefore, it is essential to clearly understand the biblical purposes of youth ministry.

The Purposes of Youth Ministry

The quality of a student ministry is strongly related to its purpose.[28] When you think about the purpose of youth ministry, you are questioning *why* it exists. Failure to address why youth ministry exists results in a ministry that is "vapid and bankrupt."[29] Cannister observes that a "clear purpose has marked student ministry from the beginning, and each time student ministry has veered off course, it has been, in part, because of confusion of purpose—not unlike the church in general."[30] He advocates for a comprehensive youth ministry that includes "both evangelistic and discipleship with worship, ministry, and fellowship."[31] If you have not clearly defined the purpose of your ministry, you will be unable to communicate that purpose to students, parents, and volunteers.

---

[27] See Tony Morgan, "4 Assumptions Hurting Your Church," The Unstuck Group, https://theunstuckgroup.com/4-assumptions-hurting-your-church/.

[28] Cannister, *Teenagers Matter*, 23.

[29] Robbins, *This Way to Youth Ministry*, 24.

[30] Cannister, *Teenagers Matter*, xx.

[31] Cannister, 35.

Doug Fields's *Purpose Driven Youth Ministry* is a popular and beneficial book on the purpose of youth ministry.[32] Fields proposes a comprehensive view of youth ministry that brings together the Great Commandment, the Great Commission, and Jesus's final words to his disciples (Matt 22:37–40; 28:19–20; Acts 1:6–8). The Great Commandment declares our motive for disciple-making—our love of God and love for people. The Great Commission proclaims our mission—to make disciples.[33] Fields states, "Everything you do for students should be an attempt to fulfill one of these biblical purposes in your youth ministry and in students' hearts."[34] The five purposes of youth ministry are evangelism, discipleship, fellowship, ministry, and worship.

Evangelism is at the heart of the church's mission. It involves sharing the good news of Jesus Christ with students and parents and inviting them into a relationship with God. The greatest need of every person is to come to faith in Christ. The church is called to proclaim the message of salvation and demonstrate God's love through compassion and service. Youth ministry has historically created opportunities for young people to hear and respond to the truth of the gospel. You do this because you realize that evangelism is part of the Great Commission (Matt 28:19–20) and that God desires for every student to repent and turn to him (John 3:17; 1 Tim 2:3–4; 2 Pet 3:9). You tell students about Jesus because he died for everyone (Heb 2:9; 1 Tim 4:10; 1 John 2:2) and, as a result, God will forgive any teenager who calls on him (Rom 10:13). Yet a student ministry will not naturally drift toward evangelism. A culture of evangelism will only happen because you provide leadership in that direction. You should faithfully share the gospel with students and invite them to respond. You must model evangelism and train leaders, parents, and students to communicate the gospel. By

---

[32] See Doug Fields, *Purpose Driven Youth Ministry: 9 Essential Foundations for Healthy Growth* (Zondervan, 1998), 43.

[33] See Dann Spader, *4 Chair Discipling: What Jesus Calls Us to Do* (Moody, 2014), 33.

[34] Doug Fields, *Your First Two Years in Youth Ministry: A Personal and Practical Guide to Starting Right* (Zondervan, 2002), 216.

engaging in evangelism, youth ministry fulfills its purpose of spreading the gospel's transformative power to lost teenagers.

Discipleship is nurturing and equipping believers to grow in their faith and become more like Christ. The goal of every believer is to be like Christ. The process of becoming like Christ is spiritual growth or discipleship. Discipleship ministries provide an environment where individuals can learn, study the Bible, and develop a deeper understanding of God's Word. Through teaching, mentoring, and accountability, a youth ministry guides its members in spiritual formation, helping them develop a personal relationship with God and empowering them to live out their faith daily. Many youth leaders struggle with the dichotomy between evangelism and discipleship. It is common for a youth ministry to emphasize one over the other. Mark Senter defines this dichotomy as a "dynamic tension in youth ministry."[35]

Evangelism ⟷ Discipleship

Figure 1: The Dynamic Tension in Youth Ministry

Figure 1 illustrates the tension between an attraction-based youth ministry approach (evangelism) and one focusing on training (discipleship). However, the tension between these two does not have to exist. Jesus did not separate the functions of evangelism and discipleship. According to Jeff Pratt and Scott Stevens, "They are opposite sides of the same coin, and biblically grounded youth ministry will include both."[36] Teenagers need regular engagement in both areas to mature spiritually. They are cyclical—evangelism leading to discipleship and discipleship informing evangelism.[37]

---

[35] Mark Senter, "A Historical Framework for Doing Youth Ministry" in *Reaching a Generation for Christ*, ed. Richard R. Dunn and Mark Senter (Moody, 1997), 111.

[36] Jeff Pratt and Scott Stevens, *Are You Developing Your Students or Your Student Ministry?* (LifeWay Press, 2010).

[37] See David Odom, "Ministry Leadership with Emerging Adults," in *Together We Equip: Integrating Disciple and Ministry Leadership for Holistic Spiritual Formation*, ed. Jody Dean and Hal Stewart (WestBow, 2018), 143.

Fellowship is the communal aspect of the church, where believers come together to build meaningful relationships, support one another, and experience a sense of belonging. The church is designed to be a community that provides its members with love, care, and encouragement. This can be especially important to teenagers. For some students, belonging precedes belief. They want to experience the love and support of others before committing to accept Jesus as their savior. Youth ministry offers a place where young people can find acceptance, share their joys and sorrows, and find support during times of difficulty. Chances are you probably already offer fellowship opportunities for teenagers, but how intentional are these gatherings? Your church should not simply be a social gathering place but a place for godly relationships to form and strengthen. True discipleship can only take place in the context of relationships. Therefore, teenagers and leaders must have opportunities to build godly relationships. In fellowship, teenage believers are united by their shared faith and become a family that loves and serves one another.

Ministry involves serving others and meeting the practical needs of the community. The church is called to be a source of compassion and assistance, addressing individuals' and society's physical, emotional, and spiritual needs. By engaging in ministry, students demonstrate the love of Christ in action. Young people need the chance to serve the youth group and the church.

> Nothing is more reflective of healthy student ministries than students who launch into the full and robust life of the church. In order for this to happen, though, the broader church must be prepared for and committed to receiving teenagers into its midst by valuing them for who they are and allowing them to contribute to the whole life of the church.[38]

In my research, I found that exemplary youth leaders report a high expectation of teen service in the church as the primary connection method. Teenagers in these churches are expected to serve in various "ministry

[38] Cannister, *Teenagers Matter*, 117.

teams." As a result, leaders spend time training and coaching students for ministry and service.

Worship is an essential aspect of the church's purpose. It is the act of praising and honoring God individually and corporately. The church gathers to express gratitude, adoration, and reverence toward God, acknowledging his greatness and sovereignty. Mark Cannister writes, "Many teenagers in the church rarely attend an intergenerational worship service, opting instead for the homogenous youth worship program that has become a church of its own within the church."[39] Perhaps your church is like many today, offering students an opportunity to gather with other teenagers for worship separate from the main congregation. Maybe your teenagers come together on Wednesday nights and are led in worship by a student praise band. Worship gatherings like this are common in youth ministry today. But your students need an opportunity to worship with older and younger believers. You might say, "But David, our church *does* offer intergenerational worship through our congregational gatherings on Sunday mornings." That's great—but do students understand the importance of worshipping with people outside the youth group? Do you? The problem with youth-only worship is that it can have the unintended consequence of teaching teenagers that worship is about them, not God. Through intergenerational worship, teenage believers encounter the presence of God, find spiritual renewal, and draw closer to him.

Fields famously illustrates the five purposes using a baseball diamond: fellowship at first base, discipleship at second, ministry at third base, and evangelism at homeplate. Worship is envisioned as encompassing everything you do in ministry; therefore, he places it on the pitcher's mound in the center of the baseball diamond. However, I believe there is another way to envision the five purposes by emphasizing discipleship. The overarching purpose of youth ministry is to make disciples who make disciples. That means that the process ends with a disciple-making teenager and a disciple-making parent. Therefore, I am a proponent of a hybrid purpose-driven model that

---

[39] Cannister, 115.

places four purposes (worship, evangelism, ministry, and fellowship) under the umbrella of discipleship. I don't mean to imply that discipleship is more important than worship, or evangelism (or ministry or fellowship). To me, it simply makes sense to think about the end result—a disciple-making disciple.[40] I say this because a disciple-making teenager worships God and tells others about Jesus. A disciple-making teenager serves others in ministry. A disciple-making teenager desires fellowship with other believers. A disciple-making parent worships God, tells others about Christ, serves others, and leads students to do the same.

Deconstructing youth ministry is about getting back to the basics—to the foundations of why we do youth ministry. Testing the assumption that your ministry is built on the biblical purposes of youth ministry is the next step in deconstruction. Start by reflecting on this question: Have your assumptions about the biblical basis of youth ministry handicapped your effectiveness?

Testing the Assumptions

An honest examination of the biblical rationale for youth ministry can reinvigorate your ministry. Begin by reflecting on this chapter by responding to the following questions. Review the questions and invite others to dialogue with you concerning each one.

Questions to Consider

1. To what extent do leaders and church members understand the biblical rationale of youth ministry?

---

[40] See Aubrey Malphurs, *Strategic Disciple Making: A Practical Tool for Successful Ministry* (Baker, 2009), 67. For Malphurs, discipleship is both the mission and the very life of the church. "It is not to be one of several programs of the church; it is the program of the church. All the activities and programs of the church work together to make disciples."

2. Is your ministry based on a specific Scripture passage such as Matt 28:19–20?
3. In what ways do you communicate that your youth ministry is part of fulfilling the Great Commission?
4. To what extent can leaders, parents, and students clearly articulate the purposes of youth ministry?
5. To what extent do parents understand their role as the most significant spiritual influence on their teenager?
6. In what ways do you needlessly separate teenagers and parents?
7. To what extent do you provide opportunities for teenagers and parents to worship and serve together?
8. In what ways do you encourage teenagers to be part of the church congregation?
9. In what ways does your ministry programming reflect the five purposes?
10. To what extent do you clearly articulate the purpose of youth ministry to parents, volunteers, and students?
11. In what ways are the purposes expressed in your mission statement?
12. In what ways are the purposes expressed in your ministry programming?
13. How do you overemphasize one or more of the purposes and deemphasize others?

For Further Reading

Several of my friends and colleagues have excellent books that discuss the topics of this chapter in greater detail. Tim McKnight's *Navigating Student Ministry*, Duffy Robbins's *This Way to Youth Ministry*, and Mike McGarry's *A Biblical Theology of Youth Ministry* offer extensive overviews of the biblical foundations of youth ministry.

CHAPTER 2

Discipleship Metrics

Measuring Spiritual Growth

I recently overheard two youth pastors talking about their ministries. The first leader asked, "How are things at your church?" The second one responded, "Things are going great! How about you? How many students do you have?" The first leader smiled and said, "We had forty-five kids at church last Wednesday night! That's the most we've had in a while. How about you?" "Things are going great for us as well," responded the leader. "We had sixty youth at our last DiscipleNow weekend!" The leaders smiled and congratulated each other before parting ways.

Perhaps you've had a similar conversation and either championed or lamented the number of teenagers attending your church and events regularly. We do this because counting people is the most straightforward form of evaluation; for most, it's the only type of assessment they conduct. The hope is that if we just get teens in the church building, they will come to Christ and grow in their faith. We tell ourselves that having more students involved in our ministry means we do a good job. Pastors and elders are happy if the students are having a good time and parents aren't complaining.

Yet measuring participation alone is not a clear indication of spiritual growth. Intuitively, we know this, so we look for other ways to affirm we're doing well. Here's what I used to do as a youth minister—highlight spiritually mature students. I would invite a few students I knew who were active in their faith to share their testimonies with the youth group. Or I would make a video of these key leaders telling how they shared the gospel with a friend or resisted some temptation. I did this because I understood the axiom—*celebrate what you want to replicate*. I wanted to encourage more students to take steps toward Christian maturity by spotlighting a few already doing it. However, spotlighting is not an accurate evaluation of our ministries. According to Clint Grider, "Spotlighting is elevating a few success stories to represent what is happening among the many."[1] It can be an effective way to communicate your goals but an ineffective way to measure them. You see, I was not only using spotlighting to encourage teenagers; I was using it to pat myself on the back and show others that our ministry was reaching teens. I was using the positive testimonies of a few to represent the whole. The problem with this type of evaluation is that it misrepresents ministry effectiveness and demonstrates confirmation bias. Confirmation bias is the tendency to look for facts that support, rather than reject, your preconceived ideas about a situation.[2] To overcome confirmation bias, you must be willing to examine all the facts, especially the information that contradicts your assumptions.

Without a critical evaluation of the spiritual growth of your students, you are left with only your best guess about their spiritual journeys, and your ministry planning is just a shot in the dark.[3] Grider observes, "The truth is

---

[1] Clint Grider, *Mind the Gap: Leading Your Church to Agility and Effectiveness in Any Environment* (B&H, 2023), 8.

[2] See Christina Schwind and Jurgen Büder, "Reducing confirmation bias and evaluation bias: When are preference-inconsistent recommendations effective—and when not?" *Computers in Human Behavior* 28, no. 6 (November 2012): 2280.

[3] See Eric Geiger and Jeff Borton, *Simple Student Ministry: A Clear Process for Strategic Youth Discipleship* (B&H, 2009), chapter 37. Geiger and Borton found

that avoiding evaluation leads churches to confuse busyness with progress and attending church with growing in Christ."[4] What you want to know is how teenagers have changed after spending six years in your youth ministry. When they graduate from your program, could they be called "mature in Christ"? Are you making disciples who make disciples? In my research and conversations with youth leaders around the country, I have found few who could confidently express the spiritual condition of more than a handful of students. I don't know about you, but I don't want to continue to assume students are growing in their faith—and you shouldn't either.

Deconstructing youth ministry involves testing your assumptions about how you lead students and discovering the true spiritual condition of teenagers and parents. This chapter will examine three assumptions: (1) *My youth ministry has clear goals and outcomes for students*, (2) *students in my youth ministry are growing spiritually*, and (3) *parents of teenagers in my church are growing spiritually*. To evaluate these assumptions and practices, we need to first examine your ministry goals and outcomes.

Assumption: My Youth Ministry Has Clear Goals and Outcomes for Students

In 1964, Supreme Court Justice Potter Stewart famously tried to define pornography and what constitutes obscenity by saying, "I know it when I see it." Many churches use the same type of explanation when defining spiritually mature teenagers. Rather than clearly describing the biblical characteristics of a mature believer, they rely on a more subjective approach—we'll know when we see it. This type of approach can hinder your ministry and its impact on students. Instead, you must clearly define your discipleship goals for students and the outcomes you desire to see in their lives.

---

that most student ministries offer programs and events "with no sense of direction and no understanding of how the programs contribute to the overall picture."

[4] Grider, *Mind the Gap*, 42.

Goal-setting may not be your favorite activity. Some people are wired in such a way that setting and achieving goals is highly enjoyable and motivating. For others, it can be another way to define their shortcomings or failures. Some youth leaders want to spend time discipling teenagers and would rather not waste time on mundane tasks such as defining goals and outcomes. Regardless of your natural inclinations or preferences concerning youth ministry, you need to define your goals and outcomes for students.

Goals and Outcomes

Goals represent a beginning step, and outcomes are the final result. According to Svetlana Whitener, "The journey to achievement starts with a goal and finishes with a desired outcome."[5] Goals are overarching statements for your ministry. A goal is a broad, general statement about what your ministry intends to accomplish. Your ministry may have several goals you seek to accomplish. For example, you might have an evangelistic goal: reach spiritually lost teenagers by sharing the gospel with them.

Outcomes define the details of the goal, and they should be specific and measurable. Outcomes are the Christlike characteristics you desire to see in young people. As Clint Grider says, they "paint the picture of a person who is being formed by God into the likeness of Christ."[6] You should have several outcomes for each goal statement. For example, if your goal is to reach spiritually lost teenagers by sharing the gospel with them, you might have several outcomes: adults and students will pray for lost students by name on a weekly basis, adults and students will intentionally develop relationships with lost students to have an opportunity to share the gospel, adults and students will be trained to use the *3 Circles* gospel presentation,

---

[5] Svetlana Whitener, "How to Understand the Difference Between Goals and Outcomes," *Forbes*, July 7, 2017, https://www.forbes.com/sites/forbescoachescouncil/2017/07/27/how-to-understand-the-difference-between-goals-and-outcomes/?sh=4ee52ed415c3.

[6] Grider, *Mind the Gap*, 52.

and adult volunteers will present the gospel in small groups once a month. You can see how each of these outcomes is specific and measurable. Small group leaders can report the names of lost students prayed for on a weekly basis. Adults and students can report the number of lost students they have connections with. Leaders can track the number of adults and students trained to use the *3 Circles* gospel presentation. Lastly, you can hold adult volunteers accountable to present the gospel in small groups once a month.

It is crucial for you to establish clear goals and outcomes. Defining goals and outcomes in youth ministry helps create a framework for intentional growth and serves as benchmarks for measuring the progress and success of your ministry. Clearly defined youth ministry goals and outcomes are the first step in assessing the extent to which youth and parents are growing toward spiritual maturity.

Youth Ministry Goals and Outcomes

The Fuller Youth Institute (FYI) asked leaders to share the top five goals for youth ministry as part of the Character and Virtue Development in Youth Ministry project. FYI surveyed hundreds of youth workers nationwide and asked them to rank each of the five goals. They received over 2,000 goals, which gave them great insights into what youth ministries are trying to do.[7] The ministry goals were broken down into six major categories:

1. Relationship with God. Approximately 25 percent of responses described students' relationship with God, faith, worship, discipleship, or something similar.
2. Relationship with others. Another 25 percent involved some form of relationship with peers, adults, the church, and the community.

---

[7] See Lisa Hanle, "What are your youth ministry goals this year?" Fuller Youth Institute, June 18, 2019, https://fulleryouthinstitute.org/blog/youth-ministry-goals-this-year.

3. Christian Education. Approximately 15 percent related to some form of learning, including Bible knowledge, theology, or skills.
4. Welcoming Environment. Twelve percent described creating a specific environment, such as safe, fun, or a place of belonging.
5. Ministry Opportunities. Service was the highest single goal, with about 9 percent of goals specifically about students serving.
6. Miscellaneous. Other goals included leadership, missions, wrestling with questions, partnering with parents, training volunteers, and evangelism.[8]

The FYI research revealed that half of youth ministry goals focused on relationships (God, peers, adults, church). Chances are your goals will reflect similar themes. Regardless of how God is leading you and your church, you must clearly state your goals. Chapter 6 will describe how your goals help you evaluate your ministry and set a course for effectively reaching students and parents.

I don't assume to know what is best for your ministry context when establishing goals and outcomes. However, I can provide some general guidance and examples to follow as you and your team write your goals and outcomes. Review the following list and use it to craft your own.[9]

1. Goal: Develop godly relationships with teenagers and parents (1 Thess 5:11; 1 Cor 11:1; Acts 2:42). To accomplish this goal, we will train volunteers to engage students and parents relationally.

---

[8] Hanle, "What are your youth ministry goals this year?"

[9] See Richard Ross, *A New Vision for SBC Student Ministry: Reaching, Baptizing, Discipling, and Sending Teenagers* (Seminary Hill, 2021), 9–10. As a member of the Student Ministry Collective formed for the creation of a list of "sixteen changes in youth ministry," I had the privilege of participating in the formation of ideas that served as the genesis for this book by Dr. Ross. The goals and outcomes listed here are based on the changes in youth ministry presented in the book.

Outcomes: Volunteers will know the names of every student and parent. Leaders will value students as persons created in God's image through active listening, verbal encouragement, and gentle correction. Adults will demonstrate appreciation for students by celebrating their accomplishments (academic, athletic, artistic, and spiritual). Leaders will value parents by seeking their input and collaboration when planning and implementing youth programs and activities. Volunteers will show support for parents through open and transparent communication. Youth workers will demonstrate the value of parents by organizing parent education sessions and workshops.

2. Goal: Share the gospel with spiritually lost teenagers (Acts 1:8–11; Rom 1:16). To accomplish this goal, we will equip adult leaders and teenagers to pray for and share the gospel with spiritually lost teenagers (Matt 28:19–20; Eph 4:12).

Outcomes: Adults and students will pray by name for lost teenagers. Adults and students will intentionally develop relationships with lost students to have an opportunity to share the gospel. Adults and students will be trained to use the *3 Circles* gospel presentation. Adult volunteers will present the gospel in small groups once a month. Leaders will celebrate student and parent salvations and baptisms.

3. Goal: Disciple teenagers in relational environments of devotion, spiritual discipline, and application of God's Word (John 15:1–8; 2 Cor 3:18). To accomplish this goal, we will train leaders to teach the Bible and relationally model spiritual disciplines (Rom 12:1–2; Eph 6:10–19).

Outcomes: Adults will demonstrate spiritual maturity through personal prayer, Bible reading, and worship attendance. Leaders

> will show they care for students by arriving early and coming prepared to engage with youth relationally. Students will demonstrate devotion to Christ by regularly praying and reading their Bible. Students will regularly experience intergenerational worship. Students will demonstrate a biblical worldview through Jesus-centered living.

4. Goal: Send teenagers on mission to fulfill the Great Commission in obedience to Christ wherever he calls them (Jer 1:7–8; Matt 28:18–20; John 15:16). To accomplish this goal, we will partner with parents to lead their teenagers toward a lifestyle of biblical mission, including mission engagement for the entire family (Ps 145:4–7; 1 Cor 11:1; 2 Tim 3:14–15).

> Outcomes: Leaders will provide opportunities for students and parents to serve together in both local and international missions. Adults will challenge students to serve through church ministers and local mission projects. Youth workers will encourage students to answer the call to full-time vocational ministry and missions.

You may state your outcomes with specific numbers or percentages in mind. For instance, if you have surveyed your students and found that 47 percent of youth regularly pray and read their Bible, you may want to see a specific increase in this percentage. Therefore, you may decide on a stated outcome of 75 percent of students regularly praying and reading their Bible.

You'll find several reflection questions at the end of the chapter to help you test the assumption that your youth ministry has clear goals and outcomes. You can start with this question: How are you and your leaders developing godly relationships with teenagers and parents?

Assumption: Students in My Youth Ministry Are Growing Spiritually

The essence of deconstruction is posing difficult questions and seeking honest answers. It begins with evaluating what youth ministry is all about and asking ourselves if we are accomplishing what we've set out to do. Deconstructing youth ministry will lead you to critically examine and question the assumptions and practices of youth ministry to get to the heart of what you seek to do—make disciple-makers of young people and parents. This involves a systematic analysis of student spiritual maturity.

Student Spiritual Maturity

Growth is the process of life: Children grow, plants grow, animals grow, and each grows in its own way.[10] God wants each teen to grow spiritually: "Like newborn infants, desire the pure milk of the word, so that by it you may grow up into your salvation" (1 Pet 2:2). But growth is not the goal—maturity is the goal. Growth is simply the means, and maturity is the end result. The goal of every believer is to become mature in Christ. Paul described the goal in Eph 4:12–13: "to equip the saints for the work of ministry, to build up the body of Christ, until we all reach unity in the faith and in the knowledge of God's Son, growing into maturity with a stature measured by Christ's fullness." Therefore, spiritual maturity is a crucial outcome of youth ministry. To measure spiritual maturity, you can keep track of various metrics, including attendance at church services or youth group meetings, participation in spiritual practices like prayer or Bible study, involvement in service projects or mission trips, self-reported spiritual development and growth, and an increased understanding of and engagement with the Bible and Christian theology.

---

[10] See Elmer Towns, *Successful Biblical Youth Work* (Gospel Light, 1966), 155.

In his book *Stages of Faith,* James Fowler describes the faith of young adulthood as "Individuative-Reflective." He describes this stage of faith as personal belief and ownership of faith. Young adults at this stage question their assumptions about faith. Of course, many students leave the church during this time of life, but those who remain come through this stage with greater maturity. Fowler describes this type of belief as maturing faith. I believe that maturing faith should be the goal of youth ministry. Therefore, if Christian maturity is the goal, how do you evaluate student progress? One answer is discipleship metrics for students.

Discipleship Metrics for Students

Beyond the metrics of tracking attendance and salvation/baptism, you can use other measures of Christian maturity. For example, you can measure the frequency of prayer and Bible reading, the number of times students share the gospel or stand up for faith amidst opposition, and biblical characteristics such as the fruit of the Spirit. The National Study of Youth and Religion suggests three types of youth ministry metrics: the content of religious belief, the conduct of religious activity, and the centrality of religion to life.[11] The content of religious belief refers to a teenager's biblical and doctrinal understanding. The conduct of religious activities is the practices associated with a teenager's faith, such as worship attendance and Bible reading. The centrality of religion to life speaks to the extent to which a teenager's faith impacts daily life.

The three types of metrics provide general guidance for the assessment of student spiritual growth. Expanding on these types, I find it helpful to use the following six specific discipleship metric categories:

---

[11] See Lisa Pearce and Melissa Denton, *A Faith of Their Own: Stability and Change in the Religiosity of American's Adolescents* (Oxford University Press, 2011), 13.

1. personal relationship with God
2. practicing spiritual disciplines
3. service to others
4. spiritual leadership of parents
5. relational connection to the youth group
6. relational connection to the church

I designed the survey questions in the appendix to assess spiritual growth within these six categories.

Personal Relationship with God

Beyond knowledge and practice is the internalization of belief. This is when it moves from "my parents' belief" to "my belief." It is ownership of faith and belief in Jesus Christ. Are students actively seeking God's purpose for their life? How often do they seek God's wisdom for problems and issues? How do youth respond to opposition to faith or criticism of their beliefs? Assessing how well youth integrate Christian principles into daily life is crucial to youth ministry evaluation.

Practicing Spiritual Disciplines

It's one thing to know what a disciple should do and another to actually do it. Discipleship entails cultivating a deep understanding of God and his Word. A disciple seeks wisdom, insight, and knowledge from the Bible, leaders, and mentors. Christian disciplines include prayer, Bible reading, worship, fasting, and evangelism. Are students dedicated to prayer and Bible reading? How often do they gather for worship and Bible study? How consistently do they share their faith with others? Examining the consistency and depth of student faith practices is one indicator of spiritual growth.

Service to Others

Ministry and service are demonstrations of faith in action. This generation of students wants to make a difference in the world. You can tap into this desire by encouraging youth to serve in the church and community. How often are students engaged in service to others? Are youth actively seeking opportunities to contribute to the community? Are teenagers building meaningful relationships with others and supporting their spiritual growth? Measuring service is another vital discipleship metric.

Spiritual Leadership of Parents

As stated earlier, parents are the primary influencers of teen faith. I was part of a research study on teenagers in 2020 called the Student Assessment of Enduring Faith Factors (SAEFF). We surveyed over five hundred teenagers from around the country. Our study found evidence of significant parental influence on the faith practices of young people. In fact, 86 percent of students consider their parents essential for their spiritual growth. Further, 66 percent had parents who were active leaders in the church. We found a strong relationship between parents as leaders and eight spiritual growth factors (part of a discipleship group, pursuing God's will, reading the Bible, helping someone understand what it means to be a Christian, talking with their parents about spiritual issues, helping someone become a Christian, talking about Jesus with a non-Christian recently, and believing God has a purpose for their lives).[12] To see these spiritual growth factors in your students, you must encourage Christian parents to lead in your church.

---

[12] See Karen Jones, "Inspecting the Scaffolding for Adult Faith: A Student Perspective," a presentation on the results of the Student Assessment of Enduring Faith Factors (SAEFF), September 13, 2022.

Relational Connection to Youth Group

True discipleship can only take place in the context of relationships. Therefore, students need to develop godly relationships with adults and students. The purpose of the fun activities you do in youth ministry is to foster lasting relationships that become the basis for student discipleship. Students need to know that youth leaders and peers care about them and are genuinely interested in their lives. When this is true for young people, they can express doubts and questions about faith and take significant steps in their spiritual journey.

Relational Connection to Church

Students need to develop relationships beyond the youth group. They need relational connections with members of your congregation. When young adults were asked why they remain in church, 42 percent said it was because of the relationships they have at church.[13] In the same study, one-third (33.4 percent) of young adults reported that a lack of relational connection was why they left the church.[14] In what ways are you helping foster godly relationships between older and younger members of your congregation? How often do you encourage youth participation in church-wide fellowships or ministry service alongside church members?

I designed the Student Spiritual Growth and Influence Survey in the appendix to help you test the assumption that students in your youth ministry are growing spiritually. Each question on the survey supports the six discipleship metric categories. In addition, you can test the assumptions about your ministry by reflecting on the questions at the end of the chapter.

---

[13] See Ebonie Davis, "Engaging Youth Discipleship through a Relational Discovery Paradigm," *Journal of Youth Ministry* 23, no. 1 (2023): 43.

[14] Davis, "Engaging Youth Discipleship," 43.

Assumption: Parents of Teenagers in My Church Are Growing Spiritually

We can't talk about student spiritual growth without discussing the spiritual health of parents. Why? Because the degree to which a parent models faith directly impacts faith in adulthood.[15] According to Kenneth Boa, "When parents model what it is to love and walk with Jesus, they develop an authenticity that gives them authority and credibility when they teach and train their children."[16]

I know what you're thinking: *David, I'm a youth pastor—I work with teenagers, not adults.* I hear what you're saying and realize that this section will be a challenge for many, but spiritually shallow parents produce spiritually shallow young adults. Therefore, to be an influential youth minister, you must do everything you can to impact the spiritual condition of parents. I believe that youth leaders are uniquely positioned to exert a tremendous amount of influence on moms and dads. So let's take a look at parent spiritual maturity.

Parent Spiritual Maturity

Grey Matter Research and Consulting studied 1,022 US adults to measure spiritual growth.[17] The researchers surveyed participants on various Christian practices and then placed them into categories that described their spiritual growth based on human development from newborn to grandparent. A newborn referred to a person with an immature faith, and a grandparent

---

[15] See Carolyn McNamara Barry et al., "Religiosity and Spirituality during the Transition to Adulthood," *International Journal of Behavioral Development* 34, no. 4 (April 1, 2010).

[16] Kenneth Boa, *Conformed to His Image: Biblical and Practical Approaches to Spiritual Formation* (Zondervan, 2001).

[17] See Grey Matter Research and Consulting, "Mature-ish Spiritual Assessment," June 2022. Dr. Bill White, Christ Journey Church in Miami, FL, commissioned this study for his book *Mature-ish: Your Mission from God, Should You Choose to Accept It . . .* (Baxter, 2021).

described an individual who intentionally shared the gospel and discipled people. For example, a person was still considered a spiritual newborn if he/she was not part of a group of believers at least once a month and didn't read the Bible at least once a month. Researchers found that 88 percent of adults had not advanced out of the "toddler" stage of spiritual development. Only 6 percent of the participants were described as "spiritual adults."[18]

The reality is that many parents are not prepared to disciple their teenagers. Even the most faithful Christian parent may struggle with how to help their teenager grow as a disciple of Christ. As a result, many parents completely "outsource" spiritual development to the church.[19] Therefore, equipping parents to effectively pass on their faith should be essential to your youth ministry leadership.

So what does that look like? How can youth leaders help parents disciple their teenagers? Researchers and authors have found several factors contributing to a parent's effectiveness in passing on faith.[20] The factors include these five:

1. parents cultivating a vibrant personal faith
2. parents modeling consistent faith practices
3. developing healthy parent-child relationships
4. parents volunteering alongside children and youth
5. parents talking about faith with their children and youth

---

[18] Grey Matter Research and Consulting, "Mature-ish Spiritual Assessment."

[19] See Jana Magruder, *Nothing Less: Engaging Kids in a Lifetime of Faith* (LifeWay, 2017). Mark Cannister, *Teenagers Matter: Making Student Ministry a Priority in the Church* (Baker, 2013), 13.

[20] See Christian Smith and Amy Adamczyk, *Handing Down the Faith: How Parents Pass Their Religion on to the Next Generation* (Oxford University Press, 2021); Christian Smith, Bridget Ritz, and Michael Rotolo, *Religious Parenting: Transmitting Faith and Values in Contemporary America* (Princeton University Press, 2020); Brian Haynes and Angela Haynes, *Relentless Parenting: The Crucial Pursuit of Your Teen's Heart* (Randall House, 2016); Kara Powell, Chap Clark, et al., *Sticky Faith: Everyday Ideas to Build Lasting Faith in Your Kids* (Zondervan, 2011); Richard Ross, *Youth Ministry That Lasts a Lifetime* (Seminary Hill, 2017).

Cultivating a Vibrant Personal Faith

According to researcher Christian Smith, "When it comes to kids' faith, parents get what they are."[21] The personal faith of parents impacts children and youth more than any other factor.[22] Faith practices led at home by "spiritually lethargic parents lead to spiritually lethargic teenagers."[23] To increase the likelihood of a teenager becoming a growing Christian, parents must have a growing personal relationship with Jesus.[24] This means that, at a minimum, parents must pray, read the Bible, and attend worship services regularly. According to Rob Gallaty, "The heart of discipleship, as Christ modeled and instituted it, is that you are not learning only for yourself. You are learning for the person to whom you will mentor in following Him."[25] In this context, parents should be motivated toward discipleship in order to disciple their own teenager. Parents should ask themselves: Do I frequently make excuses for my failure to be obedient and faithful to God's Word? In what ways am I growing in faithfulness or stagnating by being too comfortable in my spiritual life?

Modeling Consistent Faith Practices

The degree to which a parent models faith directly impacts faith in adulthood.[26] Parents must "practice their own personal religious faith, naturally, for its own sake and as role models for their children."[27] The good news is that this

---

[21] Powell and Clark, *Sticky Faith*, 24.

[22] Powell and Clark, 184.

[23] See Richard Ross, *The Senior Pastor and the Reformation of Youth Ministry* (LifeWay, 2015), 8.

[24] Smith, Ritz, and Rotolo, *Religious Parenting*, 179.

[25] Rob Gallaty, *Growing Up: How to Be a Disciple Who Makes Disciples* (CrossBooks, 2013), 14.

[26] See Barry et al., "Religiosity and Spirituality During the Transition to Adulthood," 313; Christian Smith and Patricia Snell, *Souls in Transition* (Oxford University Press, 2009), 256.

[27] Smith and Adamczyk, *Handing Down the Faith*, 33.

does not require parents to be theologians or experts on doctrinal issues; they simply need to practice what they believe faithfully. In my experience, parents grossly underestimate their spiritual influence on teenagers. They view cultural and peer influences as greater than their own. Parents need to hear from youth leaders that they still have the most significant impact on their teenager's faith. Therefore, you should lead parents to reflect on questions such as: How can I be more consistent in my faith practices? In what ways do I model a personal relationship with Jesus and spiritual disciplines such as prayer, Bible reading, church attendance, witnessing, fasting, and service?[28]

Healthy Parent-Child Relationships

The health of a parent's relationship with a child impacts how well they pass on faith. The first emotional bond children form is with their parents. The nature of these bonds influences the rest of a person's life.[29] Estranged parents can negatively impact a teen's faith. Emotionally distant and critical relationships hinder faith transmission. On the other hand, young people who experience "unconditional support" are more likely to have a strong faith.[30] Warm and affirming relations with children are crucial to faith transmission. Parents should consider the following ways to strengthen parent-youth relationships: say "I love you" often, spend quality time with youth, listen and empathize, eat meals together, and set boundaries and consequences.[31]

---

[28] See Jason Jimenez, *Parenting Gen Z: Guiding Your Child Through a Hostile Culture* (Tyndale House, 2023), 208. Jimenez suggest that parents model faith in six ways: personal relationship with Jesus, a life devoted to growing in faith and knowledge, the value of attending church, the importance of community, a servant's heart, and how to defend your faith.

[29] See Vern Bengtson, Norella Putney, and Susan Harris, *Families and Faith: How Religion Is Passed Down Across Generations* (Oxford University Press, 2017), 71.

[30] Powell and Clark, *Sticky Faith*,178.

[31] See Paige Dorn, "8 Ways to Strengthen a Parent-Child Relationship" Family Services, https://www.familyservicesnew.org/news/8-ways-to-strengthen-a-parent-child-relationship/.

Volunteering Alongside Children and Youth

Service is a crucial component of faith transmission. In my own Youth Ministry Arenas research, I found that serving in the church is the number one way for parents and leaders to help young people build connections to the church. In fact, parents who lead at church increase the likelihood that children and teens will remain in church as adults.[32] It works like this: It's easy to dismiss something a parent says like, "believing in Jesus is important," if youth never see any evidence of belief in Mom or Dad. But when a parent chooses to volunteer and serve at church or in the community, it communicates to a teen that their parent's faith really matters.

Talking About Faith with Their Children and Youth

Most parents don't talk about faith with their kids. Only one out of eight (12.5 percent) kids talk about faith with their mom, and only one out of twenty (5 percent) have a faith conversation with their dad.[33] Students also need to feel free to express doubts and questions about faith with parents. Young people who have parents willing to discuss doubts tend to have a more vibrant faith.[34] Parents talking with teenagers about religious matters (beyond just Sunday) is associated with the active faith of emerging adults and worship attendance a decade later.[35]

---

[32] See Steve Parr and Tom Crites, *Why They Stay: Helping Parents and Church Leaders Make Investments That Keep Children and Teens Connected to the Church for a Lifetime* (WestBow, 2015), 160.

[33] Powell and Clark, *Sticky Faith*, 71.

[34] Powell and Clark, 72.

[35] Smith and Adamczyk, *Handing Down the Faith*, 53.

Discipleship Metrics for Parents

Just as we did above with students, let's now examine how we can measure the spiritual growth of parents. I find it helpful to use the following five specific discipleship metric categories:

1. a personal relationship with God
2. practicing spiritual disciplines
3. church engagement
4. parent-youth relational health
5. faith conversations

I designed the Parent Spiritual Growth and Leadership Survey questions in the appendix to assess the spiritual growth of parents within these five categories.

Personal Relationship with God

Are parents actively seeking God's direction for their life and work? How do they handle a crisis of faith when someone is sick, loses a job, or dies? This metric seeks to identify to what extent a parent is cultivating a vibrant, personal faith.

Practicing Spiritual Disciplines

Just as you measure the spiritual practices of teenagers, you should assess the spiritual practices of parents: prayer, Bible reading, worship, fasting, and evangelism. Are parents dedicated to prayer and Bible reading? How often do they gather for worship and Bible study? How consistently do they share their faith with others? How well do parents encourage teenagers to grow as Christians? As parents practice these disciplines, they model consistent faith for teenagers.

Church Engagement

According to John Wilson and Darren Sherkat, families are a "commitment mechanism for the church."[36] The commitment of Mom and Dad to church participation impacts the church engagement of teenagers. To what extent are parents engaged in Bible study and worship? When it comes to ministry service, parents magnify the impact on faith when they serve alongside their teenagers. How often are parents and students serving others together?

Parent-Youth Relational Health

Parents influence the faith practices of young people. Vern Bengtson led a team that conducted the largest study of religion and family across generations. They conducted a longitudinal study spanning almost four decades, researching the faith of seven generations. In particular, Bengtson found that the pivotal factor in successful faith transmission was warm, affirming parents.[37] Relational descriptors that hinder faith transmission are cold, distant, or authoritarian parenting; ambivalent or mixed-message parenting (when a parent is sometimes warm, sometimes cold, or one parent is warm and the other is cold or distant); strained or preoccupied parenting (when a parent is distracted by marital, financial, health, or substance abuse issues).[38] According to Bengtson, "Children responded best to parents who were unconditionally supportive, who provided consistent role modeling of religious practices, and who did not force their beliefs or practices on their children."[39] The bottom line is this—the higher the quality of a parent-child relationship, the higher the quality of religiosity in young

---

[36] John Wilson and Darren Sherkat, "Returning to the Fold," *Journal for the Scientific Study of Religion* 33, no. 2 (June 1994): 158.

[37] Bengtson, Putney, and Harris, *Families and Faith*, 73.

[38] Bengtson, Putney, and Harris, 186.

[39] Bengtson, Putney, and Harris, 186.

adulthood.[40] To that end, this metric seeks to measure the health of the parent-youth relationship.

Faith Conversations

Parents can't just have a personal faith and practice spiritual disciplines; they must also have actual conversations with teenagers about faith. Parents talking with teenagers about faith and belief during the week (beyond Sunday) significantly impacts the importance of faith and church attendance in emerging adults.[41] In fact, Smith and Adamczyk found that the strongest factor influencing a young adult's faith was "parents regularly talking with their children about religious matters as part of ordinary life."[42]

I designed the Parent Spiritual Growth and Leadership Survey in the appendix to help you test the assumption that parents of teenagers in your church are growing spiritually and intentionally leading. Each question on the survey supports the five parent discipleship metric categories. In addition, test the assumptions of your ministry by reflecting on questions at the end of the chapter.

Testing the Assumptions

You can test the assumptions raised in this chapter in several ways. First, you can use the surveys found in the appendix to evaluate the spiritual growth of students and parents. You can also find electronic versions of the surveys at deconstructingym.com. You can also reflect on the following questions. Review the questions and invite others to dialogue with you concerning each.

---

[40] See Mark Regnerus and Jeremy Uecker, "Finding Faith, Losing Faith: The prevalence and context of religious transformation during adolescence," *Review of Religious Research* 47 (2006): 592.

[41] Smith and Adamczyk, *Handing Down the Faith*, 53.

[42] Smith and Adamczyk, 54.

Questions to Consider

1. Do you track any student metrics beyond attendance?
2. To what extent are you sharing the gospel with lost teenagers?
3. How well does your church disciple teenagers in relational environments?
4. To what extent do you send teenagers on mission?
5. Have you designed your youth ministry around the three arenas? (I will discuss the arenas in the next chapter.)
6. To what extent are students practicing spiritual disciplines?
7. To what extent are students developing a personal relationship with God?
8. In what ways are students given an opportunity to serve others?
9. In what ways are you helping develop the spiritual leadership of parents?
10. In what ways are you helping youth build relational connections to your youth group and church?
11. To what extent are parents practicing spiritual disciplines?
12. To what extent are parents developing a personal relationship with God?
13. In what ways are parents serving alongside their teenagers?
14. In what ways are parents displaying spiritual leadership in the home?
15. In what ways are parents encouraging relational connections to your youth group and church?
16. Do you invite volunteers to assess student spiritual maturity?

CHAPTER 3

Ministry Metrics

Assessing Youth Ministry in Three Arenas

I served as a youth minister in a church in Midland, Texas. The oil and gas industry is huge in West Texas. You can see drilling rigs and pump jacks everywhere you go. Drilling mechanics rely on enormous amounts of pressure to cut into the earth. Oil field workers use specialized pressure gauges to monitor a drilling rig for potential problems. These gauges can detect various issues, such as a washed-out drill pipe or bit nozzle problems. Without properly calibrated gauges, drilling would be more dangerous than it already is and much less effective—equipment would continue to fail without a worker knowing what happened.

We need properly calibrated gauges in youth ministry as well. You need to use ministry metrics to gauge the effectiveness of your ministry. All too often, we rely on one metric—attendance—to measure the effectiveness of our ministry. As I said earlier, tracking attendance is an essential aspect of ministry, but counting the number of people in our chairs falls short of effectively evaluating what is truly important in youth ministry: developing disciple-making disciples. How do you gauge your youth ministry success? What's your measure of effectiveness?

An early ministry experience taught me a valuable lesson on evaluation and ministry change. As a college student, I volunteered in the youth ministry of a large mega-church. The Sunday night high school ministry at this church attracted hundreds of teenagers. It was high-energy, with music, skits, worship, and games. When I returned to school after the summer break to serve again with the youth ministry, I was surprised to hear that the leadership was planning to shelve the large group gathering in favor of small home groups. I became a leader for one of the small groups that were now organized according to grade and high school. You see, the leadership had evaluated the large group gathering and found that it was not producing the intended results. The evaluation revealed that the youth ministry was not hitting the intended target. They were not seeing significant numbers of students become disciples who make disciples, so they made radical changes to reach that goal.

Aims and Targets

Archery provides a clear example of the role of aims and targets. An archer must know the location of the target. The archer first takes aim with the bow and arrow to hit the target. She releases the arrow and drives it toward the target. If the arrow misses the target, it reveals the aim was not true. She then adjusts her aim to hit the target. Like an archer, youth leaders must know what they are aiming for. The aim of youth ministry is the same as the local church—to make disciples who make other disciples. Disciple-making teenage disciples is the target of youth ministry. The aims of youth ministry are what we do to reach the target. Ask yourself: *Am I happy with the current results of youth ministry? Am I missing the target in some aspect of my ministry?*

If you're missing your target, you need to check your aim. Just like you used metrics to measure the spiritual growth of teens and parents, you can use metrics to measure the effectiveness of your youth ministry. In this way, we seek to identify the accuracy and relevance of the specific intended outcomes for each program.[1] Metrics help you check your aim.

Using metrics involves systematically analyzing the various components of your ministry to teenagers. The essence of deconstruction is posing difficult questions and seeking honest answers. This chapter will examine three assumptions: (1) *The current structures and programs of my youth ministry produce disciple-makers*, (2) *parents are prepared to lead at home spiritually*, and (3) *teenagers will naturally come to value the church on their own.* To evaluate these assumptions and practices, we need to look at the Youth Ministry Arenas.

Youth Ministry Arenas

The arenas of youth ministry are the domains in which youth leaders operate. Think of the arenas in terms of time spent doing something. For most of the history of youth ministry, the sole arena has been working with teenagers. Working solely with teenagers is the arena most commonly referred to when we think about youth ministry. After all, it is a ministry to *youth*. In many cases, the reason someone chooses to work in youth ministry is *because* they love young people and want to see them come to Christ and grow as believers. Maybe you intentionally present the gospel to lost teens personally and at outreach events. Perhaps you have small group Bible studies to engage teens in God's Word. You also encourage your volunteer leaders to disciple young people. However, your discipleship strategy should include more than just the arena of teenagers in a youth group. A new approach to youth ministry is needed that focuses not only on students in a youth group but also on families and the church congregation. The three arenas of youth ministry are: teenagers in the youth group, teenagers in families, and teenagers in the congregation.

---

[1] See Doug Fields, *Your First Two Years in Youth Ministry: A Personal and Practical Guide to Starting Right* (Zondervan, 2002), 220.

Assumption: The Current Structures and Programs of My Youth Ministry Produce Disciple-Makers

Of all the assumptions you can have in youth ministry, this one is the most damaging. You may assume the things you are doing will make a lasting impact on the lives of teenagers. You want to believe that students who are active in your youth ministry for six years will graduate from high school and be able to spiritually reproduce themselves as disciple-makers. But your ministry may not be set up to do this.

Teenagers in the Youth Group

A healthy ministry invites young people into a relationship with Jesus Christ and helps them grow toward spiritual maturity. According to Mark Cannister, "We are not simply passing on the faith to teenagers; we are cultivating the faith of teenagers as we seek to merge their story with God's story."[2] Disciple-making begins by leading young people to a saving relationship with Jesus Christ.[3] Unbelievers and seekers need opportunities to hear the gospel. The next step is providing teenagers with the spiritual food from God's Word necessary for growth. A key component in establishing disciples is Bible study. Brian H. Crosby writes, "For an increasing number of teenagers today, the church is not just another place to receive biblical guidance and instruction; it is the only place to receive biblical guidance and instruction."[4] Biblical illiteracy is common in the church today.[5] In addition, research indicates young people lack a deep understanding of their

---

[2] Mark Cannister, *Teenagers Matter: Making Student Ministry a Priority in the Church* (Baker, 2013), 9.

[3] See Richard Ross, *Student Ministry and the Supremacy of Christ* (CrossBooks, 2009), 76.

[4] Brian H. Crosby, "The Reformed View," in *Youth Ministry in the 21st Century: Five Views* (Baker Academic, 2015), 50.

[5] See Christian Smith, *Souls in Transition: The Religious and Spiritual Lives of Emerging Adults* (Oxford University Press, 2009), 291.

faith.[6] Christian Smith, the lead researcher for the National Study of Youth and Religion, found that most students could not articulate their faith.[7] In youth ministry, leaders must help students move from spiritually lifeless to spiritually fruitful. This means leading teenagers from realizing, "I am a lost teenager" to declaring, "I am a disciple-making teenager."

Ministry Metrics for Teenagers in the Youth Group

I find it helpful to use the following six ministry metric categories for teenagers in the youth group:

1. evangelistic outreach
2. discipleship environments
3. fellowship activities
4. intergenerational worship
5. leadership development
6. service opportunities

Evangelistic Outreach

The greatest need of every teenager is to come to faith in Jesus Christ. Because most Christians accept Christ before the age of twenty-one, it is vitally important to present the gospel to young people in their teenage years.[8] To that end, youth ministry leaders must personally share the gospel with students and provide evangelistic events in which teenagers will be

---

[6] See David Kinnaman, *You Lost Me: Why Young Christians are Leaving the Church . . . and Rethinking Faith* (Baker, 2011),115.

[7] Christian Smith and Melinda Lundquist Denton, *Soul Searching: The Religious and Spiritual Lives of American Teenagers* (Oxford University Press, 2009), 120.

[8] See Grey Matter Research, "The Spiritual Journey: How Evangelicals Come to Faith" (2024), https://www.infinityconcepts.com/wp-content/uploads/2024/12/The-Spiritual-Journey-Downloadable.pdf

given opportunities to respond to God's saving work. Some leaders may feel pressure to focus on ministry and programs for the current members of the youth group at the expense of reaching lost teens in the community. But leaders must not lose focus on reaching lost teenagers. Evangelistic outreach is a necessary component of youth ministry.

Discipleship Environments

Students need opportunities to grow in their faith, and leaders must provide environments for discipleship. Preston Cave reminds ministry leaders, "The 'win' isn't salvation. The 'win' is transformation."[9] Healthy churches allow teenagers to respond to the gospel and help them grow spiritually as disciples of Jesus Christ. However, today's churches often fail to produce teenage disciples with a maturing faith. Research indicates that only 10 percent of teenagers who stay active in church after high school are "resilient disciples."[10]

Churches provide opportunities for teenage spiritual growth in five types of discipleship environments: church group, youth group, small groups, micro-groups, and mentoring relationships. More than likely, you already have a church group or congregational gathering for discipleship. Your church gathers for weekly worship in which your pastor preaches from God's Word. You may also provide a youth group gathering for teenagers where leaders present a message to challenge students toward Christian growth. Small groups are gatherings of students for relational connection and studying the Bible. Small groups are typically considered open or closed. Open small groups are open to both Christian and non-Christian students. You may organize groups according to age, gender, school, or geographic location. Closed small groups are designed for committed Christians. These micro-groups of three to five students are designed for Christian growth

---

[9] Preston Cave, *Family Ministry That Counts: A Fresh, Simple Approach to Growing Your Youth and Family Ministries Through the Gospel* (Ministry Cue, 2018), 74–75.

[10] See David Kinnaman and Mark Matlock, *Faith for Exiles: 5 Ways for a New Generation to Follow Jesus in Digital Babylon* (Baker, 2019), 15.

and discipleship. Finally, mentoring environments provide youth with an opportunity for one-on-one discipleship. Perhaps you might mentor a student who senses a call to ministry. Each of these environments follows a progressive design toward fewer and fewer participants.

Large group gatherings are for everyone. Open small groups are also for anyone but require a commitment to another gathering besides the larger group. Closed small groups (micro-groups) will attract even fewer students because they require an even greater level of commitment, and micro-groups provide a more significant opportunity for transparency and accountability. By design, mentoring relationships aren't for everyone. A leader typically invites one or two students to meet weekly. Eric Geiger and Jeff Borton observe, "Discipleship is not merely information transfer; it is life transfer."[11] These environments provide opportunities for adult leaders to model Christian faith for students. In chapter 5, I provide a more detailed examination of these environments and how to evaluate them in your context.

Fellowship Activities

Fun youth group activities have been the lifeblood of youth ministry since the beginning. These include activities such as laser tag, lock-ins, and amusement park trips. The key is to be intentional about your activities and help your leaders understand the purpose of fellowship. Fellowship activities provide opportunities for your adult volunteers to build relationships with students.

Intergenerational Worship

Generational gaps widen each year. Fostering a sense of community and understanding between different age groups is more critical than ever. Teenagers need more than worship in the youth group; they need to worship alongside other members of your congregation. Intergenerational worship

---

[11] Eric Geiger and Jeff Borton, *Simple Student Ministry: A Clear Process for Strategic Youth Discipleship* (B&H, 2009), chapter 2.

is a powerful way to bridge these gaps. These worship experiences allow teens to actively engage with and learn from older generations of your local congregation. I provide a more detailed examination of intergenerational worship (church group) as the first environment discussed in chapter 5.

Leadership Development

Healthy youth ministries provide training opportunities for students and volunteers. According to Doug Fields, "The success of a program is often directly related to the quality of leadership."[12] Effective discipleship requires strong adult relationships with youth.[13] Encourage youth workers to "make better efforts to learn teens' names, to strike up conversations with teens, to make themselves available in times of trouble and crisis, to work toward becoming models and partners in love and concern and sacrifice."[14] You need to train not only your adult volunteers but also your teenagers. Richard Ross writes, "Beyond taking responsibility for their own spiritual growth, teenage disciples need to prepare to disciple someone else."[15] Chapter 8 focuses on leadership development in more detail.

Service Opportunities

According to Ross, "Youth ministry should lead teenagers to look a lot like Jesus."[16] Jesus was a servant, and when you lead students to serve, you lead them to look like Jesus. Youth need opportunities to serve their church and community. Engaging teenagers in service benefits the church and empowers them to develop life skills, strengthen their faith, and cultivate a sense of purpose.

---

[12] Fields, *Your First Two Years in Youth Ministry*, 221.

[13] Smith and Denton, *Soul Searching*, 267.

[14] Smith and Denton, 269.

[15] Richard Ross, *The Senior Pastor and the Reformation of Youth Ministry* (LifeWay, 2015), 108.

[16] Ross, 95.

I designed the Youth Ministry Arenas survey questions in the appendix to help you test the assumption that your youth ministry's current structures and programs produce disciple-makers. Each question on the survey under Teenagers in the Youth Group supports the six ministry metric categories. You can test the assumptions about your ministry by responding to questions at the end of the chapter.

Assumption: Parents Are Prepared to Lead at Home Spiritually

Growing Christian teenagers need growing Christian parents. Parents may desire to lead spiritually at home but don't know how to lead. Part of your job is to help parents understand their role in the faith development of their teen and then help them spiritually lead at home. This means expanding your view of youth ministry beyond just teenagers in the youth group to the second arena of youth ministry—teenagers in families.

Expanding the arenas of youth ministry to more than just time with students is imperative. Most notably, the arena of focus in recent years has been parent/family ministry. The single most important influence on adolescents' religious and spiritual lives is their parents.[17] Youth ministers should not only plan their week around time with students but also time with parents. The result is a deeper and broader perspective on what it means to be in youth ministry.

Teenagers in Families

One of the most important things you can do in youth ministry to reach and disciple teenagers is to focus on reaching and discipling parents.[18] The

---

[17] Smith and Denton, *Soul Searching*, 56.

[18] See Smith and Denton, 82; Merton P. Strommen and Richard A. Hardel, *Passing On the Faith: A Radical New Model for Youth and Family Ministry* (Saint

degree to which a parent models faith directly impacts faith in adulthood.[19] Michael J. Anthony states, "Although there is a place for parents to formalize teaching and training, the natural flow of their lives offers the most fertile soil for knowing God personally."[20] Anthony et al. encourage a home environment where young people learn to listen to and obey God's voice and live in the power of the Holy Spirit as modeled by their family.[21]

Youth leaders can help parents model lasting faith.[22] According to Kenneth Boa, "When parents model what it is to love and walk with Jesus, they develop an authenticity that gives them authority and credibility when they teach and train their children."[23] Preston Cave encourages ministry leaders to "influence the influencers."[24] Parents spend nearly 3,000 yearly hours with a student compared to ministry leaders who spend approximately ninety yearly hours with that same student. Equipping parents for effective discipleship is an essential part of youth ministry leadership. Youth leaders should help parents move from spiritual wanderers to spiritual leaders. This means leading parents from admitting, "I am a lost parent" to declaring, "I am a disciple-making parent."

Mary's, 2000), 85; Vern Bengtson, Norella Putney, and Susan Harris, *Families and Faith: How Religion Is Passed Down Across Generations* (Oxford University Press, 2017), 195; Scott Myers, "An Interactive Model of Religiosity Inheritance: The importance of family context," *American Sociological Review* 61, no. 5 (October 1996): 865.

[19] See Carolyn McNamara Barry et al., "Religiosity and Spirituality during the Transition to Adulthood," *International Journal of Behavioral Development* 34, no. 4 (2010): 314.

[20] Michael J. Anthony and Michelle Anthony, eds., *A Theology for Family Ministries* (B&H Academic, 2011), 184.

[21] Anthony and Anthony, 184.

[22] See Richard Ross, *Youth Ministry That Lasts a Lifetime* (Seminary Hill, 2017), 50.

[23] Kenneth Boa, *Conforming to His Image: Biblical and Practical Approaches to Spiritual Formation* (Zondervan, 2001), 385.

[24] Cave, *Family Ministry That Counts*, 97.

Ministry Metrics for Teenagers in Families

I find it helpful to use the following six ministry metric categories for teenagers in families:

1. relationships with parents
2. parents of teenagers Bible study/support group
3. family fellowship activities
4. intergenerational worship
5. parents mentoring parents
6. family service project opportunities

Relationships with Parents

You must develop relationships with parents to share the gospel and encourage Christian growth. In my research, exemplary youth leaders stated that the primary parent ministry method is simply spending time with parents. Leaders were intentional about interactions with parents. They referred to casual conversations after church, at school sporting events, teen performances, etc. This deliberate approach to engaging parents in conversation is evidence of a relational context for parent ministry. The *Growing Young* research completed at Fuller Youth Institute revealed a like-minded commitment to teenagers and their families.[25]

Parents of Teenagers Bible/Support Group

Parents need the care and support of youth leaders and the church. Your church probably already has a Bible study, or Sunday school class made up of adults who are also parents of teenagers. Have you considered ways in

---

[25] See Kara Powell, Jake Mulder, and Brad Griffin, *Growing Young: Six Essential Strategies to Help Young People Discover and Love Your Church* (Baker, 2016), 196.

which this existing class could serve as an extension of your youth ministry? You might also facilitate a monthly gathering of parents of teenagers to discuss hot topics such as dating, smartphone use, and social media. Imagine a gathering of parents of teenagers in which you weren't asking for permission slips or looking for volunteers. When parents see you as a resource and support for their efforts to raise godly teenagers, you move from being the person who hangs out with young people to a minister who genuinely cares for the entire family.

Family Fellowship Activities

If you are like most leaders, you plan all of your activities with a focus solely on teenagers. However, you also need to provide "generation-integrated" opportunities that bring parents (and grandparents) and teenagers together for Bible study, fellowship, and service.[26] I am not suggesting that every activity should be family-focused. Instead, I suggest you consider planning a few events each year focusing on families. For instance, you might plan a family bowling night or a river tubing event. Family fellowship activities move your ministry from a siloed approach to a whole-family approach.

Intergenerational Worship

Just as with teenagers in the youth group, you need to encourage parents to participate in weekly worship. Effective parent ministry means helping moms and dads understand the importance of regular worship attendance. Parents and teenagers don't have to sit together in the worship service. When a parent is in the service, it communicates to a teenager that worship is essential.

---

[26] Bengtson, Putney, and Harris, *Families and Faith*, 202.

Parents Mentoring Parents

Parents can significantly benefit from guidance and support from others who have experienced similar situations. This form of peer support can build a stronger sense of community and foster Christian growth among adults in your church. Youth leaders can liaise between parents of teenagers and other adults in the congregation—organizing relational pairings of older adults with parents of teenagers. Pairing parents of teenagers with adults willing to mentor them can lead to stronger families and disciple-making parents.

Family Service Project Opportunities

Like your fellowship activities, you may focus all your service projects around teenagers engaging in ministry. However, students benefit from opportunities to serve alongside their parents. Family service projects give moms and dads a chance to demonstrate the importance of faith in a practical way. Parents and teenagers serving together should be integral to your youth ministry strategy.

A focus on parents is shown to have a lasting impact on teenagers. Seventy-four percent of teens say they mainly participate in youth group "to gain deeper knowledge about Jesus and the Bible."[27] This statistic indicated a high level of spiritual maturity among a majority of teens in the SAEFF survey. They didn't say, "my parents make me," or "I participate to be with friends," or even just "to have something to do." However, a deeper look at the survey results revealed more at work. Students who go to youth group to gain deeper knowledge had four things in common:

- Say parents value glorifying God over a successful career
- Say parents encourage their spiritual growth

---

[27] See Karen Jones, "Inspecting the Scaffolding for Adult Faith: A Student Perspective," a presentation on the results of the Student Assessment of Enduring Faith Factors (SAEFF), September 13, 2022.

- Believe there are adults in the church they can talk with about important spiritual issues
- Indicate that their church provides opportunities for teens to talk about significant spiritual issues[28]

Leaders must help parents move from spiritual wanderers to spiritual leaders. This means leading parents from admitting, "I am a lost parent," to declaring, "I am a disciple-making parent." When you commit to ministering to teenagers in families, you indicate that you have a broader view than just youth ministry. A commitment to families indicates a long-range view of ministry. As a youth minister, you have limited time to influence teenagers—once or twice a week for a maximum of six or seven years. But families influence for a lifetime. Your investments in parents of teenagers may not show the immediate results you want, but research indicates that it will pay dividends in the long run.[29]

I designed the Youth Ministry Arenas survey questions in the appendix to help you test the assumption that parents are prepared to lead at home spiritually. Each question on the survey under Teenagers in Families supports the six ministry metric categories. Additionally, you can test your assumptions about your ministry by reflecting on the questions at the end of the chapter.

Assumption: Teenagers Will Naturally Come to Value the Church on Their Own

Don't assume that teenagers will naturally develop a love and appreciation for your church. You need to take steps to intentionally lead young people to make lasting connections with members of your congregation. These lasting connections are the focus of the third arena of youth ministry: teenagers in the

[28] Jones, "Inspecting the Scaffolding for Adult Faith."

[29] Bengtson, Putney, and Harris, *Families and Faith*, 203.

congregation. This arena involves time spent developing ways to help teenagers fully engage in the overall life of the church. Young people want relationships with adults.[30] According to Kara Powell et al., "Adults underestimate how much kids want to be with us. Kids are far more interested in talking to caring, trustworthy adults than we think they are."[31] As Joyce Ann Mercer observes, youth ministry no longer means constructing "a parallel church experience for youth that operates separately and independently of the work, worship, education, and service going on in the rest of the congregation."[32]

Teenagers in the Congregation

It is not enough to focus on teenagers and parents.[33] Young people need deep connections to your church congregation. The *Sticky Faith* research of Kara Powell and Brad Griffin revealed that a predictive factor of lasting faith is "connection to the larger congregation through participation in intergenerational relationships and worship."[34] Similarly, Mark Cannister reports how "students feel valued, empowered, and honored when other adults ask them to contribute to meaningful ventures."[35] According to Cannister,

---

[30] See Mark Yaconelli, *Contemplative Youth Ministry: Practicing the Presence of Jesus* (Zondervan, 2006), 24.

[31] Kara Powell, Marshall Shelley, and Brandon O'Brien, "Is the Era of Age Segregation Over? After 50 years of student ministry, a researcher argues that the future will require bringing the generations together," *Leadership* 30, no. 3 (June 1, 2009): 47.

[32] Joyce Ann Mercer, "Emerging Scholarship on Youth and Religion: Resources for a New Generation of Youth Ministry," *Journal of Baptist Theology and Ministry* 13, no. 1 (Spring 2016): 77.

[33] Robert Wuthnow, *After the Baby Boomers: How Twenty- and Thirty-Somethings Are Shaping the Future of American Religion* (Princeton University Press, 2007), 13.

[34] Kara Powell and Chap Clark, et al., *Sticky Faith: Everyday Ideas to Build Lasting Faith in Your Kids* (Zondervan, 2011), 146.

[35] Mark Cannister, "Thinking Ecclesiologically: Teenagers Becoming Part of the Church," in *Adoptive Youth Ministry: Integrating Emerging Generations into the Family of Faith*, ed. Chap Clark (Baker Academic, 2016), 142.

"Transformation happens most deeply in the lives of teenagers when they are engaged in the broader life of the church and connected to a network of caring adults."[36]

In fact, the development of lasting faith is "not primarily about teenagers, it is about the entire church."[37] Many congregations are comprised of four or five generations. Hayden Shaw believes the local church should embody generational differences and model mutual encouragement to benefit the building of God's church.[38] The Effective Christian Education study found "a high correlation between caring adults and mature faith, growth in faith, congregational loyalty, and denominational loyalty among youth."[39] When teenagers see adults in their church as supportive and responsive to their needs, they are more likely to view God in the same way.[40] Mark Devries agrees, noting the essential nature of connectedness among teenagers and the church:

> If our goal is to create mature Christian adolescents, then maybe we should focus only on moms and dads. But our goal is not adolescent disciples. It is adult disciples. And adult disciples are shaped, as they move into adulthood, not simply by their parents' faith. When I asked groups of adults, "How many of you had at least one

---

[36] Cannister, "Thinking Ecclesiologically," 137.

[37] Brad Griffin and Jacob Mulder, "Churches Engaging Young People: Preliminary Research Findings and Implications for Youth Ministry Education" presentation at Association of Youth Ministry Educators, 2015.

[38] Hayden Shaw, *Sticking Points: How to Get 5 Generations Working Together in the 12 Places They Come Apart* (Tyndale, 2020).

[39] Merton Strommen and Richard Hardel, *Passing on the Faith: A Radical New Model for Youth and Family Ministry* (Saint Mary's, 2000), 215; Kenda Creasy Dean, *Almost Christian: What the Faith of Our Teenagers Is Telling the American Church* (Oxford University Press, 2010), 6.

[40] See Erin Smith and Robert Crosby, "Unpacking religious affiliation: Exploring associations between Christian children's religious cultural context, God image, and self-esteem across development," *British Journal of Developmental Psychology* 35, no. 1 (March 2017): 76–90.

person in your life, outside your mom and dad, who had as much or more influence on your faith than your parents did?" Always more than half the room raise their hands. An exclusive focus on the faith maturity of "teenagers" during their teenage years can be short-sighted.[41]

Andrew Root admonishes the integration of teenagers into the full life of the church. Root states, "Because we want our young people to hold onto their faith, we must provide them with opportunities to participate in the multigenerational life of the whole congregation."[42] The question is, How effective are your efforts to engage young people in the full life of your church? To answer that question, you need a final set of ministry metrics.

Ministry Metrics for Teenagers in the Congregation

I suggest using the following four ministry metric categories for teenagers in the congregation:

1. valuing the church as the body of Christ
2. building intergenerational relationships
3. church-wide fellowships
4. service opportunities

Valuing the Church as the Body of Christ

Youth leaders typically do a great job of leading teenagers to fall in love with the youth group; however, we don't usually do a great job helping them fall in love with the church. Students must develop a positive attitude toward

---

[41] JDFM Forum, "Interview with Mark Devries—Family-Based Youth Ministry: Then and Now" *Journal of Discipleship and Family Ministry* 4, no. 2 (Spring/Summer 2014).

[42] Andrew Root, *Revising Relational Youth Ministry: From a Strategy of Influence to a Theology of Incarnation* (InterVarsity, 2007), 214.

the church. They need to see the value of being part of the body of Christ. You need to express a positive attitude about your church to teenagers and lead your church to value teenagers. According to Mark Cannister, "In order for students to become connected to the whole church, the whole church must highly value community."[43]

Building Intergenerational Relationships

Healthy intergenerational relationships are the context for teen connection to the congregation. Leaders must actively seek to build relationships between young people and other age groups. The emphasis is on "bringing generations together" and helping teens "get to know adults." In my research study, exemplary leaders indicated "silo" ministries that operate with little connection to other ministries or members of the congregation were barriers to an effective connection of teenagers to the church family.

Church-Wide Fellowships

Teenagers need to participate in church-wide fellowships with believers of all ages. Engaging in these activities offers opportunities for both social and emotional development. These gatherings provide a unique environment that nurtures the spiritual growth of teenagers and fosters a sense of connection to the entire body of believers.

Service Opportunities

Youth need opportunities to serve alongside members of the congregation. In the exemplary churches I researched, if students are not involved in serving in some way, they are less likely to develop a connection to the congregation. Service opportunities allow leaders to help teenagers move from

---

[43] Cannister, *Teenagers Matter*, 119.

consumers to contributors. That means leading teenagers from saying, "I love my youth group," to declaring, "I serve Christ at my church."

I designed the Youth Ministry Arenas survey questions in the appendix to help you test the assumption that teenagers will naturally come to value the church on their own. Each question on the survey under Teenagers in the Congregation supports the four ministry metric categories. Review the questions at the end of the chapter to help you test the assumptions about your youth ministry.

What I Believe About Youth Ministry:

1. Youth ministries emphasizing discipleship in a caring and welcoming community provide opportunities for spiritual growth among teenagers.
2. Youth ministries that consider parents the most influential factor in shaping a student's faith prioritize intentional family connections.
3. Youth ministries emphasizing connection to the larger church body provide opportunities for intergenerational relationships.

David Baysinger, youth pastor at First Baptist Church, Corinth, Texas, led his team of volunteers to take the Youth Ministry Arenas Assessment. It provided valuable insights and helped affirm several needs David had previously identified. Areas the assessment led him to address included developing a clear disciple-making strategy, providing a smaller ratio of disciple-making relationships such as micro-groups, and a need to equip more leaders and parents.

The deconstruction of your ministry starts by considering how effective your church is in each arena. I encourage you to take the Youth Ministry Arenas Assessment in the appendix or online at deconstructingym.com. Taking an online assessment will automatically assign an overall score and scores for each of the three arenas. Scores are ranked high, medium, and low. If you score between 80–100, you are in the exemplary (high) category.

An exemplary score indicates that you perceive yourself to operate at a high level in the arena and have a highly effective ministry. A 60–79 score places you in the average (medium) category. An average score indicates proficiency in some elements of ministry but room for improvement in others. If you score 59 or lower, you are in the struggling (low) category. This means you understand the need for drastic improvement in the ministry arena. When you take the assessment online, you can download a free detailed report explaining your scores and giving you suggestions for improvement.

Try not to be too discouraged by your score. The assessment is meant to help you identify areas of strength and weakness. The focus should be on improvement. That's what this book is all about, helping you make improvements that lead to greater ministry success.

Testing the Assumptions

Test the assumptions about your youth ministry by responding to the following questions. Review the questions and invite others to dialogue with you concerning each.

Questions to Consider

1. In what ways are you leading effective evangelistic outreach?
2. To what extent do your discipleship environments produce disciple-makers?
3. How do you intentionally use fellowship activities to help your leaders build relationships with teenagers?
4. In what ways do you encourage intergenerational worship?
5. How are you fostering the leadership development of adult volunteers and students?
6. In what ways do you provide service opportunities for students?
7. In what ways are you intentionally developing relationships with parents?

8. How might you organize a parents of teenagers Bible study/support group?
9. In what ways are you providing family fellowship activities for youth and parents?
10. In what ways do you encourage intergenerational worship?
11. In what ways do you encourage parents mentoring parents?
12. In what ways do you provide family service opportunities for students and parents?
13. In what ways do you help students value the church as the body of Christ?
14. In what ways do you encourage youth participation in church-wide fellowships?
15. How are you encouraging healthy intergenerational relationships among students and the congregation?
16. In what ways do you provide service opportunities for students and members of the congregation?

CHAPTER 4

PROCESS METRICS

EVALUATING YOUR DISCIPLESHIP PATHWAY

Years ago, I led a youth discipleship weekend at my church called *Metamorphosis*. This DiscipleNow-type event featured fun activities, tons of food, discipleship groups, and a mission project. The young people stayed in host homes, and college students led the discipleship groups. Students experienced a weekend of intensive discipleship, and the event was a springboard opportunity for them to get involved in ongoing discipleship after the event. Metamorphosis weekend was a fantastic event for teens, yet events have limited impact if not strategically linked to ongoing discipleship.

The word translated as "transformed" in Rom 12:2 is *metamorphousthe*, from which we get the English word *metamorphosis*. It means "to change the form or essential nature of something."[1] It's the word we use to describe a

[1] See Frederick William Danker, ed., *A Greek-English Lexicon of the New Testament and Other Early Christian Literature*, 3rd ed., BDAG (University of Chicago Press, 2000), 639–40. Danker also notes that *metamorphousthe* refers "to change inwardly in fundamental character or condition."

caterpillar's process to become a butterfly. When the Bible speaks of transformation, it means radical change. Metamorphosis is not merely an outward change but a change in our very being. We were not only transformed in the past, but God is also working in us today.

In youth ministry, we have the privilege of being part of what God is doing in the lives of young people. Youth ministry plays a crucial role in shaping the spiritual foundation of young individuals. It provides an opportunity for students to come to know Jesus as savior, grow in their faith, and become active members of their church community. When your church has a clear discipleship process, you allow students and parents to see a way to experience spiritual transformation.

Deconstructing youth ministry involves testing the assumptions you have about the way you disciple students and parents. Although most leaders believe they prioritize disciple-making, participation in discipleship does not reflect this pastoral emphasis.[2] This chapter will lead you to examine your discipleship process for teenagers and parents by addressing the following assumptions: (1) *My church recognizes the need for discipleship*, (2) *my church understands the roles of a disciple and disciple-maker*, (3) *my church has a clearly defined discipleship process*, and (4) *my church communicates our discipleship process*. To evaluate these assumptions and practices, we must first examine the need for discipleship.

Assumption: My Church Recognizes the Need for Discipleship

We often interchange terms such as *spiritual formation* and *discipleship*, yet there are differences between the two. According to Dallas Willard, Christian spiritual formation is "the Spirit-driven process of forming the inner world of the human self in such a way that it becomes like the inner

[2] See Barna, *State of Discipleship: A Barna Report Produced in Partnership with The Navigators* (The Navigators, 2015), 66.

being of Christ himself."[3] It is the work of the Holy Spirit in the life of a believer. Spiritual formation is conformity to Christ (Rom 8:29; 12:2; 2 Cor 3:18; Gal 2:20; Eph 4:24; Col 3:10). My favorite definition of spiritual formation is from Robert Mulholland. Spiritual formation is "a process of being conformed to the image of Christ for the sake of others."[4] It is a process, like human growth, of moving from immature to mature. The goal of the process of spiritual formation is conformity to Christ. Conforming to Christ's image is the Holy Spirit's work of transformation (Rom 12:2). But conformity to Christ is not the endpoint of spiritual formation. The final result of formation in Christ is—"for the sake of others"—being a disciple-maker. As Rob Gallaty says, "The gospel came to you because it was heading to someone else."[5] I was saved from my sin by the gospel of Jesus Christ, not just for me, but also for those with whom I would share. The same applies to you and your students, parents, and volunteers. God has brought them the message of redemption so they would also declare that same message to others.

The word *discipleship* is not expressly found in Scripture. A word containing the suffix "ship" refers to a "state of being." Therefore, discipleship is the state of being a disciple. It refers to the present experience of a believer. When we talk about discipleship, the key ingredient is the presence of a disciple-maker. For me, spiritual formation refers to the personal work of God in the life of a Christian, and when a disciple-maker gets involved in a Christian's life—that's discipleship. A follower of Jesus experiences discipleship in a relationship with a disciple-maker. The Great Commission's task is for disciple-makers to make disciples, so the objective of your youth ministry is to help students and parents become disciples who make disciples.

---

[3] Dallas Willard, *Renovation of the Heart: Putting on the Character of Christ* (NavPress, 2021).

[4] M. Robert Mulholland, *Invitation to a Journey: A Road Map for Spiritual Formation* (IVP, 1993), 15.

[5] Rob Gallaty, *Growing Up, Revised and Updated: How to Be a Disciple Who Makes Disciples* (B&H, 2022), 1.

Pastors, authors, and theologians have described discipleship in various ways. Some are from the perspective of the end goal, and others are from the disciple's point of view.[6] Here are a few definitions.

A disciple is:

- one who follows Christ—Robert Coleman[7]
- one who adheres to Christ—Dietrich Bonhoeffer[8]
- someone who desires above all else to be like Christ—Dallas Willard[9]

---

[6] See Bob Dukes, *Maturity Matters: The Priority and Progress for Disciple Building in the Church* (Worldwide Discipleship Association, 2014), 43. I like Dukes's definition for its emphasis on an intentional process and the ministry of the church: "Discipleship is an intentional process, entrusted to the Church, where mature leaders help others progressively grow to Christlike maturity." Brandon Guindon, *Disciple-Making Culture: Cultivate Thriving Disciple-Makers Throughout Your Church* (Harrington Interactive Media, 2020), 19. Guindon defines discipleship as "the process of growth for the one being discipled, and disciple-making is the process that disciple-makers engage in when they invest into the lives of those God calls them to disciple." Gary Kuhne, "Follow-Up—An Overview," in *Discipleship: The Best Writing from the Most Experienced Disciple Makers* (Zondervan, 1981), 117. Kuhne refers to a disciple-maker as a multiplier. He says, "A multiplier is a disciple who is training his spiritual children to reproduce themselves." LeRoy Eims, *The Lost Art of Disciple Making* (Zondervan, 1978), 61. For Eims, the goal of discipleship is for believers to become "dedicated, mature, and fruitful disciples." Bobby Harrington and Alex Absalom, *Discipleship That Fits: The Five Kinds of Relationships God Uses to Help Us Grow* (Zondervan, 2016), 16. Harrington and Absalom state, "Being a disciple of Jesus simply means that you are modeling your life—your thoughts, your words, your actions, your everything—after the example and teaching Jesus has given us. And the related word *discipleship* simply refers to the process through which Jesus turns us into people who trust and follow him."

[7] Robert Coleman, *The Master Plan of Evangelism*, 2nd ed. (Revell, 2010), 33.

[8] Dietrich Bonhoeffer, *The Cost of Discipleship* (SCM Press, 2001), 17.

[9] Dallas Willard, *The Great Omission: Reclaiming Jesus' Essential Teachings on Discipleship* (HarperCollins, 2006), 24. Willard also says (303), "If I am Jesus' disciple that means I am with him to learn from him how to be like him," and Willard laments (40), "The most telling thing about the contemporary Christian is that

Discipleship is:

- the ongoing life of a disciple (believer in Christ) that involves following the Savior and becoming more like him—Aubrey Malphurs[10]
- an intentional relationship in which we walk alongside other disciples in order to encourage, equip, and challenge one another in love to grow toward maturity in Christ—Greg Ogden[11]
- someone who is following Jesus, being changed by Jesus, and is committed to Jesus's kingdom mission—Bobby Harrington and Alex Absalom[12]

Definitions of discipleship help us clarify our mission. They assist us in communicating with others what we are trying to do. Definitions of discipleship articulate in a few words what we desire to accomplish in a lifetime of service. I synthesized several definitions of discipleship into my own: *Discipleship is a lifelong relational journey toward Christlike maturity.*

Discipleship is lifelong. The journey toward Christlikeness takes a lifetime. On earth, there is never a sense that we have completely arrived at being like Christ. As a youth leader, you help teenagers begin this journey by inviting youth to accept Christ as their savior. Discipleship is walking alongside students as they pursue obedience to Christ. What about after high school or college? We must help teenagers understand the need to continue this pursuit into adulthood. Young people tend to be short-sighted, rarely looking to or planning for the future. Part of your job as a disciple-maker of young

---

he or she simply has no compelling sense that understanding of and conformity with the clear teachings of Christ is of any vital importance to his or her life, and certainly not that it is in any way essential."

[10] Aubrey Malphurs, *Strategic Disciple Making: A Practical Tool for Successful Ministry* (Baker, 2009), 34.

[11] Greg Ogden, *Transforming Discipleship: Making Disciples a Few at a Time* (InterVarsity, 2003), 129.

[12] Harrington and Absalom, *Discipleship That Fits*, 16.

people is to encourage students to continue the journey of faith after youth group, into young adulthood, and beyond.

Discipleship is relational. It is easy to think of discipleship as something you do. We often refer to discipleship as a program or ministry component in church work. However, discipleship is always relational.[13] It begins with a personal relationship with Jesus Christ and continues within the context of relationships with other believers. This dual focus on relationships enables believers to grow in their faith and fulfill the Great Commission.

In youth ministry, we don't want students to fall in love with our programs—we want them to fall in love with Jesus. We want to see teenagers come to faith in Jesus and grow in their knowledge and understanding of who he is. We intentionally lead students in discipleship because we know that an intimate relationship with Jesus transforms their lives. Simultaneously, we help students integrate into the church because relationships with peers and adults nurture them and prepare them for lifelong discipleship. Discipleship, therefore, is deeply relational, rooted in a vibrant relationship with Jesus and nurturing relationships with fellow believers.

Discipleship is a journey. Discipleship is progressive and ongoing. Paul writes about the journey in Phil 3:13, describing how he is "reaching forward to what is ahead." Discipleship is a continuous process of striving toward Christlike maturity. It is a dynamic journey rather than a static state. It is the picture of constant forward motion as believers learn and grow. I tend to describe discipleship in a linear fashion, but most people don't experience the life of a disciple in a straight-line path. Discipleship is full of ups and downs, twists and turns. We take great strides forward as we live in obedience to God's Word and take steps backward when we succumb to temptation and fall into sin.

---

[13] See Harrington and Absalom, 38.

The discipleship journey is not always easy. The path toward Christlike maturity requires perseverance. We face challenges, trials, and persecution. We experience loss, disappointment, and betrayal. James 1:2–4 encourages us, "Consider it a great joy, my brothers and sisters, whenever you experience various trials, because you know that the testing of your faith produces endurance. And let endurance have its full effect, so that you may be mature and complete, lacking nothing." The journey is an endurance race, not a sprint. The trials and difficulties we face are God's way of strengthening our faith, leading to greater maturity and completeness in Christ.

Discipleship is directional. Although the word *direction* does not appear in my definition, it is implied with the word *toward*. We are on a journey toward someone—Jesus. Our GPS is set to Christlikeness, and each day, we choose to either continue the journey toward Jesus or stray off the path. The directional nature of the journey is also pictured in our repentance from sin. The word *repent* means to "turn around" or change direction. It refers to making a U-turn. Before we were saved, you and I were on a journey toward death and destruction. But Christ intervened, and when we repented of our sins, he changed the direction of our lives toward himself. At times, it is a seemingly gradual and arduous journey. Paul talks about the gradual transformation taking place in 2 Cor 3:18, "We all, with unveiled faces, are looking as in a mirror at the glory of the Lord and are being transformed into the same image from glory to glory; this is from the Lord who is the Spirit." Our gradual transformation is the work of the Holy Spirit. The Spirit empowers us to overcome sin and develop Christlikeness.

We all know students and adults who believe in Christ, yet seem far from God. Either by their words or actions, they demonstrate a level of spiritual immaturity that sometimes causes us to doubt the genuineness of their conversion to Christ. However, just because someone isn't as far along the path as we are doesn't mean they aren't heading in the same direction. Disciple-makers must trust the work of the Holy Spirit. Even when we can't clearly see progress along the journey, we must trust that God is at work. Daniel Im says, "Disciples are formed *while moving* toward Christ."[14] Despite their present location, all believers are disciples who have embarked on a journey toward Christlike maturity.[15]

Discipleship's goal is Christlike maturity. The ultimate goal of our discipleship journey is to be like Christ. Paul reminds us of this goal in Eph 4:13, "until we all reach unity in the faith and in the knowledge of God's Son, growing into maturity with a stature measured by Christ's fullness." Christlike maturity means our thoughts, actions, character, and attitudes mirror the thoughts, actions, character, and attitudes of Jesus. This is obedience to Christ and God's Word. Jesus highlighted the importance of obedience in John 14:23, "If anyone loves me, he will keep my word. My Father will love him, and we will come to him and make our home with him." Discipleship is not merely knowing the teachings of Jesus but living out Christ's teachings. It means that we daily align our thoughts and actions with his Word. Through obedience to Christ, we demonstrate our love for him and allow the Holy Spirit to transform us into his likeness. In Eph 4:15, Paul urges believers to "grow in every way into him who is the head—Christ." Christlike maturity involves aligning every aspect of our lives with the character of Jesus.[16]

Christlike maturity means loving others and pursuing holiness. In John 13:34–35, Jesus said, "I give you a new command: Love one another. Just as I have loved you, you must also love one another. By this everyone will know that you are my disciples, if you love one another." People will know we are Christ's followers by our genuine, sacrificial love. It is a love that goes

---

[14] Daniel Im, *No Silver Bullets: 5 Small Shifts That Will Transform Your Ministry* (B&H, 2017), 33.

[15] See Michael J. Wilkins, *Following the Master: A Biblical Theology of Discipleship* (Zondervan, 1992), 221.

[16] Malphurs, *Strategic Disciple Making*, 34. Malphurs says, "To talk about Christian discipleship properly, we must use the term to refer to the growth of a disciple (Christian) in every area of his or her life."

beyond words to tangible actions that serve the needs of others. It's not the world's definition of love, but a love reflected in the life and death of Christ himself. In addition, Christlike maturity involves a commitment to holiness. Peter exhorts believers, "But as the one who called you is holy, you also are to be holy in all your conduct; for it is written, Be holy, because I am holy" (1 Pet 1:15–16). Christlike maturity means believers strive to live a life marked by purity and righteousness. The pursuit of holiness is not about perfection, but a sincere and continuous effort to obey God and his Word.

Youth ministry aims to help teenagers and parents be like Christ. You are inviting them on a lifelong relational journey toward Christlike maturity. Everything you do in ministry should lead to this. As you deconstruct your youth ministry, you should critically examine discipleship in your church. You can test the assumption that your church understands the need for discipleship by responding to the questions at the end of the chapter.

Assumption: My Church Understands the Roles of a Disciple and Disciple-Maker

My wife and I have raised two girls. Both of my daughters are now strong believers, and we are very proud of them. But raising them wasn't easy. It took hard work and dedication. And it took time. Raising a child is at least an eighteen-year commitment with lessons to be taught and caught, and mistakes to be made. Progress comes slowly, just a little bit at a time. But over time, an infant becomes a toddler, a child turns into an adolescent, and a young adult emerges from chaos.

Parenting children to adulthood is a great metaphor for discipleship—we desire to see students grow toward Christlike maturity. Spiritual parenting was one of the apostle Paul's favorite metaphors for discipleship. He used developmental language to describe spiritual growth in Ephesians 4. He refers to new believers as infants and children and declares that the goal of a Christian is to "grow in every way" toward maturity (Eph 4:13–15; 1 Cor 3:1–3; Col 1:28–29). Maturity is the "end product" that Paul is attempting to produce.[17] Paul clarifies what he means by maturity by saying that the purpose of existence is to be "conformed to the image of [God's] Son" (Rom 8:29).

Two Perspectives of Discipleship

I want to examine discipleship from two perspectives: disciple-maker (parent) and disciple (child). From the disciple-maker perspective, we seek to provide a process that helps teenagers grow toward Christlike maturity. From the disciple perspective, teenagers and parents must own their role in discipleship as they submit to Christ's authority and work in their lives.

Disciple-Maker

Discipleship mirrors the maturation process that occurs as humans grow from infancy to adulthood. Just as a parent nurtures and guides a child's growth, a disciple-maker commits to the Christian growth of a disciple. The parents' role is to meet the physical, emotional, and intellectual needs of a child. Parents also model behavior for their children. A child learns by observing and imitating his or her parent's actions and words. The parents' example serves as a blueprint for the child's thoughts, behaviors, and beliefs. Through time and relational investment, parents come to know their children and understand their unique needs and challenges. The result is a parent-child bond that shapes both lives.

Similarly, a disciple-maker's role is to lead a person to faith in Jesus Christ and nurture growth toward Christlike maturity. A disciple-maker also models Christlikeness for the disciple and echoes the apostle Paul's admonition, "Imitate me, as I also imitate Christ" (1 Cor 11:1). A disciple observes and learns from the disciple-maker's journey. The role of a disciple-maker

---

[17] See Ogden, *Transforming Discipleship*, 103.

requires a "life investment" in which a believer becomes a living testimony of God's work.[18]

Disciple

The role of a disciple is similar to a child's role in a relationship with a parent. When a child receives care and unconditional love from a parent, strong bonds form. As parents demonstrate dependability and listen to the concerns of a child, trust builds between the two. Trust forms the foundation of how a child receives instruction and correction. If a child trusts a parent, he or she will more likely respond in obedience. Children learn that even when they don't understand or agree with a command, they can trust that their parents want what is best for them.

The word *disciple* means "learner." A disciple is "an intentional learner from Jesus,"[19] and the role of a disciple is to learn from Christ through the example of a disciple-maker. Trust plays a vital role between disciple-makers and disciples. Trust holds everything together. Over time, a disciple learns to trust the guidance and instructions of a disciple-maker. A disciple learns by example what it means to grow toward Christlike maturity. Paul describes his journey toward Christlike maturity when he states, "When I was a child, I spoke like a child, I thought like a child, I reasoned like a child. When I became a man, I put aside childish things" (1 Cor 13:11). Disciples are born to reproduce. Ultimately, a disciple must decide to take steps toward becoming a disciple-maker.

The Bible teaches that all believers in Jesus experience redemption through his sacrifice on the cross. When Paul refers to some of the Corinthians as "infants in Christ" and others as "mature," he is not talking about unbelievers and believers (1 Corinthians 2–3). He is making a distinction between growing Christians and those who are new to the faith. There is no mention of various classes of Christians in the Bible. According

---

[18] Ogden, 109.

[19] Harrington and Absalom, *Discipleship That Fits*, 17.

to Aubrey Malphurs, "Scripture does not draw a line in the sand between ordinary Christians and active Christians. The reality is that all Christians are living at some point along the discipleship or maturity continuum."[20] Therefore, every believer is a disciple of Jesus, whether they realize it or not.

Understanding the roles of a disciple and disciple-maker is crucial for an effective discipleship process. You need volunteers and parents who understand what it means to be disciple-makers to help teenage disciples grow toward Christlike maturity. As you deconstruct your youth ministry, you can test the assumption that your church understands these roles by reflecting on the questions at the end of the chapter.

Assumption: My Church Understands the Need for a Discipleship Process

Most churches do not have a clear process for Christian maturity and few churches are disciple-making churches. Finding a church with a well-thought-out, clearly communicated pathway for reproducing disciple-makers is rare. Churches are reaching teenagers and leading them to faith in Christ, but few are leading those teens to become disciple-makers. Disciple-making teenagers certainly exist in many churches today, but few churches have an intentional process to develop more of them.

Grey Matter Research conducted a study for Discipleship.org, which studied the characteristics of churches in the United States.[21] The study used five church categories:

- Level 1—churches are in decline
- Level 2—plateauing churches
- Level 3—churches adding members

---

[20] Malphurs, *Strategic Disciple Making*, 31.

[21] See Grey Matter Research, *National Study on Disciple Making in USA Churches: High Aspirations Amidst Disappointing Results*, Discipleship.org and Exponential (March 2020).

- Level 4—reproducing churches
- Level 5—multiplying churches

They found evidence that Level 4 churches that regularly reproduce disciples and emphasize disciple-making exist, but they are rare. Just under 5 percent of churches qualified as Level 4. Most troubling, they could not find any churches that qualify as Level 5.[22] The bottom line: Most churches are not reproducing disciples.

The Engel Scale

James F. Engel introduced his scale in his book *What's Gone Wrong with the Harvest?* to understand the steps a person goes through to become a disciple-maker.[23] It illustrates how everyone who becomes a Christian progresses through several steps on a journey from no awareness of God to becoming a disciple-maker. The scale is helpful as an evaluation tool for evangelistic strategies, but it can also help churches hone their discipleship process. For example, if your first step assumes individuals come to your church ready to accept Christ, the scale should prompt you to deconstruct the process by testing that assumption.[24] The Engel Scale appears in various forms describing each step, but they follow this basic pattern:

1. No awareness of God
2. Some awareness of God
3. Contact with Christians

---

[22] Grey Matter Research, *National Study on Disciple Making in USA Churches.*

[23] See James F. Engel and Wilbert Norton, *What's Gone Wrong with the Harvest?* (Zondervan, 1975).

[24] See Tony Morgan, "Developing an Effective Discipleship Strategy: The Ultimate Guide," The Unstuck Church (October 24, 2022), https://theunstuckgroup.com/developing-an-effective-discipleship-strategy-the-ultimate-guide/. Morgan says, "Even though our spiritual journeys don't begin when we put our trust in Jesus, most churches act like they do."

4. Interest in Jesus Christ
5. Decide to investigate Jesus
6. Grasp the truth about Jesus
7. Understand the implications of faith in Jesus
8. Acceptance of Christian truth
9. Acceptance of the implications
10. Decision to surrender to Christ
11. Gaining confidence in their decision
12. Experiencing change in their life
13. Learning the basics of their faith
14. Learning the Christian disciplines
15. Sharing their faith with others[25]

The scale can be reduced to broad categories for developing a discipleship process. For example, the following five categories summarize the fifteen steps: (1) No interest in God, (2) understanding the gospel, (3) believing, (4) learning basics/growing Christian, and (5) disciple-maker. I'll use the five categories below to describe the discipleship processes in the three arenas.

Discipleship is essential. As a youth leader, you understand this, but your students, parents, and volunteers may not. Deconstructing youth ministry means challenging the assumptions your church has about discipleship. You can test the assumption that your church understands the need for a discipleship process by responding to the questions at the end of the chapter.

Assumption: My Church Has a Clearly Defined Discipleship Process

When I consult with youth leaders, one of the first questions I ask concerns their discipleship process for students and parents. In these conversations,

---

[25] See Evangelical Alliance, "What Is the Engel scale?" https://www.eauk.org/great-commission/what-is-the-engel-scale; Engel and Norton, *What's Gone Wrong with the Harvest?*

few can clearly articulate their discipleship process. Are you ready to clarify your process? Let's start with the end in mind.

Characteristics of Christlike Maturity

When developing a discipleship process for teenagers and parents, you must keep your goals in mind. What should eighteen-year-old believers look like, spiritually speaking, when they graduate from high school? How should parents act toward their teenagers and others? What are the Christlike characteristics you seek to develop in students and parents? An excellent place to start is the fruit of the Spirit. Paul tells us in Gal 5:22–23 that the results of the Holy Spirit's work in our life are as follows: love, joy, peace, patience, kindness, goodness, faithfulness, gentleness, and self-control. The fruit of the Spirit is the work of God in our lives, and your ministry should encourage students and parents to demonstrate each one. But you may have additional characteristics in mind. You should create your own list, but here are a few characteristics to consider.

Faithful amid Opposition

When I think of a spiritually mature student, I have in mind a young person who stands up for their belief, no matter the consequences. I think about the countless students I've spoken with over the years who lamented being ostracized, ridiculed, or rejected because they stood for Christ. When a young person decides to speak or act based on their Christian beliefs, regardless of the consequences, it is a mark of maturity.

Evangelistic

Similarly, when a student or parent regularly shares the gospel with someone, they demonstrate a deeper level of spiritual commitment. An evangelistic teen or parent obeys Christ's command to "make disciples." They also demonstrate an understanding of Scripture and the basics of how to help a person come to faith in Christ. Speaking to someone about sin, death, forgiveness, Christ's sacrifice on the cross, and the need for repentance shows that you clearly understand the Christian faith. An evangelistic teen or parent demonstrates Christlike maturity.

Follow Christ's Teachings

You want students and parents to follow the teachings of Jesus obediently. In John 8:31–32, Jesus declares that true disciples follow his teachings. "Then Jesus said to the Jews who had believed him, 'If you continue in my word, you really are my disciples. You will know the truth, and the truth will set you free.'" The phrase "To continue in my word" means that believers agree with Christ's teachings and live in obedience to them.[26]

These and other characteristics should form the basis of your "end product"—students and parents as disciple-makers demonstrating Christlike maturity. I suggest you gather several students, parents, and leaders to help you develop your list. You might also involve your deconstruction team (chapter 6).

The Discipleship Process

In Eph 4:12, Paul uses the Greek word *katartismos*, translated as "training." The word refers to "adjustments that result in a complete preparedness."[27] The preparedness necessary to complete a complex task requires time, knowledge, dedication, and experience. In the same verse, Paul uses the word *oikodomeen*, translated as "build up." This word refers to construction or the "act of building a house."[28] Like preparedness, construction takes

---

[26] Malphurs, *Strategic Disciple Making*, 55.

[27] See Timothy Friberg, Barbara Friberg, and Neva F. Mille, *Analytical Lexicon of the Greek New Testament* (Trafford, 2006), 221.

[28] See *Strong's Exhaustive Concordance*, οἰκοδομή, https://Biblehub.com/greek/3619.htm.

time. A builder brings various pieces and parts together over time. Paul uses these words to demonstrate that discipleship is a process—a process that takes time and is progressive.

Examples of processes are all around us today. From baking a cake, developing a budget, triaging a patient, cleaning a room, and changing the oil in a car—each requires specific steps to complete the task. A process is a series of progressive and interdependent steps by which an end is attained. A discipleship process seeks to move people from one step to the next. Each step encourages progressively deeper spiritual growth. One step of the process builds on the previous step. A discipleship process is interdependent because each step is connected to the others.

Eric Geiger and Jeff Borton's *Simple Student Ministry* is one of the best and most helpful books on creating a discipleship process for youth ministry. Geiger and Borton outline the basics of a discipleship process using four keywords: clarity, movement, alignment, and focus.

> The process should be crystal clear (clarity) and move students to greater levels of spiritual commitment (movement). All of your programs and leaders should be aligned (alignment) to the process God gives you. And you should leverage (focus) all your energy and resources on your discipleship process.[29]

For Geiger and Borton, a discipleship process begins with a purpose or mission statement. They declare, "Your purpose should be a process."[30] A mission statement describes the purpose of your ministry in a single sentence. It answers the question of why your ministry exists.[31] Your discipleship process is like a blueprint for your ministry. Aubrey Malphurs says, "From a discipleship perspective, the church's mission involves both making disciples

---

[29] Eric Geiger and Jeff Borton, *Simple Student Ministry: A Clear Process for Strategic Youth Discipleship* (B&H, 2009), 19.

[30] Geiger and Borton, 208.

[31] Malphurs, *Strategic Disciple Making*, 88.

(evangelism) and maturing them (edification)."[32] Your church or youth ministry may have a mission statement, but does it articulate your process? It may be biblical, but does it communicate how you intend to accomplish the mission? Here's an example of a weak mission statement without a clear process:

Our youth ministry exists to make disciples of Jesus Christ.

This is a solid, biblical statement but lacks any indication of process. How does your youth ministry intend to make disciples? What are the steps to becoming a disciple of Jesus Christ? How are the various environments and programs connected to your purpose?

Writing a Discipleship Process Within a Mission Statement

If your youth ministry does not have a mission/process statement, then you should prioritize developing one. Writing a youth ministry mission statement that describes your discipleship process requires careful reflection. I suggest involving your deconstruction team (chapter 6) in this process. First, you need to take your list of characteristics of Christlike maturity and synthesize them into categories. Next, consider how you might develop these characteristics in students and parents. Write a few phrases that capture the essence of your goals. Place these phrases in an order reflecting your understanding of how Scripture describes spiritual growth.[33]

Here's an example of a youth ministry mission statement:

Our youth ministry wants to get to know teenagers and invite them to become Christians so they can grow closer to God and tell others about him.

Although it is a little wordy, this mission statement does an excellent job of describing the ministry's intentions. This youth group desires to build

[32] Malphurs, 78.

[33] Geiger and Borton, *Simple Student Ministry*, 42.

relationships, share the gospel, help believers grow spiritually, and encourage them toward Christian service. These are excellent process points. We can strengthen the statement with action verbs. A little fine-tuning of the phrases can lead to this statement:

> *We exist to help teenagers discover Jesus, connect with believers, grow in Christ, and multiply disciples.*

We can use the action verbs in the statement to summarize the steps of the process. The key verbs in the statement are *discover*, *connect*, *grow*, and *multiply*. Form follows function. The steps of your process should correspond to the discipleship environments of your ministry.[34] Do you have worship and small groups? If so, your mission statement should describe how these environments connect to help students grow toward Christlikeness. In the example statement above, we want to connect the four verbs with existing or new environments or programs in our youth ministry. What environments or events do you have that help students discover who Jesus is and help them understand the gospel? Chances are your main worship gathering accomplishes this step. Do you have a program that helps teenagers connect relationally with others to study God's Word? Your youth group gathering probably fits the bill. What environments help teenagers grow toward Christlikeness? You probably have several in mind, but you should select one to be the primary focus of this step. Perhaps small groups become the main focus of discipleship at this step. Finally, what do you do to help students multiply as disciple-makers? If you offer monthly service opportunities, those projects become your process's final step.

Your youth ministry structure should be built around the discipleship process, with everyone working together to encourage movement. When all of your environments, events, and programs connect, believers see a clear

---

[34] See Tony Morgan, *The Unstuck Church: Equipping Churches to Experience Sustained Health* (Thomas Nelson, 2017), 105.

path toward Christlike maturity. Each becomes a tool to move students through the process. When you have a clear discipleship process, the one message that gets communicated above all others is how people can take the next step in their spiritual journey.[35]

Discipleship in Three Arenas

The uniqueness of deconstructing youth ministry is developing a discipleship process through the lens of the three arenas. You are not just building a discipleship process for teenagers, you are working with others in your church to develop a discipleship process for parents. For the third arena, you are partnering with church leaders to help students establish connections to the church congregation as a whole. To illustrate how you can begin to think of discipleship within the three arenas, I will use the descriptions of each arena from chapter 3, along with the Engel categories and mission statement action verbs from above.

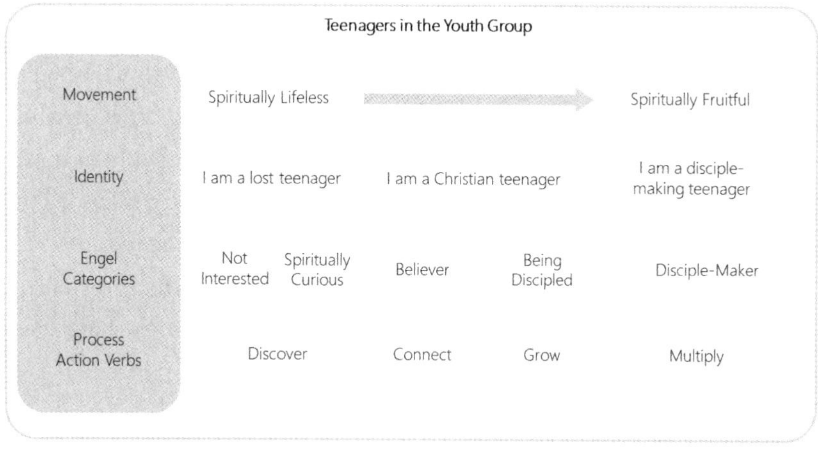

FIGURE 2: TEENAGERS IN THE YOUTH GROUP

[35] Morgan, 135.

Discipleship with Teenagers in the Youth Group (Figure 2) is about moving students from spiritually lifeless to spiritually fruitful. You can identify students in three broad categories. Lost teenagers are spiritually lifeless while disciple-making teenagers are spiritually fruitful. In between are growing Christian teenagers. The Engel Scale descriptions help you further define students in each category. Finally, the mission statement action verbs *discover*, *connect*, *grow*, and *multiply* correspond to each category. You will have different action verbs for your discipleship process, but this example should give you a picture of discipleship with teenagers in the youth group. Think about where you would place your students. How many would you put in the lost teenager category? How many teenagers would you consider disciple-makers? What are you doing to help students move from spiritually lifeless to spiritually fruitful? The next chapter will help you think about how your environments, events, and programs can help accomplish this task.

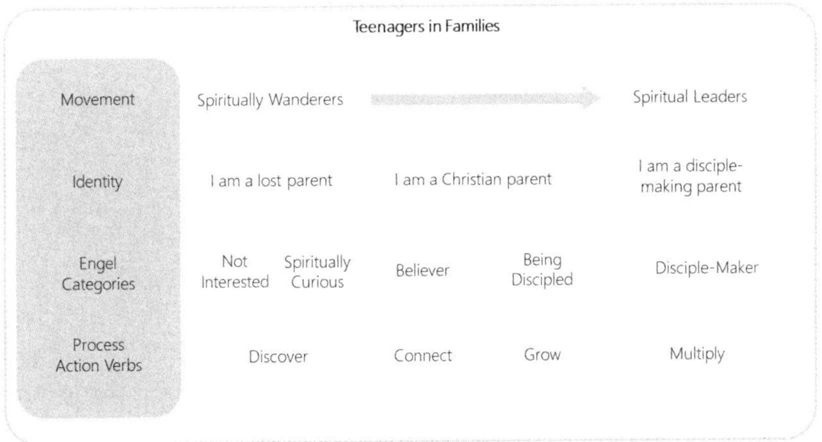

FIGURE 3: TEENAGERS IN FAMILIES

Discipleship with Teenagers in Families (Figure 3) involves moving parents from spiritual wanders to spiritual leaders. You can identify parents in three broad categories. Lost parents are spiritual wanders, while disciple-making parents are spiritual leaders. In between are growing Christian parents. As with Teenagers in the Youth Group, the Engel Scale descriptions help you further understand parents in each category. Finally, the mission statement action verbs (you'll want to insert your own) also correspond to the parent category. I use *discover*, *connect*, *grow*, and *multiply* for this example. This chart should help you better understand parents' spiritual growth and identify where they are in the process. Do you know the spiritual condition of parents? How many parents would you consider spiritual wanderers? How many disciple-making parents do you have? In what ways are you encouraging parents toward Christlike maturity? Who are you partnering with in your church to help parents grow?

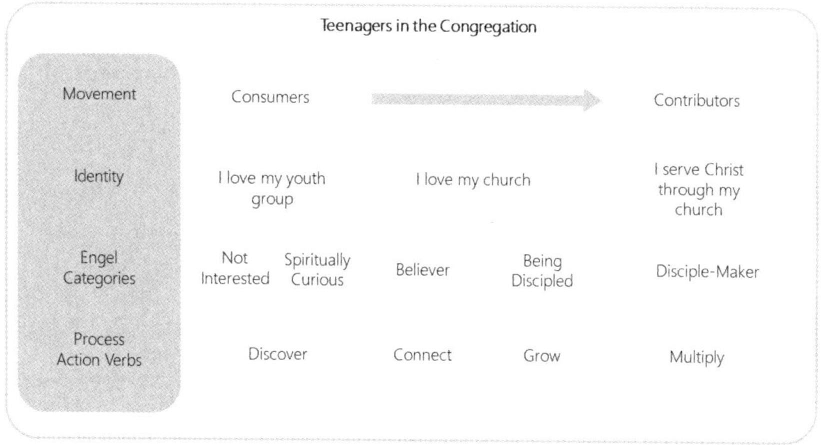

FIGURE 4: TEENAGERS IN THE CONGREGATION

Discipleship with Teenagers in the Congregation (Figure 4) focuses on moving students from consumers to contributors. You can identify teenagers in three broad categories. Students who love the youth group but have little connection to the rest of the congregation are consumers. Young people who desire to serve Christ through service in the church, community, and world are contributors. In between are teens who are growing to love your church. The Engel Scale descriptions help you see the nuance of each category.

Finally, the mission statement action verbs—*discover*, *connect*, *grow*, and *multiply*—take on a new meaning in Teenagers in the Congregation. For example, you are excited when a teen accepts Christ and falls in love with your youth group because of relational connections. However, part of your job is also to help young people *Discover* how your youth group relates to the congregation as a whole. You not only want young people to *Connect* with peers and youth volunteers, but you want students to develop relational connections with members of your congregation. Christian *Growth* happens in the youth group context, but you also want to foster relationships with other adults so students grow to see their place in the congregation. Finally, you rejoice when students desire to *Multiply* as disciple-makers through service projects with teenagers in the youth group. However, you must also provide opportunities for youth to serve alongside members of your church. This chart should help you expand your view of youth discipleship and challenge you to identify where your students are in this process. How many young people in your youth group would you consider consumers? How many are contributors? In what ways are you encouraging teens to move forward in this process? Who are you partnering with in your church to help connect teenagers to the congregation?

Barna Research revealed that "exemplar leaders say that having a clearly articulated plan is a key factor in a thriving discipleship program—and this is an area where many church leaders see room for improvement."[36] The goal is disciple-making teenagers, disciple-making parents, and teenagers and parents who serve Christ through the church. In chapter 9, I will show you how to connect your environments, events, and other elements to the discipleship process in each arena. Deconstructing youth ministry means evaluating your discipleship process. You can test the assumption that your church has a discipleship process by responding to the questions at the end of the chapter.

---

[36] Barna, *State of Discipleship: A Barna Report Produced in Partnership with The Navigators* (The Navigators, 2015), 66.

Assumption: My Church Communicates Our Discipleship Process

A clear discipleship process is worthless if no one knows about it. You must communicate your process so that people understand where they are in the process and how to take the next step. According to Ken Braddy, "Remember, if we want to make disciples, not only should we (the leaders) know the process, but the members of our churches must know it too. If people don't know the next step to take, they'll stall out in their discipleship process."[37]

The most successful process-oriented churches constantly talk about the next steps. It requires total buy-in from staff and volunteers to communicate your process. Your process should appear everywhere at your church. You should see references to your process in your youth room, on social media, on your website, in small group gathering spaces, on signage, on coffee mugs, and backpacks.

In your youth group gatherings each week, someone on stage or video should reference at least one part of your process. Many churches use a monthly calendar to dedicate time to one aspect a week. For example, you would talk about *Discover* on the first Sunday of the month. On the second Sunday, you'd emphasize *Connect* and so on. One reason to reduce your process to a few key action verbs or short phrases is to help it be memorable. According to Peter Drucker, you want your process to be short enough to "fit on a T-shirt."[38]

Illustrate Your Process

Young people today are image-driven. Images matter to teens. Students use images every day to communicate via social media. That means you

---

[37] Ken Braddy, "5 Steps to Create a Discipleship Plan," Lifeway Research, February 11, 2022, https://research.lifeway.com/2022/02/11/5-steps-to-create-a-discipleship-plan/.

[38] Peter Drucker and Jim Collins, *The Five Most Important Questions You Will Ever Ask about Your Organization* (Jossey-Bass, 2008), 13.

should pay attention to how you communicate your process. I suggest you develop a series of images or icons to correspond to each process step. To illustrate what I mean, let's return to the four action verbs from above. The *Discover* step of the process might utilize a simple icon of an open Bible, with a cross prominently displayed in the center of the open pages. For *Connect*, you might use an icon depicting two simplified human figures shaking hands, indicating fellowship and friendship. The *Grow* graphic might use an icon of a plant with leaves growing upward. Finally, *Multiply* could be illustrated with an icon of two hands gently holding a heart. Chances are you and your team can come up with better graphic ideas to communicate your process. I suggest enlisting several students to assist with this process. These young people will appreciate the opportunity to contribute, and you will benefit from using images and graphics that pass the "cool" test.

Discipleship Process Examples

As you consider your discipleship process, it can be helpful to learn from others. Here are a few examples of youth ministry mission statements and how they describe their discipleship process. Note the various ways leaders communicate a similar process described in this chapter.

The HUB Student Ministry at Houston's First Baptist Church

The vision of the HUB Student Ministry is to see students Gather, Grow, Give, and Go to see students have King Hearts and live Kingdom Lives.

First West Monroe Student Ministry

The discipleship process of First West Student Ministry is the same as the church: Worship, Reach, Equip, and Multiply.

Lakepointe Church Student Ministry

The process for the student ministry is the same as the church as a whole: Know God, Find Freedom, Discover Calling, and Make a Difference.

First Baptist Church of LaPlace

We at LPFBC exist to Reach people for Christ, to Disciple people in Christ, and to Send people out to impact generations in His name. The keywords that express our mission are: Reaching, Discipling, and Sending.

New Zion Baptist Church

The mission statement of New Zion's youth ministry is to Be One with Christ and Be One as a Community. The core values are *Belonging Together, Believing Together, and Becoming Together.*

Testing the Assumptions

Deconstructing youth ministry means evaluating your discipleship process. You can test the assumptions raised in this chapter by reflecting on the following questions. Review the questions and invite others to dialogue with you concerning each.

Questions to Consider

1. Does your ministry produce new disciples? Does it produce disciple-makers?
2. Do believers in your church understand the definitions of a disciple and discipleship?
3. To what extent do students, parents, and volunteers in your church understand the goal of discipleship?
4. How do you model Christlikeness and encourage others to be like Christ?

5. To what extent do young people, parents, and volunteers understand the definitions of a disciple and disciple-maker?
6. Who are you currently discipling?
7. To what extent does your youth ministry communicate the goals and outcomes of discipleship?
8. Do you use the term *disciple* to describe believers? Why or why not?
9. Do your students, leaders, and parents of teenagers understand the necessity of discipleship?
10. In what ways do you make discipleship a priority in your youth ministry?
11. Does your church have a straightforward discipleship process?
12. In what ways might you use the Engel scale to evaluate your youth ministry environments and events?
13. Do your people know the characteristics of a mature believer and how your ministry helps them develop those characteristics?
14. Do you have a discipleship process for your youth ministry?
15. Does your mission statement describe your process?
16. Does your discipleship process apply to all three arenas?
17. How well can youth, parents, and volunteers articulate your discipleship process?
18. In what ways do students, parents, and volunteers see examples of your process in your building?
19. In what ways do graphics and icons help you communicate your process?

For Further Reading

Geiger, Eric, and Jeff Borton. *Simple Student Ministry: A Clear Process for Strategic Youth Discipleship*. B&H, 2009.

Malphurs, Aubrey, *Strategic Disciple Making: A Practical Tool for Successful Ministry.* Baker, 2009.

Morgan, Tony. *The Unstuck Church: Equipping Churches to Experience Sustained Health*. Thomas Nelson, 2017.

CHAPTER 5

ENVIRONMENTAL METRICS

ASSESSING YOUR DISCIPLESHIP ENVIRONMENTS

I love living in South Louisiana. There are wonderful people here, and I love the New Orleans cuisine. But one of my favorite things is the climate. We are a zone 9 climate on the USDA Cold Hardiness Map. For reference, south Florida is zone 10, and Hawaii is zone 11. These three zones represent the warmest climates in the United States. The Gulf Coast region in which I live enjoys a subtropical climate. Tropical plants that would struggle in other parts of the country can thrive here. My backyard boasts banana trees and palm trees. I'm not an expert gardener. I just like looking at plants, but I know that certain plants can only grow in specific regions where climate conditions are just right. For most plants to thrive, they need an optimal environment.

In his book *Transforming Disciples*, Greg Ogden shares the illustration of a hothouse. A hothouse is a type of greenhouse designed for growing plants requiring high heat and humidity. Ogden says, "Hothouses maximize the environmental conditions so that living things can grow at a rate greater than would exist under normal circumstances."[1] These specialized structures require precise temperature and humidity for tropical plants. The hothouse produces the optimal environment for tropical plants to thrive in climates with colder conditions.

What is the point of this little horticultural segment? Your students need optimal environments for discipleship. The culture in which teens live today is cold and dry. On their own, most teens will struggle to grow spiritually. But when your church provides discipleship environments, teens can thrive spiritually and grow toward Christlike maturity. You don't want to merely help students spiritually survive—you want to see them thrive! Discipleship environments are the avenues by which spiritual growth occurs. To move students and parents to become disciple-makers, you need discipleship environments. The five discipleship environments discussed in this chapter are the church group, youth group, small groups, micro-groups, and mentoring relationships. Which environment is best or ideal? There are no silver bullets for discipleship. The truth is Jesus used a variety of environments. He trained disciples in large groups and smaller gatherings. Jesus taught the multitudes and the Twelve—and sometimes just Peter, James, and John. The point is that discipleship can take place in a variety of environments.

Deconstructing youth ministry is about critically examining your ministry to students and their parents. It includes questioning why you do what you do in youth ministry and the environments your church offers. In my conversations with youth leaders around the country, it won't surprise you to learn that every one of them shared that their church provides congregational worship (church group) and some form of Bible study program (small group). But why? Why are these two environments the status quo?

As you deconstruct your ministry, you should question everything, including the most basic elements. I'm not saying you should do away with congregational worship and small groups, but I suggest you examine why

---

[1] Greg Ogden, *Transforming Discipleship: Making Disciples a Few at a Time* (InterVarsity, 2003), 153.

you offer these environments and what you might do to improve them as elements of your discipleship process. I also want you to consider the possibility that if you are not getting the desired results using only one or two environments, you should consider one of the other ones discussed in this chapter. Discipleship environments should be the centerpiece of your ministry to youth and parents. If they are not, you should make radical changes to provide specific opportunities for Christian growth.

Deconstructing youth ministry involves testing your assumptions about the effectiveness of your discipleship environments for youth and parents. This chapter will lead you to examine your discipleship environments by addressing the following assumptions: (1) *My volunteers understand the need to build godly relationships with teenagers and parents*, (2) *my ministry provides discipleship environments for optimal spiritual growth,* and (3) *the entry points of my ministry effectively connect people to our discipleship environments.* To evaluate these assumptions and practices, we first need to examine the importance of relationships.

Assumption: My Volunteers Understand the Need to Build Godly Relationships with Teenagers and Parents

People are messy. They're not perfect, so they make mistakes. As a result, some leaders avoid developing relationships. Perhaps you've felt this way (or currently feel this way) because of damaging relationships in the church. A student you saw as a spiritually mature leader may have been caught in a public sin. Perhaps you're still bruised from a hurtful conversation with a parent, which has you questioning everything about your call to ministry. Your relationship with your senior pastor may be strained, and you are considering leaving the church. The fact is relationships are hard. But just because something is hard doesn't mean we should avoid it.

One of the ways youth leaders avoid building relationships is by focusing on programs instead of people. Programs are easy—well, at least easier than people. You can plan extraordinary gatherings and spend lots of time on your messages and curriculum without being bothered by people. But we are in the people business. Loving and caring for people and leading them to Jesus and Christlike maturity is what ministry is all about. However, ministry leaders are not the only ones who may struggle to build relationships. According to Lifeway Research, two-thirds of churchgoers believe they can walk with God without other believers.[2] This means that most of the people in your congregation may not value relationships with fellow believers. They don't see a connection between truly knowing someone (and being fully known) and their own spiritual growth. As a result, many Christians are apathetic about church attendance and involvement in discipleship ministries.

So, before I look at discipleship environments, I want to discuss the importance of relationships. To begin, I have two questions for you:

- How do you demonstrate a value for relationships with teenagers and parents? (Or put another way, can others tell through your words and actions that you value relationships with teenagers and parents?)
- In what ways do you intentionally spend time in your week focused on developing and maintaining relationships? (Not planning, administration, or sermon prep—but genuine relationships with real people?)

You may intuitively know that relationships are vital to your ministry, but you may not give attention to intentionally developing and maintaining relationships with young people and members of your congregation. Even if you do understand its importance, perhaps your volunteers do not. Your youth workers may assume that their priority should be "getting through the small group lesson material on time" rather than getting to know their students. Have you communicated through your actions or words that you simply need them present in a room for "crowd control" instead of relational

---

[2] See Scott McConnell, *Together: The Power of Groups* (Lifeway, 2020), 12.

intimacy? If you're anything like me, I need constant reminders that ministry must be relational to be effective. The best place to be reminded of this is in Scripture.

When Jesus called his first disciples, he said, "Follow me" (Matt 4:19; Mark 1:17). This call to "follow me" was a relational call. Jesus was inviting the disciples into a relationship with him. Throughout his earthly ministry, Jesus was committed to relational ministry.[3] In John 3:22, we read that Jesus "spent time" with his disciples. *Diatribo* is the Greek word translated here as "spent time with." It means "to rub between or wear away."[4] It's a word picture of sandals rubbing between your toes. It carries a connotation of becoming comfortable in your shoes. You know how uncomfortable a new pair of shoes can be. But once you wear them a few times and break them in, they no longer bother you. You become comfortable with them over time. It's the same with relationships; we become comfortable with people when we spend time with them. Jesus spent time with his disciples, not just in formal settings or occasional gatherings—he was present with them constantly.

Jesus could have chosen any strategy, and he decided to relationally pour himself into a group of individuals.[5] He did this because he knew they needed him more than anything else. Greg Ogden states, "As important as Jesus' teaching was, it was his person that became the vehicle for the transmission of his life to his disciples."[6] For example, in the Gospel of Mark, we see how Jesus built meaningful relationships with the disciples. Jesus went

---

[3] See Dann Spader, *4 Chair Discipling: What Jesus Calls Us to Do* (Moody, 2014), 14.

[4] See *New American Standard New Testament Greek Lexicon*, "Diatribo," https://www.biblestudytools.com/lexicons/greek/nas/diatribo.html; Frederick William Danker, *A Greek-English Lexicon of the New Testament and other Early Christian Literature*, 3rd ed. (The University of Chicago Press, 2000), 211. Danker notes that idiomatically *diatribo* refers to spending time with someone on a trip or journey.

[5] See Eric Geiger and Jeff Borton, *Simple Student Ministry: A Clear Process for Strategic Youth Discipleship* (B&H, 2009), 22.

[6] Ogden, *Transforming Discipleship*, 76.

to their homes (Mark 1:29), met their families (Mark 1:31), ate with them (Mark 3:20), and celebrated holidays with them (Mark 14:12).[7]

The greatest need of teenagers and parents is a relationship with Jesus. When your church provides discipleship environments, you give them an opportunity to come to faith in Jesus and grow toward Christlikeness. As I describe the five discipleship environments in this chapter, your first thought might be to just add programming elements to your schedule with the assumption that the programs themselves will result in spiritual growth. This is flawed thinking. It's not about the programs or even the environments themselves that matter; it's the relationships. As Greg Ogden says, "Discipleship is fundamentally a relational process."[8] People are discipled by God through relationships with other people.[9] As a result, true discipleship can only take place in the context of relationships. Therefore, your students need relationships with godly adults to grow toward Christlikeness.[10] Likewise, the parents of your teenagers need relationships with growing Christians to do the same.

You may have noticed that throughout the beginning of this chapter, I have constantly used the qualifier *godly* to describe relationships with teenagers and parents. It's an important distinction to make in light of reported cases of the sexual abuse of children and teenagers by pastors, youth ministers, and/or adult volunteers. In addition, there are reports of ministry leaders having extramarital affairs with ministry assistants or other adults. These are not godly relationships. We must do everything we can to protect children and teenagers in our care. We must also remember God's standards of conduct in our relationships with adults. I highly recommend that you require sexual abuse awareness training in your ministry. This means that

---

[7] Geiger and Borton, *Simple Student Ministry*, 22–23.

[8] Ogden, *Transforming Discipleship*, 67.

[9] See Bobby Harrington and Alex Absalom, *Discipleship That Fits: The Five Kinds of Relationships God Uses to Help Us Grow* (Zondervan, 2016), 29.

[10] Geiger and Borton, *Simple Student Ministry*, 20.

no one, including yourself, can volunteer in your church without completing the training. In addition, you should enact policies that prohibit adults from being alone with students. For example, follow the "two-person rule" that prohibits a student from being alone with an adult.[11] One-on-one conversations must take place in public spaces. You want anyone who sees you talking with a male or female student to clearly see that you are simply having a conversation—nothing inappropriate is happening. When you and I model this behavior with teenagers, we help set the standard for appropriate *godly* relationships.

Even if you or your volunteers struggle to get to know youth and parents, it is a skill that can be developed. Consider adding relational skills development to volunteer leader training. Here are a few tips on building relationships with teenagers and parents.

Relationships with Teenagers

Relationships with students may begin with superficial information such as grade and school, but you should seek to know more about them. Depending on your personality and how you are wired, you may find relational ministry with students easy or more difficult. For example, if you are extroverted, conversations with students may flow naturally. If not, you have to be more intentional with your conversations and work to develop relationships with youth. Here's a starting list of things to learn about your young people—not in formal interviews, but through casual conversations over time. There is no need to rush it—deep relationships take time to develop. Share this list with your volunteers to help "prime the pump" in conversations.

- What do you enjoy doing in your free time?
- Tell me about your family.

---

[11] See Jody Dean, *Protect: A Youth Worker's Guide to Navigating Risk, Second Edition* (YouthMinistry360, 2024), 19.

- How can I pray for you? Do you have a test or tryouts coming up? Are there family issues or health concerns that I can pray for?
- What are your hopes and dreams for the future?
- Are you a Christian? Tell me about when and how you came to faith in Christ.

I try to find at least one area of connection with every student. As students respond to these and other questions, it enables me to know how to engage them the next time we talk. The next time I see the student, I can follow up on conversations about family, prayer requests, or areas of interest. Even if I'm unfamiliar with a particular interest or hobby, I can ask questions and show genuine interest in learning about the subject and the student's involvement in the activity.

Relationships with Parents

Chances are you know your students pretty well. But how well do you know their parents? The greatest need of your youth ministry may be better relationships between you and the parents of teenagers. You're probably more comfortable engaging students than parents, but that doesn't mean you shouldn't try. You know from previous chapters how vital parents are to the faith development of students, so you need to make a concerted effort to build relationships with moms and dads. It's not overstating to say that your relationships with parents could be some of the most important to build. It can be challenging to develop relationships with parents if you are a young adult and don't yet have children. But I want to encourage you to stay the course and continue to prioritize getting to know the parents of your teenagers. Below is a list of conversation starters with parents. Share this list with your volunteers to help them initiate conversations with parents.

- What do you do for work?
- How did you meet your spouse?

- What are your biggest struggles with raising a teenager?
- How can I pray for you?
- Have you accepted Christ as your savior? Tell me about when and how you came to faith in Christ.

An important aspect of developing relationships with parents is not asking for help every time you speak with them. You need to have conversations about the topics above without asking parents to volunteer for something. This takes effort. You may genuinely need help with something. You may desperately need sponsors for an event or a host home for DiscipleNow. But if you haven't spoken to a parent before or it's been some time since you connected with them, I advise you not to make the ask. You must intentionally build relationships with parents without expecting something in return. Parents will see through this if you only speak to them when you need something.

You need to go where parents are. Hang out before and after church where you will likely run into parents. Get to know the leaders of the small group that parents attend. Ask to be invited to social events like Sunday school parties at Christmas or July 4. These social gatherings allow you to connect with parents in an informal setting.

You must connect with parents beyond the church for these relationships to develop. Go to football games, attend concerts, show up at recitals, watch practices—and when you do, talk to your students, but also make a point to engage with parents. Sit with them at the games, concerts, and recitals. Beyond these events, consider visiting with parents in their homes, attending churchwide activities, and attending community events.

Testing the assumption that your church understands the need for godly relationships is a crucial next step in deconstruction. You can start by reflecting on the questions at the end of the chapter. Invite a volunteer or ministry friend to discuss the questions with you.

Assumption: My Church Provides Discipleship Environments for Optimal Spiritual Growth

Discipleship is complex, and no single environment can provide spiritual growth for every individual. It is a myth that you can have an effective "one-size-fits-all" approach to discipleship. Bobby Harrington and Alex Absalom say, "God uses people to disciple us differently in different relational contexts."[12] In fact, Jesus discipled in a variety of environments. He preached to the multitudes (the crowd), led a small group (the Twelve), focused on a few (his inner circle), and interacted one-on-one with people.[13] We see a similar pattern in the book of Acts. Peter preached to the multitudes (the crowd). The early church met in large homes (large groups) and smaller homes (small groups). Members of the early church ministered one-on-one.[14]

The environments discussed in this chapter are the church group (public space) for the whole congregation, youth group (social space) for all young people, small groups (personal space) for seven to twelve people, micro-groups (transparent space) of three to five people, and mentoring (one-on-one space) relationships.[15] Each environment increases in relational depth and connection. Although I encourage you to consider these five environments as you deconstruct your youth ministry, the list is descriptive and not prescriptive. It represents the types of discipleship environments youth leaders effectively use in youth ministry today. Not all environments are necessary for every youth ministry context. Instead of trying to provide for each of them, I encourage you to evaluate your current environments to offer as high a relational environment as possible for your ministry context.

---

[12] Harrington and Absalom, *Discipleship That Fits*, 30.

[13] See Aubrey Malphurs, *Strategic Disciple Making: A Practical Tool for Successful Ministry* (Baker, 2009), 57.

[14] Malphurs, 72.

[15] Harrington and Absalom, *Discipleship That Fits*, 50. I have adapted Harrington and Absalom's discipleship spaces to youth ministry.

Environment 1: The Church Group

We generally think of gathering for corporate worship when considering going to church. In fact, of all the discipleship environments discussed in this chapter, the church group environment is the one you most likely already experience every week. It is the one practice believers have participated in from the beginning of the church in Acts 2. The Barna Group notes, "An overwhelming majority of senior pastors (87%) and youth pastors (84%) describe attending all-church worship services as a youth group activity, meaning they value the presence of teenagers in the worshipping community."[16] You may not consider your corporate worship gathering part of your discipleship strategy for youth and parents. However, I believe placing the youth group in context within the church group is essential. Your ministry to teenagers should not stand alone and separate from the church. As such, you may need to reconstruct your youth ministry with a greater emphasis on corporate gatherings. Let's examine the goals of the church group environment.

The church group environment is about participation in a shared experience of our identity as believers in Jesus Christ. Harrington and Absalom refer to this environment as the *Public Space*.[17] The church group environment provides a place for teenagers and parents to come to faith in Jesus and take steps toward Christlike maturity. Today, we still practice what we read about in Acts 2:42, "And they devoted themselves to the apostles' teaching, to the fellowship, to the breaking of bread, and to the prayers." In the church group environment, discipleship is accomplished through building community (fellowship), preaching the gospel of Jesus Christ (apostles' teaching), and engaging in intergenerational worship (breaking of bread and prayers).

---

[16] The Barna Group, *The State of Youth Ministry: How Churches Reach Today's Teens—and What Parents Think About It* (Barna Group, 2016), 39.

[17] Harrington and Absalom, *Discipleship That Fits*, 52.

Teenagers in the Church Group

Your students need an opportunity to worship with older and younger believers. Don't allow youth-only worship gatherings to become a substitute for intergenerational corporate worship. Teenagers in the church group benefit both young people and the congregation. The participation of young people in corporate worship adds a refreshing dynamic to the experience, and teenage involvement in corporate worship sets the stage for a lifetime of worship. If you minimize intergenerational worship, you risk communicating to young people that church, apart from the youth group, doesn't matter. Think about your church group environment with the end in mind. Eric Mathis remarks, "Who do we pray teenagers might be on the eve of their twentieth birthdays? How do we hope the worship practices they have engaged in during their teenage years have formed them?"[18]

The church group environment aims for teenagers to become lifelong worshipping disciples of Jesus Christ. As such, young people need opportunities to lead worship in the church group environment—and not just on special "youth service" days. When young people experience leading in worship, it consistently predicts their religious identity and faith practices in the future.[19] Young people need opportunities for meaningful and public roles in the church group. Involvement includes not only worship leaders, musicians, and public speakers but also greeters and ushers. Youth pastors should encourage worship leaders to involve young people as much as possible. Mentoring students to lead worship in various ways can have a lasting impact on young people.[20]

---

[18] Eric Mathis, *Worship with Teenagers: Adolescent Spirituality and Congregational Practice* (Baker Academic, 2022), 83.

[19] See Marjorie Lindner Gunnoe and Claudia DeVries Beversluis, "And a Teen Shall Lead Them: The relationship between worship experiences and youth religiosity in the Panel Study of American Religiosity and Ethnicity (PS-ARE)," *Journal of Psychology and Christianity* 28, no. 3 (Fall 2009): 236–47.

[20] Mathis, *Worship with Teenagers*, 28.

Parents in the Church Group

An aim of the church group environment for parents, like teenagers, is for parents to become worshipping disciples. Parents must build relational connections, hear the gospel, and worship with students. According to the Barna Group, Christian parents of Generation Z overwhelmingly say that "attending church together is one of the most important family activities in which they engage."[21] Most teenagers share the religious beliefs of their parents, and most report attending religious services with either both (40 percent) or one (25 percent) of their parents.[22] Even if teenagers attend worship because parents make them, 79 percent say they get at least "some enjoyment from it."[23] Parents may prefer their teenagers sit with them in corporate worship, but it is common for young people to gather in a separate section of the sanctuary. Whether or not teenagers sit with their families in the church group environment is not the primary issue. The point is that families are in the same congregation, singing the same songs and hearing the same message. This shared experience in worship allows parents to discuss the worship experience later with teenagers.

The church group has limits to its effectiveness as a discipleship environment. Harrington and Absalom observe that Sunday worship services are "the most common size of church gathering—which leads to the problem of

---

[21] The Barna Group, *Gen Z: The Culture, Beliefs, and Motivations Shaping the Next Generation* (Barna Group, 2018), 34.

[22] See Jeff Diamant and Elizabeth Podrebarac Sciupac, "10 key findings about the religious lives of U.S. teens and their parents," Pew Research (September 10, 2020), https://www.pewresearch.org/short-reads/2020/09/10/10-key-findings-about-the-religious-lives-of-u-s-teens-and-their-parents/. Teen religious practices in "U.S. Teens Take After Their Parents Religiously, Attend Services Together and Enjoy Family Rituals" (September 10, 2020), https://www.pewresearch.org/religion/2020/09/10/u-s-teens-take-after-their-parents-religiously-attend-services-together-and-enjoy-family-rituals/.

[23] Diamant and Sciupac, "10 key findings."

wrongly expecting Sundays to deliver most of our discipling."[24] However, as Leroy Eims says, disciples cannot be "mass produced."[25] In-depth discipleship does not happen in a large group setting. People don't enter the church group program and emerge as fully formed disciples at the end of the production line.[26] One reason is that the church group environment represents the lowest level of relational connection (Figure 5). Remember this as you test the assumption that the church group is an optimal discipleship environment and look for ways to encourage relational connections with teenagers and parents.

You can test the assumption that your church group is an optimal discipleship environment by utilizing the survey instruments in the appendix. The Student Spiritual Growth and Influence survey and the Parent Spiritual Growth and Leadership survey include worship and church-wide participation questions. You'll find a complete list of questions at the end of the chapter to help your evaluation.

Discipleship Environments

Environments	Context	Size	Goals	Relational Level
Church Group	Congregation/Public	Entire Congregation	Community Preaching Worship	Low
Youth Group	Fellowship/Social	All youth	Belonging Proclamation Service	Medium
Small Groups	Friendship/Personal	6 to 12	Devotion Disciplines Application	High
Micro Groups	Accountable/ Transparent	3 to 5	Intimacy Accountability Ministry	Higher
Mentoring Relationships	Apprentice/Training	1-on-1	Challenged Leadership Life-on-Life	Extremely High

FIGURE 5: DISCIPLESHIP ENVIRONMENTS

[24] Harrington and Absalom, *Discipleship That Fits*, 60.

[25] Leroy Eims, *The Lost Art of Disciple Making* (Zondervan, 1978), 45.

[26] See Daniel Im, *No Silver Bullets: 5 Small Shifts That Will Transform Your Ministry* (B&H, 2017), 33.

Environment 2: The Youth Group

The youth group is the environment most commonly associated with youth ministry. The youth group environment allows teenagers to engage with peers and adult leaders in a social space.[27] A desired outcome of the social space or youth group environment is for teenagers to become faithful disciples of Jesus Christ. Faithful disciples in the youth group environment are developed through belonging, proclamation, and service. This environment should provide opportunities for teenagers to build a sense of belonging within the context of the youth group. Teenagers will also hear the gospel and be exposed to the truth of God's Word. Finally, the youth group environment provides an opportunity for teenagers to serve on mission for Christ.

Teenagers in the Youth Group

When most people think of youth ministry, they think of gatherings of teenagers. As you read this book, I hope you will develop an expanded view of youth ministry that includes more than this. Yet, the youth group gathering remains a hallmark of ministry to teenagers. The youth group environment aims for teenagers to become faithful disciples for a lifetime. Being part of a youth group emphasizing belonging, gospel proclamation, and ministry service can have profound implications for students. The youth group offers young people a place to experience worship and Bible study among peers. According to Eric Mathis, "When youth ministry began in the early nineteenth century, it did so by supplementing worship in the sanctuary with worship in the youth room, an age-specific ministry that did not include adults."[28] It's now common for youth groups to have their own worship service with a student-led praise band and a topical sermon by the youth pastor.

---

[27] Harrington and Absalom, *Discipleship That Fits*, 52.
[28] Mathis, *Worship with Teenagers*, 52.

An unfortunate side effect of this practice is that we have raised a generation of young people "who now expect worship to be catered especially to them and their needs."[29] Don't let worship in the youth group environment be a substitute for intergenerational worship in the church group.

Parents and the Youth Group

Your church probably doesn't provide parents with a "youth group" experience, but many churches offer large group Bible studies and social activities for adults. The goal of the social space for parents, like the goal for students, is to become faithful disciples. You can encourage Christian growth in parents by challenging them to connect with other adults at your church. For parents, one of the benefits of the youth group is that it offers significant support and encouragement to them as primary spiritual influencers. Knowing their teenagers have a safe, nurturing space for relational connection and discipleship can reassure parents. The emphasis on the gospel and Bible teaching in the youth group complements what Christian parents teach at home. When teenagers actively serve in ministry and missions, parents experience pride and confidence that their young people are growing into compassionate, service-oriented individuals. These acts of service can, in turn, encourage parents to get involved in ministry service. In fact, you should encourage parents to participate in ministry and missions alongside their teenagers.

The youth group environment has its limits. If you rely only on a large group discipleship environment, you are probably not effectively producing disciples. Although the level of relational connection is higher than in the church group, Figure 5 demonstrates that other environments can provide greater levels of relational intimacy. As you deconstruct your youth ministry,

[29] Randall Bradley, "Desegregating Worship," *Creator* 36, no. 2 (2014), https://issuu.com/creatormagazine/docs/creator_magazine_1402_for_web.

consider ways to enhance the relational connections of the youth group environment.

The survey instruments in the appendix are a great way to test the assumption that your youth group is an optimal discipleship environment. The Student Spiritual Growth and Influence survey and the Parent Spiritual Growth and Leadership survey include questions related to the youth group. Additionally, you can test the assumptions of your youth ministry by responding to the questions at the end of the chapter.

Environment 3: Small Groups

The Gospel accounts show us that Jesus poured his life into a small group of disciples known as the Twelve (Matt 10:2–4; Mark 1:16–20; Luke 6:12–19). The early church met in house churches in the homes of Mary, the mother of John (Acts 12:12) and Lydia (Acts 16:40). The apostle Paul mentions the churches that met in the homes of Aquila and Priscilla (Rom 16:3–5; 1 Cor 16:19), Nympha in Laodicea (Col 4:15), and one at Philemon's house (Phlm 2). These biblical examples of small groups help ground modern ministry to first-century practices.

Most churches offer some form of small group ministry for teenagers and adults. Small group environments provide a more personal space for Christian growth.[30] A desired outcome of small groups is for teenagers and parents to become growing disciples of Christ. In small groups, six to twelve (or more) participants gather relationally, and discipleship occurs through devotion, discipline, and application of the Bible. This environment should allow teenagers and parents to own their faith through a deeper devotion to Christ. Small groups also allow teens and parents to practice spiritual disciplines. Finally, the small group environment provides an opportunity for teenagers and parents to apply the Bible to real life.

---

[30] Harrington and Absalom, *Discipleship That Fits*, 52.

Open and Closed Small Groups

There are two types of small groups: open and closed. Each type serves a different function and seeks to reach different audiences. As you deconstruct your youth ministry, I encourage you to evaluate the use of both open and closed groups as part of your discipleship strategy.

Open Small Groups. Small groups in which anyone is welcome are referred to as open. This means they are open to church members, non-members, Christians, and non-Christians. In fact, non-members and non-Christians are typically encouraged to attend.[31] Another way small groups can be considered open is in the nature of the Bible study structure. Although the curriculum or topics of study may be sequential, participants are not required to have attended previous sessions to be welcome to join a current gathering. The typical Sunday school class is open because anyone can participate anytime. Open small groups often go by names like LIFE Groups or Connect Groups. Scott McConnell, executive director of Lifeway Research, noted in his book *Together: The Power of Groups* that 47 percent of group members joined because the leader or member invited them. McConnell notes, "Almost half of church-goers who participate in a small group or class joined that group because the leader (17%) or member of the group (30%) invited them."[32] Welcoming guests and unbelievers is part of the expectation.

Closed Small Groups. Small groups are considered closed because they are designed exclusively for those committed to deeper spiritual growth. As such, non-believers or uncommitted members are not invited. In my experience, many leaders are hesitant to offer any type of closed group for fear of the appearance of favoritism. These leaders believe the false assumption that everything we do in ministry must be open to everyone. They think all environments and programming elements must be designed for anyone—Christian and

---

[31] See Ken Braddy, *Breakthrough: Creating a New Scorecard for Group Ministry Success* (B&H, 2022), 158.

[32] McConnell, *Together*, 16.

non-Christian, members and non-members, committed and uncommitted. But the truth is that you have teenagers and parents all along the spectrum of spirituality, and you need environments for all of them. So, if you only offer open small groups in your youth ministry, I encourage you to consider starting a closed group for committed Christians. Perhaps start with a small group of juniors and seniors that focuses on defending their faith or responding to questions and doubts. The fourth environment, micro-groups, is a type of closed group, and I'll discuss this environment in detail below.

Teenagers in Small Groups

Small groups of youth are common in churches today, and according to Pew Research, as many as 60 percent of young people in the US participate in religious education programs.[33] Leaders gather young people in small groups in various ways, including by grade, sex, school, and geographic location. Small group leaders use a variety of learning methodologies, such as working in pairs, playing music, watching videos, moving around the room, going outside, reflecting on Scripture, and having group discussions. Small groups encourage teenagers to practice spiritual disciplines such as prayer and Bible study. However, Lifeway Research found that prayer is the only spiritual practice most teenagers take into adulthood.[34] As you deconstruct your youth ministry, evaluate how students are organized into groups, how leaders use various learning methodologies, and how youth practice spiritual disciplines.

When Small Groups Are Not Small Groups

When I talk with youth leaders about small groups, I frequently hear them describe them in this way: "After my sermon to the youth group, students

---

[33] Diamant and Sciupac, "10 key findings."

[34] See Lifeway Research, "Young Adults Keep Christian Label, Shed Many Practices," (January 31, 2019), https://research.lifeway.com/2019/01/31/young-adults-keep-christian-label-shed-many-practices/.

break into small groups for thirty minutes." Making smaller groups out of large groups is an effective teaching methodology, but these are not true small groups, as described in this chapter. The issues are two-fold: organization and time. Many leaders who practice this type of small group invite youth to gather with whoever is seated around them. Who students sit with and where they sit might change from week to week. As such, this organizational method of gathering students into a small group does not allow for consistent relational connections. In addition, thirty minutes is not an optimal amount of time for small groups. Youth may take a few minutes to settle into the group before the leader can meaningfully engage with students. In this scenario, leaders now have less time to facilitate a Bible study lesson and make relational connections with teens. A better approach is to lengthen the overall time for your student gathering. For example, if your programming allowed for an hour-and-a-half gathering, you could lead a half-hour large group and then dismiss to small groups for an hour.

As a youth pastor in Texas, I did the "small groups from a large group" approach. We used an ample space, and students gathered at round tables with at least one leader. Students were not assigned a table and sat wherever they wanted. After I preached a short message, leaders facilitated "table-talk time" for about twenty minutes. Sound familiar? The difference is that our "table-talk time" was not a substitute for small groups. Our small groups met on a different day and time. I get the appeal of this type of approach but don't make the mistake of thinking that it is a genuine expression of small groups or that students will benefit from it the same way they would in a different context.

Parents in Small Groups

Most churches have some form of prayer and Bible study already happening regularly in small groups for adults.[35] Small group Bible studies create a

---

[35] McConnell, *Together*, 15.

sense of community that is difficult to replicate in the church group environment. As members explore God's Word together and discuss their faith journeys, participants forge close bonds. These groups become places where participants can share their joys and struggles. Community building in small groups extends beyond the weekly gathering when leaders spend time with participants outside regular meetings.

As the Student Pastor at First Baptist Church, DeSoto, Missouri, Hayden Carter has responsibilities over all aspects of the youth ministry, but he also leads a parent small group. On Sunday evenings, after he teaches the youth group, students separate into small groups, and he leads the parent group. Even though Hayden does not yet have teenagers of his own, he humbly leads the group of parents to study God's Word and discuss issues related to parenting teenagers. Hayden's parent small group ministry is one example of how youth leaders can encourage moms and dads into smaller environments, but it's not the only one. For example, youth leaders should view adult Sunday school classes and small groups as extensions of their ministry to youth. These adult small groups provide Bible study and fellowship for parents of teenagers. You should get to know these leaders. You should hang out where these groups meet. You should ask for an invitation to social gatherings. Why? Because these adult groups provide small group experiences for parents of teenagers without you doing a thing. You should become a vocal advocate for adult small groups—encouraging parents to get involved.

The old scorecard for small groups measures just one thing: attendance.[36] Deconstructing youth ministry encourages you to move beyond measuring how many people are involved to discover to what extent people are growing toward Christlike maturity. You can test the assumption that your small groups are an optimal discipleship environment by utilizing the survey instruments in the appendix. Both the Student Spiritual Growth and Influence and the Parent Spiritual Growth and Leadership surveys include

---

[36] Braddy, *Breakthrough*, xii.

questions related to small groups. You can also reflect on the questions at the end of the chapter to assist with your evaluation.

Environment 4: Micro-Groups

In the New Testament, we see that Jesus not only discipled the Twelve but also poured his life into an inner circle—Peter, James, and John. Jesus led this inner circle of disciples up a mountain where they witnessed his transfiguration (Mark 9:2–13). They were the only disciples to see Jesus raise Jairus's daughter from the dead (Luke 8:49–56). His inner circle accompanied him away from the other disciples as he prayed in the garden of Gethsemane (Matt 26:36–38). These three men were with Jesus at some of his most celebrated events, but they also witnessed his most desperate moments. They were his closest friends. According to Greg Ogden, "Jesus focused on a few because that was the way to grow people and ensure transference of his heart and vision to them."[37] Focusing on a few is the basis of micro-groups.

Micro-groups have emerged as a dynamic and effective environment for deepening discipleship. The micro-group environment delivers a more intimate space for discipleship.[38] The goal of micro-groups is for teenagers and parents to become mature disciples. Micro-groups are considered "closed groups" because they are available only to believers. Many churches call their micro-groups "D-groups" (Discipleship Groups), and Greg Ogden prefers the term "triad" to describe groups of three.[39] Randall Braddy notes, "People who participate in these micro-groups are at a place in their growth as disciples where they highly value a deeper walk with Christ."[40] In closed micro-groups, three to five same-gender individuals

---

[37] Ogden, *Transforming Discipleship*, 73; Harrington and Absalom, *Discipleship That Fits*, 134.

[38] Harrington and Absalom, 52.

[39] Rob Gallaty, *Growing Up: How to Be a Disciple Who Makes Disciples*, rev. ed. (B&H, 2022); Ogden, *Transforming Discipleship*.

[40] Braddy, *Breakthrough*, 165.

gather relationally, and discipleship occurs through relational intimacy, mutual accountability, and ministry service. Relational intimacy allows group members to share their personal struggles, victories, and faith journeys in a way that might not occur in a larger environment. In micro-groups, members hold each other accountable for their Christian practices, personal goals, and moral decisions. Members develop a sense of responsibility and commitment to one another. As micro-group members grow toward Christlike maturity, they seek ways to make a tangible impact on the kingdom. Engaging in ministry and missions alongside group members is a powerful way to live out the gospel.

Forming Micro-Groups

A key aspect of micro-group success is how groups are formed. These close relationships should emerge organically among those who already have an existing relationship. Sunday school classes and small groups are the "seedbeds" for micro-group relationships.[41] According to Braddy, "Forming these smaller groups within a group is a clever way to help people move into even smaller and tighter relational spaces."[42] Rather than assigning participants to a group, leaders encourage existing small group members to form micro-groups on their own. Micro-groups are not meant to be another program for leaders to manage, but a discipleship culture to cultivate within the church.

Teenagers in Micro-Groups

Leaders invite young people to participate in micro-groups in various ways, including creating smaller groups from existing groups, accountability groups for guys and girls, and groups organized around topics or curricula.

---

[41] Gallaty, *Growing Up*, 4.

[42] Braddy, *Breakthrough*, 147.

In my experience, leadership is the main difference between youth and adult micro-groups. In most adult micro-groups, the group members share the leadership responsibility, but in most youth micro-groups, the leader is an adult volunteer. This can create issues when volunteers are asked to lead both small groups and micro-groups. As you deconstruct your youth ministry, evaluate how micro-groups are formed, the curriculum used, and the impact on leaders.

When Matthew Smith, children's and youth pastor at New Zion Baptist Church, surveyed his students, he found that a majority (59 percent) of his students desired to become more spiritual. New Zion's youth discipleship team recommended youth micro-groups to address this need. They chose to use Rob Gallaty's D-Group model in which groups commit to developing a disciple's MARCS (missional, accountable, reproducible, communal, and scriptural). D-Groups commit to meeting weekly, reading Scripture, praying, memorizing Scripture, and journaling.

Parents in Micro-Groups

There are probably parents in your church who would be eager to join a micro-group. Adults currently involved in Sunday school or small groups are prime candidates. Start by talking with the leaders of adult small groups at your church and explain the concept of micro-groups. Encourage these leaders to invite adults to form micro-groups. However, avoid turning micro-groups into a program by allowing groups to form organically. You can talk about micro-groups and train leaders, but don't announce a general sign-up or registration for anyone interested in joining.

Focus on a Few

If you're on the fence about micro-groups as a youth leader, consider this: The best ministry happens with just a few. Robert Coleman observes, "Better to give a year or so to one or two men who learn what it means to conquer for

Christ than to spend a lifetime with a congregation just keeping the program going."[43] My advice to a youth pastor looking to start micro-groups is to begin by leading the first group yourself. Prayerfully invite a few key adult or student leaders to join you for one year. After one year, challenge them to start their own micro-groups. This approach requires a long-term vision and strategy. It can also be challenging initially because some may view this as "playing favorites" and not including everyone in discipleship. You can address concerns by clearly communicating the goal of building a replicating discipleship process. Use the descriptions of micro-groups and the supporting Scripture passages in this chapter to convey the biblical basis of this approach.

Deconstructing youth ministry means thinking critically about the discipleship of youth and parents. You can test the assumption that micro-groups are an optimal discipleship environment by responding to the questions at the end of the chapter.

Environment 5: Mentoring Relationships

The term *mentor* comes from Greek mythology and Homer's *Odyssey*. Before going away to fight the Trojan War, Odysseus sought a man who would care for his son Telemachus. Odysseus wanted a man to raise his son just as he would if he were there. He found a man who did just that. The man's name was Mentor. Today, mentoring refers to a relational process between a more knowledgeable or skilled person and someone wanting to learn the knowledge or skill. An apprentice follows the instructions of the mentor. Heather Quiroz states, "A mentor takes their apprentice past the pages of a book and into the halls of their own hearts. Mentors share their lives with those they mentor—their hurts, pains, joys, and stories of redemption."[44]

---

[43] Robert Coleman, *The Master Plan of Evangelism* (Revell, 2006), 101.

[44] Heather Quiroz, *First-Century Youth Ministry: A Look Back for the Way Forward in Youth Ministry Discipleship* (YM360, 2024), 99.

The Bible does not explicitly mention mentoring, but several leaders demonstrate the characteristics of a mentor. God chose Joshua to succeed Moses (Num 27:18). Moses mentored Joshua, teaching (Exod 32:17–20) and encouraging (Deut 31:7) him to lead. Moses's mentoring eventually prepared Joshua to lead the people of Israel into the Promised Land (Deut 34:9). God chose Elisha to succeed Elijah (1 Kgs 19:16). Elisha followed his mentor until it was time to pick up Elijah's cloak and become the next prophet of God (2 Kgs 2:14–15). Jesus did not have ongoing mentoring relationships with individuals. However, he counseled and instructed people one-on-one. For example, Jesus spoke privately with Nicodemus (John 3) and directly to Peter (John 21). Later in the New Testament, we see an example of two generations of mentoring as Barnabas mentors Paul (Acts 11:25–26), and then Paul mentors Timothy (2 Tim 1:2). Paul saw in Timothy someone who had endeavored to follow his mentor's leadership: "But you have followed my teaching, conduct, purpose, faith, patience, love, and endurance" (2 Tim 3:10). Mentoring was also a crucial job of a rabbi.

> To follow a rabbi meant something radical: It meant that you wanted to be just like the rabbi, in every way possible. A rabbi was someone whose life was worth following because of how they loved God and his Word. Discipleship was not a program; it was about learning and doing life together. Mentoring was deeply rooted in the Scriptures and mentoring was how ministry was passed on from one individual to another.[45]

From a Christian perspective, mentoring is one-on-one discipleship. According to Paul Stanley and Robert Clinton, a Christian mentor is a "godly, mature, follower of Christ who shares knowledge, skills, and basic philosophy on what it means to increasingly realize Christlikeness in all

[45] Quiroz, 16.

areas of life."[46] The goal of mentoring relationships is for teenagers and parents to become disciple-makers—it is disciple-makers mentoring disciples to become disciple-makers. In mentoring relationships, discipleship occurs through spiritual challenge, leadership development, and life-on-life sharing. A Christian mentor's role is to encourage a mentee to move beyond the current state of spiritual development and experience a more profound commitment to faith. Mentors facilitate leadership development by involving mentees in ministry service. In this way, a disciple is like an apprentice.[47] The apprentice serves alongside a mentor who provides practical ministry experience for mentees to learn organizational skills, teamwork, and confidence. In discipleship, a Christian seeks to reproduce his or her life through the life of another. This is life-on-life discipleship. Alicia Britt Cole suggests, "Life is not the offspring of program or paper. Life is the offspring of life. Jesus prioritized shoulder-to-shoulder mentoring because His prize was much larger than information; it was integration."[48]

I've had several mentors in my life. Each one has provided significant guidance in my personal and professional life. I've also mentored (and currently mentor) ministry leaders. I've mentored students called to ministry, volunteers in my youth ministry, and seminary students. My mentoring involves life-on-life sharing, studying Scripture, reading a leadership book together, praying for one another, and modeling Christian leadership. My practice is to simply invite a mentee to join me in whatever I am already doing—making a hospital visit, sharing the gospel with someone, eating dinner with my family, or watching sports on TV.

---

[46] Paul Stanley and Robert Clinton, *Connecting: The Mentoring Relationships You Need to Succeed in Life* (NavPress, 1992), 48.

[47] Harrington and Absalom, *Discipleship That Fits*, 20.

[48] Alicia Britt Cole, "Purposeful Proximity—Jesus' Model of Mentoring," *Enrichment Journal: A Journal of Pentecostal Ministry* (Spring 2001), https://enrichmentjournal.ag.org/-/media/Enrichment/Issue-PDFs/2001/EJ_2001_02_Spring.pdf; Geiger and Borton, *Simple Student Ministry*, 21.

Teenagers in Mentoring Relationships

Everett Fritz argues that in youth ministry, "we try to *program* our teens instead of *mentoring* them."[49] Yet since the beginning of time, young people have learned to become adults by "observing, imitating, and interacting with grown-ups around them."[50] Teenagers need mentors who will model Christlikeness. Students are capable of more than we think. Mentors should challenge teens to think deeply about their faith and to put faith into action through ministry service. Life-on-life sharing provides young people with a guiding presence to help them through the struggles of adolescence.[51]

Parents in Mentoring Relationships

Parents of teenagers need older mentors who will help them navigate the complexities of raising adolescents. Seek out older parents who have raised their children to be Christian young adults. Ask if these older parents would consider mentoring parents of teenagers. Then, connect these mentors with willing parents. By establishing mentoring relationships, you demonstrate your desire to be an encouragement to parents of teenagers.

In addition to mentoring parents, youth leaders should consider discipling their staff or volunteers. Invite leaders to join you in your daily rhythms of life, such as having dinner with family, ministering to teenagers, and sharing hobbies. Challenge your mentees by making mutual commitments like memorizing Scripture, regularly sharing the gospel, and eating healthily.

---

[49] Everett Fritz, *The Art of Forming Young Disciples: Why Youth Ministries Aren't Working and What to Do About It* (Sophia Institute, 2018), 17.

[50] Chap Clark, *Hurt 2.0: Inside the World of Today's Teenagers* (Baker Academic, 2011), 38.

[51] See Andrew Root, *Revising Relational Youth Ministry: From a Strategy of Influence to a Theology of Incarnation* (InterVarsity, 2007), 87. Root declares, "We have offered them trips to Disneyland, silly games, and 'cool' youth rooms, not companionship in their darkest nights, their scariest of hells."

Deconstructing youth ministry means thinking critically about the one-on-one discipleship of teenagers and parents. You can test the assumption that mentoring relationships are an optimal discipleship environment by responding to the questions at the end of the chapter.

So you might be thinking, Do I need all five environments? No, I don't believe you need every environment as part of your ongoing ministry. As I stated earlier, this list is more descriptive than prescriptive. Instead, you should offer the environments you believe will best disciple your teenagers and parents in your context. But that doesn't mean that you must have five separate programming elements every week. A normal-sized church with fifteen teenagers might offer the traditional small groups on Sundays and a youth group gathering on Wednesday nights. In addition, this church might also offer a micro-group for juniors and seniors on Sunday nights. And finally, the youth pastor of this church might mentor one of the volunteers.

In chapter 9, I'll discuss how to incorporate these environments into your discipleship process. You can test the assumption that your church provides optimal environments for spiritual growth by responding to questions at the end of the chapter.

Assumption: The Entry Points of My Ministry Effectively Connect People to Our Discipleship Environments

Once you select the discipleship environments you believe will help your students and parents grow toward Christlike maturity, you must provide open doors for your people to enter these environments. These open doors are called entry points. An entry point is an event or short-term program designed to lead students and parents into a discipleship environment. Deconstructing youth ministry involves evaluating how effective your entry points are at connecting students and parents to your discipleship environments. Three entry point categories to assess are *connect*, *discipleship*, and *service*.

Connect Entry Points

Events and activities designed to help students and volunteers develop relational connections are known as connect entry points. Many young people today want to belong before they believe. They desire relational connections, enabling them to feel accepted, loved, and wanted. Connection entry points are an open invitation into this type of relationship. These entry points include traditional youth ministry events such as disc golf, laser tag, movie nights, and fifth quarters. Events such as these are not meant to simply provide fun activities for teens. Connect entry points should be designed to allow young people to build connections with peers and help volunteers intentionally develop godly relationships with students. They are not merely invitations to attend the church but opportunities for deeper relationships. For example, when an adult volunteer meets a guest at a youth mini-golf tournament, she can spend time getting to know the student and the friends who invited her. The volunteer talks with the guest about school, family life, and her relationship with God. Before the activity ends, the volunteer can invite the guest to attend the small group she leads.

Discipleship Entry Points

Youth ministry events designed to challenge students toward Christlike maturity are known as discipleship entry points. DiscipleNow (DNow) and youth camp are examples of a discipleship entry point. At a DNow weekend, young people gather in the homes of church members for small group discipleship, participate in group games, and serve others in a ministry project. The focus of DNow is youth discipleship, but instead of this being an isolated event, wise leaders make sure it becomes an entry point to further discipleship. For example, following DNow, a leader might launch a small group for new Christians, start a new sermon series on discipleship, or invite students to join micro-groups.

Service Entry Points

Youth group service projects such as packing weekend meal packets for food insecure students are examples of a service entry point. The focus of service projects is on meeting needs by becoming the hands and feet of Jesus. However, instead of planning isolated projects, wise leaders make an effort to make these events entry points for continued service. For example, after a weeklong mission trip, a youth pastor might organize a missions and ministry fair for students to see how they can regularly serve the congregation and community.

Deconstructing youth ministry means thinking critically about how students get involved in discipleship environments. It means thinking differently about youth ministry events and activities and developing an approach emphasizing discipleship. You can test the assumption that your entry points effectively connect teenagers to your discipleship environments by responding to the questions at the end of the chapter.

Testing the Assumptions

You can test the assumptions about your discipleship environments by reflecting on the following questions. Review the questions and invite others to dialogue with you concerning each.

Questions to Consider

1. In what ways do you demonstrate a value for relationships with teenagers and parents? Can others tell through your words and actions that you value relationships with teenagers and parents?
2. In what ways do you intentionally spend time in your week focused on developing and maintaining relationships?
3. Do your volunteers understand the biblical rationale for developing godly relationships with youth and parents?

4. In what ways do you help your volunteers understand their role in your discipleship process as it relates to your environments for teens and parents?
5. Do your volunteers have the necessary relational skills to build godly relationships with youth and parents?
6. How well does your church disciple teenagers in relational environments?
7. What percentage of teenagers and parents at your church attend intergenerational worship?
8. In what ways do you encourage intergenerational worship with your teenagers?
9. In what ways does your church help teenagers and parents feel like they belong?
10. How might gospel proclamation in your church group be more tailored to specifically address teenagers and parents?
11. In what ways can you involve students in congregational worship?
12. In what ways do you wrongly expect the church group environment to deliver most of your discipling of teenagers and parents?
13. In what ways do you help teenagers develop a sense of belonging with the youth group?
14. How are you crafting your preaching and teaching to clearly present the gospel and invite young people to respond?
15. What is your plan for systematically teaching the Bible to teenagers?
16. In what ways do you lead students to serve in your church, community, and the world?
17. In what ways do you wrongly expect the youth group to deliver most of your discipling of teenagers?
18. In what ways do your small groups help members develop a deep devotion to Christ?
19. How well do small groups encourage teenagers and parents to practice spiritual disciplines?

20. To what extent do small groups help your people apply God's Word to daily life?
21. How evangelistic are your small groups?
22. In what ways are your volunteers prepared to respond to questions and doubts?
23. Do your volunteers understand the differences between open and closed small groups?
24. In what ways might your church benefit from additional open or closed small groups?
25. In what ways do your micro-groups help members develop relational intimacy?
26. To what extent do micro-group members experience mutual accountability?
27. In what ways do micro-groups encourage ministry and missions service?
28. What are the possible implications of starting micro-groups at your church?
29. Who are you mentoring?
30. Do you encourage volunteers to mentor teenagers?
31. In what ways do you facilitate mentoring relationships between older and younger parents?
32. To what extent are you developing leaders by mentoring volunteers?
33. How might life-on-life mentoring of teenagers and parents impact your ministry?
34. Do you know of specific examples in which young people have participated in an entry point event and then joined a discipleship environment?
35. Do your students and volunteers understand the purpose of youth group events and activities?
36. Are your volunteers trained and prepared to relationally engage with students at events?

37. In what ways do your discipleship entry points connect teens to discipleship environments?
38. To what extent are your service projects helping connect youth to ongoing ministry service opportunities?

For more information on sexual abuse awareness training, visit MinistrySafe (ministrysafe.com). For further reading on creating safe environments for children and teenagers, check out my friend and colleague, Dr. Jody Dean's book, *Protect: A Youth Worker's Guide to Navigating Risk*.

CHAPTER 6

SURVEY WORK

APPLYING THE METRICS TO YOUR YOUTH MINISTRY

Building a new house is one of your biggest life decisions. It requires a significant investment of finances, time, and effort. Therefore, each step of the process must be meticulously planned before construction begins. When I was a youth minister in Midland, Texas, my wife and I built a house. We worked with a local builder who had just begun the development of a new subdivision. We picked out a floor plan, and our builder went to work. One of the first steps involved a land survey to determine the exact boundaries and property lines for the lot we had picked to build our home. While some properties have clear boundaries like roads and landscapes, our lot did not. To ensure that our house's foundation was built within the parameters of the lot, the survey crew used a specialized device called a *theodolite*. A theodolite is a precision instrument with a moveable telescope mounted so that it can rotate around horizontal and vertical axis to provide angular measurements. Measurements are taken by the surveyor, who adjusts the telescope's vertical and horizontal orientation so the cross-hairs align with a sighting point. These measurements provide the builder with precise boundary markers and elevation statistics. Without the survey work, builders would have no way of knowing whether or not they have the proper positioning of the house within the lot.

Similarly, you need to survey the terrain of your youth ministry to evaluate how well it is positioned to disciple students and parents. This requires the application of the metrics from chapters 1–5. A critical analysis of your youth ministry will give you a clear picture of the state of your ministry—both positive and negative.

According to Barna, less than 1 percent of leaders report using a survey or other evaluation instrument to assess their programs.[1] Most churches do not evaluate the effectiveness of their discipleship ministries—either out of fear of the results or lack of understanding of how to evaluate. I challenge you to face your fears and use the tools described in this chapter to deconstruct your youth ministry.

In chapters 1–5, I reviewed the mission and purpose of youth ministry, discussed how to measure the spiritual growth of your students and parents, explained the assessment of the three arenas of youth ministry, discussed how to evaluate your discipleship process, and explained how to assess five discipleship environments—now what? Now it's time to act. You should complete your survey work in three steps: gathering a deconstruction team, collecting and analyzing data, and communicating your findings. However, before starting the process, you must complete a preliminary step—Pray. Think. Dream.

Survey Work Preliminary Step: Pray. Think. Dream.

As a preliminary step toward deconstructing your youth ministry, I want to encourage you to do three things: pray, think, and dream. This process

---

[1] See Barna, *State of Discipleship: A Barna Report Produced in Partnership with The Navigators* (The Navigators, 2015), 12.

should not be entered into lightly. You must resist the urge to apply everything you read in this book immediately. Your first reaction might be to hastily enact some of the suggested changes. Stop. Don't do that. You need to first pray about deconstructing your youth ministry. Then, I suggest you think about what that might entail. And finally, you need to take time to dream about what God might do through your ministry to reach and disciple teenagers and parents.

Pray

As with everything in life, you should pray about it. Prayer is the foundation of transformative change in ministry. This is the Lord's work. The church you serve is his church. The youth group you lead is his youth group. Those are his students and his parents. Prayer aligns your heart with God's will. So, before making any changes, dedicate time to seek God's guidance through prayer. Through prayer, you invite the Holy Spirit into the process. Pray for the Lord's wisdom and discernment as you seek to critically examine your youth ministry. Pray for God to clarify what should change and what should remain. Pray for peace about the direction you are headed. Pray for the Lord to empower you with the strength to make difficult decisions. Pray for humility as you lead change. Through prayer, you acknowledge that God is in control and that successful ministry is ultimately his work through you.

Think

Thinking critically about your youth ministry is crucial. This involves an honest evaluation of your ministry's current practices, programs, and outcomes for teenagers. The first step to acting strategically is thinking strategically. You must give yourself time—days, weeks, months—to think critically about implementing the suggested changes. Thinking critically about your ministry helps you clarify your mission and vision and uncover underlying issues. You must approach this process with an open mind and a willingness to challenge assumptions and embrace new practices. All of this requires deep, contemplative thought. And after you've thought about deconstructing your youth ministry, you need to pray some more. Pray and think. Think and pray. At this point, all the changes you imagine enacting are merely a thought experiment. I suggest you take some time to "live within" this thought experiment. You've not yet shared your thoughts with anyone—this is between you and God. As you think about deconstructing your youth ministry, you should let your thoughts move toward a possible future—dream about what God might do.

Dream

Dreaming about the future of your youth ministry allows you to envision what God might do through your efforts. Dreaming may not come naturally to you. Perhaps you had dreams and plans when you first started in ministry. Time and the realities of life may have darkened those dreams. As you pray, ask God to renew a clear vision for your ministry. Ultimately, you should seek his dream for you and your ministry—not yours. Pray for discernment.

One way to typically distinguish your dreams from God's is the size of the dream. We serve a big God with big dreams. As you pray and think about your youth ministry, you may tend to dream small. You pray about today and next week. You think about your next Bible study and event. But things change when we invite God into the equation, including dreams. Therefore, rather than focusing only on today or next week, ask God to help you dream about the possibilities next year and beyond. Instead of just your youth group, ask God to help you dream about the possible influence on your church and community. Rather than dreaming about how changes might impact your students and parents, pray for kingdom impact! What would it look like if every teenager in your community felt loved and was discipled? What might happen if parents of teenagers were mentored and encouraged toward Christlike maturity? How might your ministry impact families and your whole congregation? Dreaming can help motivate and inspire you to make the necessary changes to drive your ministry forward. Through dreaming, you can see the potential for transformation and the lasting ways God can work through you.

After you pray, think, and dream, there is one more preliminary step—talk. Once you've spent time praying, thinking, and dreaming about deconstructing your youth ministry, it's now time to talk with others about it. Talking about deconstruction is where you slowly begin to share with others what you've been praying, thinking, and dreaming. Maybe you start with your spouse or a trusted friend. Then, talk with your pastor and key leaders. An essential aspect of this step is to focus on meaningful conversations about possible changes. These initial conversations should focus on ideas first instead of action. You are inviting others to pray, think, and dream with you. Again, you are not rushing to do away with all of your existing ministries and establish new programs. You are just talking. As you speak with people in your church about your youth ministry, begin praying about who you might invite to join you in this conversation. Talking with others about the state of your youth ministry should lead you to establish a deconstructing team.

Survey Work Step 1: Gathering a Deconstruction Team

Don't do ministry alone or attempt to deconstruct your youth ministry alone. Regardless of the size of your church or youth group, you should seek to walk this journey of deconstruction with others by your side. Even if you can only find one or two others, let this small team assist you with your survey work. Gather a team of individuals who will help you accomplish the survey work. You may already have a youth leadership committee or team—enlist these folks to assist you. If you serve a large church, you may have additional staff and interns to help with the survey work. These individuals become your deconstruction team. However, the term *deconstruction* is controversial, so you may choose another title, such as "renovation team" or simply "youth leadership team."

If you need to gather a team from scratch, you are looking for what Thom Rainer calls an "eager coalition" of people who support youth ministry and desire to see your church effectively reach and disciple teenagers.[2] Your team should consist of enthusiastic supporters who believe in your vision and are willing to influence others. Your eager coalition will serve as the backbone of your change initiative.[3] Clint Grider calls this group "metapartners" because these individuals represent people who have a "more comprehensive commitment" to your ministry.[4] Involving these metapartners means you are leveraging the broader support of your church. Support from your church will be crucial to implementing sustainable change.

Team members should include people of influence within your church, individuals in key positions, and supportive parents. A diverse group helps ensure a comprehensive overview of your youth ministry. This mix of parents, volunteers, and church staff provides varied perspectives on your existing ministry. The diversity helps you avoid blind spots and ensures that multiple aspects of your ministry are considered. They will help you identify the strengths of your program and areas of needed improvement. Their commitment and enthusiasm can influence others to embrace your deconstruction efforts. With a dedicated and diverse team by your side, you are ready to begin the deconstruction process. I'll share more about the importance of a team as I discuss leading change in chapter 7.

Deconstruction Process

The deconstruction process will use metrics, outcomes, and assessments to evaluate your youth ministry. The metrics (biblical, discipleship, ministry, process, and environmental) described in chapters 1–5 provide the

---

[2] Thom S. Rainer, *Who Moved My Pulpit?: Leading Change in the Church* (B&H, 2016), 61–62.

[3] Rainer, 61–62.

[4] Clint Grider, *Mind the Gap: Leading Your Church to Agility and Effectiveness in Any Environment* (B&H, 2023), 203.

foundation you need to conduct your survey. Chapter 2 provides the structure to create your list of desired outcomes, such as a relationship with Christ, Christian transformation, ministry service, and making other disciples. The assessments found in the appendix will assist you with your evaluation.

Your initial meeting with the deconstruction team should focus on defining why the team exists. This means clearly defining your youth ministry's mission, purpose, and objectives. What do you hope to achieve, and what values guide your work? This foundational step sets the framework for your evaluation. Use the discussion questions from chapters 1–5 to guide your discussions. Figure 6 describes the deconstruction process.

Metrics

As stated earlier, we use metrics to measure ministry progress. These metrics or key performance indicators (KPIs) are crucial for evaluating and assessing ministry. They provide an objective way to measure the achievement of outcomes and provide a benchmark against which we can measure progress. Review with your team the types of metrics you seek to measure. You want to track attendance and the number of student and parent baptisms, but you want to move beyond these. Biblical metrics relate to the extent to which your ministry operates with a scriptural foundation. Ask your team members to what extent your youth ministry has a strong biblical mission and purpose. Can youth and parents clearly state the purpose? Discipleship metrics focus on student and parent journeys toward Christlike maturity. Review the categories of Christian growth you wish to measure (relationship with Jesus, spiritual disciplines, service, etc.). Ministry metrics evaluate effectiveness within the three arenas of teenagers in the youth group, teenagers in families, and teenagers in the congregation. Invite your team to discuss the three arenas and to what extent your youth ministry needs to address a specific arena. Process metrics assess the efficacy of your discipleship pathway. Discuss your process with your team to determine how to proceed. Environmental metrics evaluate the strengths and weaknesses of your discipleship program. Review the environments (church group, youth group, small groups, micro-groups, and mentoring relationships) you wish to evaluate.

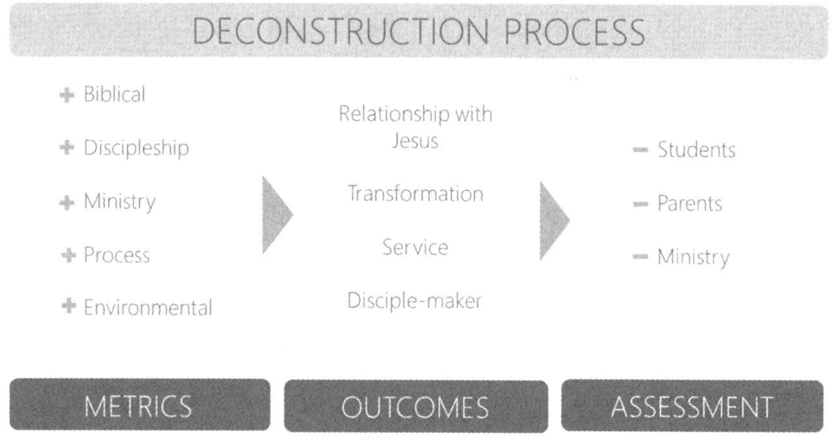

FIGURE 6: DECONSTRUCTION PROCESS

Outcomes

The final result of your discipleship efforts is measured as outcomes. Outcomes are the Christlike characteristics you desire to see in young people. Outcomes should be specific and measurable. For example, if your goal is to send teenagers on mission to fulfill the Great Commission, you might have several outcomes such as leaders will provide opportunities for students and parents to serve together in both local and international missions; adults will challenge students to serve through church ministries and local mission projects; and youth workers will encourage students to answer the call to full-time vocational ministry and missions. Each outcome represents faith in action. Work with your team to develop a list of outcomes you desire to see in teenagers and parents. They may represent small steps toward Christ and huge commitments. They might be up-front and on stage or behind the scenes. Here are a few outcomes to consider:

- Relationship with Jesus: Have youth and parents responded to the gospel and followed in baptism?
- Transformation: In what ways can teenagers and parents demonstrate evidence of a life transformed by Jesus? Outcomes might include practicing spiritual disciplines like prayer and Bible reading, sharing the gospel with others, and displaying the fruit of the Spirit.
- Service: In what ways are young people and parents engaged in ministry and mission service? Service may include volunteering in the local church and community and mission service nationally and internationally.
- Disciple-maker: In what ways are youth and parents demonstrating themselves to be disciple-makers? A disciple-maker leads individuals to personal faith in Jesus and helps them grow toward Christlike maturity.

Your youth ministry may have additional outcomes in mind for students and parents. Discuss all of the potential outcomes you envision for your people. Defining these outcomes helps focus your ministry efforts and provides a framework for evaluating success.

Assessment

Once you've determined the metrics you wish to measure and defined the outcomes you seek, it's time to assess. The surveys in the appendix will assist you with the deconstruction of your ministry. I designed them to help you test the assumptions and outcomes of your ministry. Review the list of assessments and determine which you wish to administer. Establish a systematic method for collecting data related to your chosen KPIs. Regular assessments enable you to track progress over time and make informed decisions. Through metrics, outcomes, and assessment, the deconstruction process provides a comprehensive approach to evaluating your ministry.

Survey Work Step 2: Collecting and Analyzing Data

Collecting your data is a crucial step in the deconstruction process. Your goal is to gain insight into your teenagers' and parents' diverse and personal faith experiences. I suggest you use a combination of three forms of data collection: surveys, team discussions/evaluations, and personal interviews/conversations with youth and parents.

Surveys

Surveys can be distributed in various ways, including online forms, paper copies, or in-person interviews. Consider using digital tools (such as those found at deconstructingym.com) for convenience. Choose the method that best suits your church preferences. Make sure to provide ample time for respondents to complete the survey. The Student Spiritual Growth and Influence Survey, Parent Spiritual Growth and Leadership Survey, and the Youth Ministry Arenas Assessment can be reliable KPIs for your youth ministry. Perhaps you'd like to customize the assessments for your context—we can help with that. The Youth Ministry Institute at New Orleans Baptist Theological Seminary will help you tailor an assessment to meet your specific needs.

Decide on the frequency of your evaluations. Quarterly or annual evaluations are common, but the timing should align with your ministry's objectives and activities. To encourage honesty and openness, assure respondents that their answers will remain confidential. Emphasize that the purpose of the survey is not to judge but to understand and support their spiritual journeys.

Team Discussions/Evaluations

Invite your team to complete a SWOT analysis of your youth ministry and programs (see appendix). A SWOT analysis is a strategic planning tool, used to identify and evaluate a program's Strengths, Weaknesses, Opportunities, and Threats.[5] In a youth ministry context, a SWOT analysis can help leaders assess the current state of the ministry and provide a framework for growth. I suggest you consider your overall ministry, discipleship process, and environments. Therefore, you should complete the SWOT analysis considering the youth ministry as a whole and then analyze each component.

Identify Strengths

The first step is to review your youth ministry's positive aspects. What does your youth ministry do exceptionally well? What resources do you have that others do not? Responses might include dedicated volunteers, positive attendance numbers, or successful events. Strengths are typically experiences and resources within the control of the church.

Identify Weaknesses

The next step is to focus on issues that could be improved. What are some areas in which your youth ministry struggles? What concerns do you have about your ministry or programs? Responses might include poor attendance, lack of parent support, or outdated resources. Weakness could involve administrative, operational, or relational issues within your ministry.

Identify Opportunities

The third step is to consider external factors that could be leveraged to encourage growth toward Christlike maturity among students and parents. What current youth culture trends could be addressed in your ministry?

[5] SWOT has no universally accepted creator, but the strategy is historically credited to Albert Humphrey.

Are there local organizations or other churches you could partner with? Opportunities may include previously untapped resources within your church and those outside your congregation.

Identify Threats

The final step of your SWOT analysis is to identify those external factors that pose risks to the Christian growth of students and parents. What cultural changes could impact our ministry? What changes in your community could affect growth? Are there societal trends that need to be identified as threats to Christian flourishing?

Use the chart in the appendix to summarize the discussion of each category. Populate the four quadrants (strengths, weaknesses, opportunities, threats) with responses. Discuss possible ways to celebrate strengths and take advantage of opportunities. Invite your team to address possible solutions to weaknesses and ways to eliminate threats. The SWOT analysis can be a valuable tool in the deconstruction process. Inviting open and honest conversations regarding your youth ministry can pave the way for growth and improvement.

Interviews/Conversations

Conducting interviews with teenagers and parents is crucial to deconstructing your youth ministry. While the surveys provide you with quantitative data (numbers-based data such as how many, how much, and how often), interviews give you qualitative information (interpretation-based data such as descriptions and relationships). These qualitative responses help you understand the quantitative data by going beyond surface-level observations. Engaging directly with students and parents enables your team to hear firsthand about congregants' challenges, successes, and Christian growth. Invite your team members to initiate conversations with teenagers and parents in your congregation.

Interviews and conversations with teenagers and parents provide a unique perspective for your team to consider as you deconstruct your youth ministry. Teens can share how well specific aspects of your youth ministry assist them in their journey toward Christlike maturity. Parents can reflect on your ministry's influence on teenagers and how the church helps their own Christian growth. These conversations can help you identify how effectively your ministry partners with parents to nurture the faith of teenagers. In addition to interviewing students and parents who are strong Christians and actively attend your church, consider conversations with non-believers and non-members. Consider the following questions to guide conversations:

- How do you describe your relationship with Jesus?
- What is God teaching you this week?
- What is your biggest struggle right now?
- What is the greatest hindrance to your Christian growth?
- In what ways does our youth ministry encourage your Christian growth?
- In what ways can I pray for you?

You may focus only on qualitative research by talking with leaders, parents, and students without using survey data. This type of evaluation can give you good but limited feedback, and you must carefully avoid confirmation bias. On the other hand, incorporating conversations and interviews into the evaluation process ensures a more holistic approach to deconstructing your youth ministry. These conversations can enhance your ministry's effectiveness and build stronger relationships within the church. As your team reflects on these conversations, it can promote a sense of shared responsibility in the Christian growth of youth and parents.

Administer the Surveys

Now that your team has determined the proper metrics, outcomes, and assessments, it's time to lead them in administering the surveys. If you serve a normal-sized church of 150 or fewer members, you may choose to survey and interview your entire group. In a larger church, you might select specific age groups for assessment. For example, on an annual basis, you might survey and interview sixth and ninth graders. These two grades would represent your youth group and provide a snapshot of ministry effectiveness. In addition, you may choose to survey your group every two or three years instead of annually. Remember, most churches don't conduct any type of discipleship assessment. Your willingness to evaluate places you and your church in a rare group.

Let me share some examples to help you see the potential impact of surveys on your ministry. A youth pastor of a medium-sized church in the southwest took the Youth Ministry Arenas Assessment and found that although he scored high in the arenas of teenagers in the youth group and teenagers in families, he scored low in teenagers in the congregation. Although his church provided many opportunities for teenagers to serve, he did not have a strategy to connect teenagers with the overall congregation. Because he realized that relationships are the key to connection, his efforts focused on bringing generations together. He worked with leaders in other ministries to actively seek to build relationships between young people and different age groups. The biggest takeaway he experienced was a renewed focus on helping young people establish significant connections to the congregation. He began to evaluate everything he did through the lens of assisting students to foster relationships with younger and older members of his church. He shifted his view of youth ministry beyond the teenage years and extended his ministry goals toward helping students develop lifelong faithfulness to Christ.

A medium-sized church in a suburban neighborhood in the south had forty-two teenagers complete the Student Spiritual Growth and Influence survey, and sixty-eight parents complete the Parent Spiritual Growth and Leadership survey. The surveys revealed some encouraging statistics, such as a strong correlation between attendance and spiritual growth among students (61 percent of students who occasionally attend scored in the low range, and 81 percent of those who regularly attend scored in the high range on spiritual growth). In addition, they found that 74 percent of parents volunteered in the church. But the news wasn't all rosy. They found students scored lowest in spiritual disciplines and service to others. Parents scored the lowest in church engagement. Some of the most concerning statistics were that 67 percent of youth had not talked about Jesus with a non-Christian in the last few months, and one-third of students did not feel free to express doubts at church. As a result, the youth leadership team developed a plan to challenge youth to be bold witnesses and train students to share their faith with friends. In addition, the team initiated a plan to train adult volunteers to build deep relationships with youth and prepared leaders to answer questions and doubts comfortably. The surveys also revealed a relational need between fathers and their children. Thirty-one percent of youth admitted they did not have a close relationship with their father. The leadership team shared these stats with the church deacons and worked together to formulate a strategy to train men to be godly fathers and role models. Let these stories encourage you and your team to press on.

Analyze the Data

The survey results give you valuable information you wouldn't otherwise have access to. Once you've collected the survey responses, it's time to analyze the data. Look for trends, patterns, and areas where the ministry is excelling or facing challenges. Analyze the data in at least these four ways: compare results to goals and outcomes, identify strengths and weaknesses, consider the destination or direction of youth and parents, and synthesize the data into themes.

Compare Results to Goals and Outcomes

Begin by comparing your collected data with your ministry's defined objectives. Assess whether you are achieving your goals and outcomes, and if not, identify areas that need improvement. For instance, if one of your goals is to disciple teenagers in relational environments of devotion, spiritual discipline, and application of God's Word, analyze responses related to stated outcomes. One outcome related to this goal might include adults modeling spiritual maturity through personal prayer, Bible reading, and worship attendance. How did parents score in the category of spiritual disciplines? Which spiritual discipline was the lowest and highest for parents? Another outcome might be students demonstrating devotion to Christ by regularly praying and reading their Bible. How did students score in the spiritual disciplines? Which spiritual discipline was the lowest and highest? The key aspect of this part of the analysis is to assess whether the responses align with your expectations. If the results show that your outcomes are being met or exceeded, it reinforces the effectiveness of your current discipleship strategy. On the other hand, if there is a significant gap between your stated outcomes and survey results, this indicates an area of needed improvement. This comparative analysis helps you measure progress, set benchmarks, and adjust your discipleship strategy to lead students and parents toward Christlike maturity.

Identify Strengths and Weaknesses

Based on the data and feedback, pinpoint the strengths and weaknesses of your youth ministry. This involves examining the data to determine what works well and needs attention. Strengths might be identified through high composite scores on the student and parent surveys. Lower scores would indicate a weakness. For example, the Composite Spiritual Growth Scores for youth and parents can be an important metric to analyze. The composite scores can be ranked high (80–100), medium (60–79), and low (59 and below). Here are some scores to consider:

Categories (Relationship with God, Spiritual Disciplines, etc.). What was the average score for Relationship with God? Does this indicate a high, medium, or low score?

Composite Scores (Spiritual Growth, Spiritual Influence, Spiritual Leadership). What was the composite score for Spiritual Growth? Does this indicate a high, medium, or low score? What was the composite score for Spiritual Influence? Does this indicate a high, medium, or low score?

Highs and Lows. In what areas of relationship with God did students score the highest? In what areas of spiritual disciplines did students score the lowest?

Comparison to Demographics. Compare Relationship with God scores between girls and boys. Compare parent frequency of attendance to Spiritual Disciplines and Church Engagement. Compare Parent Influence scores reported by students to Faith Conversations scores reported by parents. Demographic questions include sex, grade, and for parents—marital status.

Comparison to Frequency. Compare the frequency of Bible reading to the Relationship with God score. How might these scores relate? Frequency questions include church attendance, the reason I attend, prayer, Bible reading, parent attendance, and parent ministry/mission involvement.

Identifying these strengths and weaknesses allows you to build on your success and address areas that need attention. These areas will help you prioritize resources and budget considerations. When you prepare to present your data to others, the category of strengths and weaknesses will help your congregation identify some of the key results of your surveys.

Determine Destination or Direction

The task of discipleship is generally approached in two ways: a focus on a destination (Christlike maturity) or direction (movement toward Christ).

According to Daniel Im, "When it comes to developing a process for discipleship, most churches fall somewhere along this first spectrum."[6] Each approach reflects a different understanding of what Christian growth looks like and how it should be measured. Both approaches offer unique perspectives on the goals and processes of discipleship (Figure 7).

Focus on Destination ⟷ Focus on Direction

FIGURE 7: THE TENSION BETWEEN A FOCUS ON DESTINATION VS. DIRECTION

Destination. The destination approach to discipleship is based on the attainment of a specific set of Christlike characteristics. This approach views Christian maturity as a definitive point to be reached. It focuses on specific outcomes that mirror the life of Christ. To some degree, the goals and outcomes in chapter 2 represent a destination mindset toward discipleship. For example, a church may feel that discipleship has occurred when they see evidence of students regularly praying, reading their Bible, participating in intergenerational worship, and Jesus-centered living.

In this approach, discipleship programs are designed to cultivate these outcomes, and success is measured by how many teenagers consistently exhibit these qualities.[7] The advantage of this approach is the clarity of specific discipleship metrics. Leaders can set clear goals and outcomes (as described in chapter 2), and progress can be assessed against these predetermined criteria. This approach provides a clear discipleship pathway for students and parents.

However, the destination approach can also be limiting. This approach implies that the disciple has reached the Christian maturity goal once these characteristics are evident. This can lead to complacency and the false concept

---

[6] Daniel Im, *No Silver Bullets: 5 Small Shifts That Will Transform Your Ministry* (B&H, 2017), 23.

[7] See Im, 23.

that one can be a fully mature Christian on this side of glory. Moreover, it risks reducing the Christian faith to a series of achievements. Discipleship can become more about doing than being—emphasizing behavior modification over life transformation.

Direction. Discipleship is a lifelong relational journey toward Christlike maturity. Therefore, in contrast to the destination approach, the directional approach focuses on the journey of faith rather than a specific endpoint. This approach centers on the idea of continual growth toward Christlike maturity. The emphasis is on a trajectory rather than a final arrival point.[8] According to Eugene Peterson, discipleship is "a long obedience in the same direction."[9] As such, churches with a directional approach view Christian maturity in relation to Jesus. Although the goals and outcomes described in chapter 2 have a destination component (end result), the reality is that measuring these metrics demonstrates a directional approach. This is because teenagers (and adults) are a work in progress. They have not fully attained Christlike maturity, but they are in the process of growing toward Christ. This is a directional approach. Your team will use information from the interviews and conversations to determine to what extent students and parents are on a journey toward Christlike maturity. For example, for each of the interviews, your team could place students and parents in one of three directional categories: away from Christ, toward Christ, don't know. The first category indicates that the individual is either an unbeliever or not pursuing a relationship with Jesus. The second category indicates that the teenager or parent is either a believer and/or growing in their relationship with Jesus. This category would include a broad spectrum from new believers to disciple-makers. The final category would indicate persons whom your team does not know the spiritual condition.

---

[8] Im, 23.

[9] Eugene Peterson, *A Long Obedience in the Same Direction: Discipleship in an Instant Society* (InterVarsity, 1980).

This process can be a powerful motivational tool not only for your deconstruction team but for your volunteers as well. For instance, I suggest inviting Bible study leaders to examine a list of students in their class and perform this evaluation based on their relationship with the students. You could challenge leaders to indicate whether each student is moving away from Jesus, toward Jesus, or I don't know. This type of assessment can empower leaders to pray and lead based on the specific spiritual needs of students. The ones that leaders mark as "I don't know" should encourage them to find out the spiritual condition of teens by having conversations with students related to faith in Jesus.

Synthesize the Data

The assessment of your ministry produces a wide range of information about what's going on in your youth ministry. You need to help your team make sense of everything they've discovered without becoming overwhelmed and discouraged. Your final step is synthesizing the data to capture overarching themes and insights. This step involves looking beyond the individual responses to identify broader patterns and trends. Synthesizing the data into themes helps you see the bigger picture. By grouping similar responses, you can distill complex data into actionable trends. This step takes time and effort. Lead your team to examine the survey results and work individually to identify possible themes. Then, invite team members to share possible themes with the group. Challenge your team to come to a consensus on the themes discovered in this process. You are going to find confirmation of some of the things you have suspected to be true, and you will uncover other aspects that will be disappointing. For instance, you might find a common theme related to a lack of ministry and mission service among students and parents. The thematic analysis leads to a series of actionable items that can provide strategic direction for your ministry.

As you analyze the data, ask questions such as:

- Which of the three spiritual growth areas (relationship with God, practice of spiritual disciplines, and service to God) is the strongest? Why?
- In which of our current environments do we expect teenagers to produce a growing relationship with God?
- In which of our current environments for teenagers did we expect to produce evidence of practicing spiritual disciplines?
- Which of our current environments did we expect to result in increased service to God?
- In what ways do we currently encourage a strong connection to the youth group?
- In what ways do we currently encourage a deep connection to the congregation?
- In what ways do we currently encourage strong relational connections between teenagers and parents?
- Which environment for teenagers should be revised?
- What new environment might produce our stated outcomes?
- In what ways can we better equip and train our volunteers based on these findings?
- What is at least one action step we can take to address these findings?

Summary Table

Combine your data into a summary table containing your survey work's average scores and statistics. You want a one- or two-page summary sheet that places all the data in one place. Use Figure 8 to assist with your work.

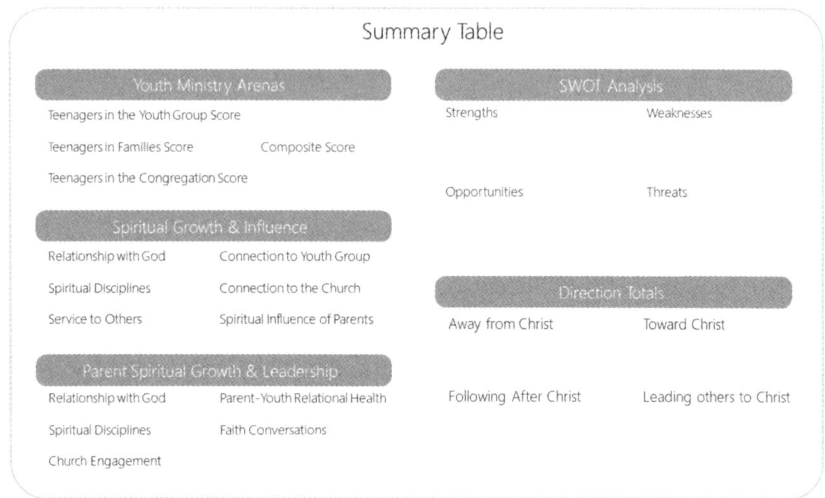

FIGURE 8: SUMMARY TABLE

Survey Work Step 3: Communicate Results

As your team completes its work, you should prepare to share the results with others. If some of the work reflects negatively on you and your ministry, your natural reaction will be to hide or minimize the results. Resist this temptation by doing the opposite—own it. Accept the results for what they are—a snapshot of the spiritual growth of your people and your current ministry. If the news is good, don't ease up on your efforts toward greater effectiveness. If the news is bad, don't give up and resign; instead, allow it to energize you to embrace the reconstruction process (next section of this book). Regardless of the findings, I encourage you to be transparent about the results. Openly sharing the results of your team's work can build trust and demonstrate accountability. Begin by sharing the results with your pastor. Invite his feedback and comments. Then, plan a meeting with parents, church leadership, and volunteers.

On a side note, you might consider presenting your data as "preliminary findings." Preliminary findings mean that you share the results of the survey work under the condition that you and your team are still at work analyzing the results and working on an action plan. If you intend to continue this process by moving from deconstructing your youth ministry to reconstructing it (next section), this approach might be helpful. In this scenario, you and your team would present the findings without any detailed response or action plan. You might say, "Our team is continuing to review and analyze the results and develop a comprehensive action plan for going forward. In the meantime, here is a summary of what we found." You have the raw data; now let's talk about what do with it to communicate to your people.

Create Presentations and Handouts

Creating clear and engaging presentations and handouts is essential when sharing survey results with the congregation. Use charts, graphs, and infographics to represent the data. If you are unfamiliar with creating this type of presentation, enlist the help of others, such as a church member or outside organization. These visual tools help make complex information easier to understand. Handouts should summarize the data clearly and concisely. Your handouts could include some of the same visuals from your presentation. The handouts provide a "take home" version of the data.

Write a Narrative Summary

A narrative summary encapsulates the survey findings and illustrates the results. It should provide a snapshot description of your youth ministry. I recommend writing a summary using some of the terms discussed earlier (highs and lows, strengths and weakness, and destination vs. direction). You may be asking yourself what the point of a narrative summary is. The short answer is stories connect with people. Describing your data in a narrative format helps communicate it in an easily digestible form.

Evaluating the survey findings will allow you to make informed decisions about your youth ministry. This might involve refining existing programs, reallocating resources, or introducing new ministry programs to address weaknesses and enhance strengths. In chapter 9, I will discuss a detailed process for rebuilding your youth ministry.

Survey Work Completion

You can complete the deconstruction process by gathering a deconstruction team, collecting and analyzing data, and communicating your findings. Review the following questions as you work with your church to deconstruct youth ministry:

Questions to Consider

1. Have you spent time in prayer about the deconstruction process?
2. Which step of pray, think, dream do you need to return to before proceeding?
3. Who do you need to enlist to join your deconstruction team?
4. Is your team a diverse representation of your congregation?
5. In what ways does your team represent an "eager coalition"?
6. In what ways do you need to prepare for the initial meeting of the deconstruction team?
7. Which surveys will your team use to collect data?
8. Who will you survey and interview?
9. Have you given ample time for your team to review and reflect on the analysis of the data before reporting?
10. What are your initial recommendations based on the survey results?
11. How can your team communicate the survey results to your church?

PART 2

Reconstruct Your Youth Ministry

CHAPTER 7

LOCAL RECONSTRUCTION

LEADING CHANGE IN YOUR CHURCH

When I was fifteen, my dad accepted a pastorate back to my home state of Mississippi. At the time, my dad was on staff at a church in Orlando, Florida. I loved living in Orlando. I loved the climate; it was close to beaches and, of course, Disney World. Like many of my friends, I anticipated getting my driver's license at sixteen and working at Disney. When my dad broke the news to my brother and me, I was devastated. I had great friends, and I loved my school—I couldn't believe we were leaving Florida. But simultaneously, as a Christian and someone already called to ministry, I understood. My dad was doing what he knew to be God's will for him and our family. I didn't know what a struggle this decision was for my dad. I mean, of course, it was. He was moving his family hundreds of miles away. But as a teenager, my thoughts were primarily about my heartbreak over the move.

Change is hard. Changing jobs is hard. Changing schools is hard. Changing zip codes is hard. Whether you are changing relationships, time zones, email addresses, or churches—change is hard. Because change is hard, we generally don't look forward to change. Lifeway Research found 29 percent of respondents left their church because the church changed in a way they didn't like.[1] When asked what changes they didn't like, 53 percent said too many things had changed "in general."[2] This chapter is about change—specifically, being a change leader.

Reconstructing youth ministry involves leading change within your church. This chapter will help youth leaders understand how to effectively lead the changes discussed in this book. Ministry practices addressed in this chapter are: being a change leader in youth ministry and leading change in four phases.

Ministry Practice: Being a Change Leader in Youth Ministry

Deconstructing youth ministry is about change. Change requires leadership. Leaders see things before others. A change leader is a catalyst for change. Being a change leader means confronting the reality of your current situation, communicating the needed changes to others, and doing these things with a sense of urgency.[3]

The Deconstruction Stage (chapters 1–6) dealt with confronting reality in your youth ministry. The metrics led you to evaluate your ministry in a variety of ways. Inevitably, they revealed necessary changes. You've taken the first steps of communicating the needed changes with others. You've gathered a team of leaders to assist you. Now in the Reconstruction Stage (chapters 7–9), I'll help you implement changes. This chapter is about preparing you to be a change leader.

---

[1] See Aaron Earls, "Church Switchers Highlight Reasons for Congregational Change," Lifeway Research (November 7, 2023), https://research.lifeway.com/2023/11/07/church-switchers-highlight-reasons-for-congregational-change/.

[2] Earls, "Church Switchers Highlight Reasons."

[3] See Thom S. Rainer, *Who Moved My Pulpit?: Leading Change in the Church* (B&H, 2016), 52.

The Vision of a Change Leader

In chapter 6, I discussed asking God to renew a clear vision for your ministry as you pray, think, and dream. I want to return to this theme because praying for a clear vision should be a part of your daily prayers. Much of this chapter on leading change revolves around helping others to see the vision God has given you for your youth ministry. Why? Because the first step of being a change leader is seeing the changes needed before anyone else.

A well-defined vision articulates the direction of your ministry and what you hope to achieve. It is a picture of what your youth ministry will look like after changes occur. Your vision should help accomplish the Great Commission and your church's mission. The vision starts with the change leader, but it grows through the input and reflection of others. Therefore, you'll need to involve key leaders, such as your reconstruction team (chapter 9), in the visioning process.

Change leaders align everything around the vision. The discipleship process, environments, and entry points should all support the vision. Change leaders seek to align the efforts of volunteers, parents, and staff around accomplishing the vision. You'll need buy-in from all of these people to see the vision become reality. Change is disruptive, and leaders rely on others to navigate the challenges.

The Challenges of a Change Leader

The vision of a change leader is crucial for navigating the challenges that often accompany change. Addressing these challenges paves the way for change and encourages others to join. Each church is unique, but most leaders face at least three challenges: resistance to change, aversion to uncertainty, and sustaining momentum for change. Pray for wisdom and discernment as you face these challenges as a change leader.

Resistance to Change

Generally speaking, people don't like change. Church members grow accustomed to how things are and how they've always been. Your volunteers, parents, students, and staff may feel attached to existing programs and ministry elements. You will face deniers, blamers, and critics who oppose the changes you suggest.[4] A denier is a person who does not believe anything needs to change. They believe the church is fine just as it is, and nothing needs to change. Blamers would rather blame others for the problems at your church than accept responsibility. For them, the issues in your church are someone else's fault—you, the senior pastor, the culture, or another church in town. The critics in your church are like the blamers, but rather than merely being resistant to change, critics take issue with everything in the church. As a result, the critics can be draining for pastors and staff who constantly attempt to address each area. Thom Rainer says that as many as 45 percent of your church members may be resistant to change.[5]

Despite the resistance to change, change leaders should continue to communicate the reality of the actual health of the church. One way to overcome resistance to change is by building trust, which takes time to build. Your people need to see your faithfulness over time. As you demonstrate consistency and unconditional love, church members will grow to trust you and your leadership. Openness and honesty throughout the deconstruction and reconstruction process lead your people to have faith in you.

Aversion to Uncertainty

Fear of the unknown is a powerful deterrent to change. Change inherently brings uncertainty. Keeping things the way they are maintains stability, but

---

[4] Rainer, 18.

[5] Rainer, 83.

change introduces unpredictability. Stress and anxiety are common results of uncertainty related to change. The deniers, blamers, and critics will voice plenty of uncertainty. Change leaders must be willing to address uncertainty by communicating a clear path forward. When it comes to change, you cannot overcommunicate. Your interpersonal skills will be put to the test as you seek to clearly articulate your plans. Prepare for meetings, one-on-one conversations, phone calls, group texts, PowerPoint presentations, video explanations, and more meetings. Your confidence in the process and your plan's potential results can create a sense of stability even amidst changes. The "eager coalition" of influencers in your church will assist you with both those who are resistant to change and those who fear uncertainty. This underscores the need to enlist people to your cause who will help you overcome these challenges.

Sustaining Momentum

A final challenge I want to address is the problem of momentum. You gain momentum in the deconstruction process as you test assumptions and signal your desire to improve your youth ministry. Some members will be excited, and others will maintain a "wait and see" attitude. Regardless, your willingness to act and make changes creates excitement. However, initial enthusiasm for your new initiatives can quickly wane. Church members can lose motivation if they do not see immediate results. To sustain momentum, a change leader must continually reinforce the vision and celebrate small wins. I'll discuss small wins below as I discuss ways to maintain change. Your communication skills are needed to keep the momentum of change going. Regular progress updates via newsletters, email, in-person conversations, and presentations help maintain high levels of engagement.

You may tend to address challenges and issues related to change from a purely logical and cognitive (thinking) perspective. However, change is more likely to occur when you connect it to an emotional experience.[6] Your survey's narrative summary report (chapter 6) is a great example of an emotional connection. Stories connect with people. Describing your data in a narrative format helps illicit an emotional response.

Related to a narrative summary report are narrative scenarios. A narrative scenario is a story describing the possible outcomes of the change initiative. These are not grandiose declarations of earth-shattering results but personal accounts of the potential difference to be made in the lives of students and families. Your scenarios can be fictitious, but the best ones are based on reality. For example, think of students at each stage of your discipleship process and write a scenario aimed at reaching their friends at the same stage. Start by addressing lost teenagers, then progress to those growing in their faith, and finish by describing disciple-making youth. End your scenario by explaining that the suggested changes are about reaching students like these. To make it more personal, when addressing a group of volunteers, leaders, and parents, you might refer specifically to some of your students by name. For example, "We are doing this to reach Camilla's friends and the students on Jacob's team." Bringing the emphasis back to teenagers and families and away from abstract notions helps leaders navigate the challenges of change.

Ministry Practice: Leading Change in Four Phases

Although I've addressed change throughout the book, I have not yet provided you with steps to implement the changes. Perhaps you are excited to deconstruct your youth ministry but don't know where to start. This section will help you develop a plan for leading change in your church.

Countless leadership books exist to assist you in ministry, but two of the most influential writers on change are John Kotter and Thom Rainer. Kotter's book on *Leading Change* is a foundational text on leading organizational change. Rainer applied Kotter's principles to the church in *Who Moved*

---

[6] See Todd Adkins, *Leading Change in Your Church* (Lifeway, 2019), 6.

My Pulpit?. Based on my own experience leading change and combining Kotter and Rainer, I suggest the following four phases, each with two goals:

1. Intentional Phase: Inspire and Rally
2. Leadership Phase: Empower and Act
3. Design Phase: Plan and Train
4. Multiplying Phase: Launch and Evaluate

Although you can begin these phases at any time in the deconstruction process, and there will certainly be overlap with what you may already have accomplished, I suggest beginning these phases after completing the deconstruction stage (chapters 1–6). The following phases will be most helpful in the reconstruction stage. This process will help you as you implement the changes you envision in chapter 9. The first step is to complete the Intentional Phase.

Intentional Phase: Inspire and Rally

As the name suggests, the first phase is about intentional leadership toward change. When you decide to act upon the things you've read in this book and begin the process of deconstruction, you are being intentional. The first phase has two goals: inspiring vision and rallying support with a sense of urgency. As I stated earlier, a leader sees things before others do. Therefore, your first task is to help your members see what you see. Start with prayer. Pray for a clear vision. Your vision should be based on the results of the survey work as outlined in chapter 6. So far, the processes I've described have been very analytical. Most of the metrics evaluate your ministry from a cognitive-thinking perspective. However, moving forward, to produce lasting change in your church and ministry, you will need to rely on the affective or emotional aspects of ministry. You need to make people feel in order for them to see the need for change.

You should begin by inspiring leaders, students, parents, and volunteers to embrace the change you feel must happen. This means clearly articulating a bold vision that addresses the pressing need or opportunity for ministry in your church. This vision should ignite passion and a sense of purpose, making the case for change both compelling and urgent. Your vision should focus on a potential end result. You inspire people by asking a question such as, "What might happen in our church *if* . . . ?" What might happen if more of our teenagers were reading the Bible and praying regularly? What might happen if more of our students were serving in our church? What might happen if more of our parents talked about their faith with their teenagers?

You may already have a mission or vision statement for your church or youth ministry. However, this vision should articulate the rationale for the specific changes you wish to make. For example, if you feel led to begin micro-groups for students, your vision statement might be: "Our youth ministry desires to cultivate an intimate, transformative discipleship experience, where three to five students embark on a journey of faith, mutual support, and accountability." Change begins by casting a clear vision that directs, aligns, and inspires action in your people.

In *Leading Change*, John P. Kotter declares that the biggest mistake leaders make when trying to change organizations is to move ahead "without establishing a high enough sense of urgency" for the needed change.[7] Deconstructing youth ministry is about a sense of urgency. You must convey a sense of urgency as you inspire and articulate your change plan. The urgency comes from students and parents needing the gospel and opportunities to grow in their faith. Can we go another year without change? Can we graduate another group of students without addressing concerns? A sense of urgency can be demonstrated by sharing the results of the discipleship surveys or the Youth Ministry Arenas Assessment. When your church understands the spiritual condition of youth and parents and the impact of your ministry, they will be more likely to embrace the changes you suggest.

---

[7] John P. Kotter, *Leading Change* (Harvard Business Review, 2012), 4.

I recommend spending at least three months in the Intentional Phase. Your first thought might be to rush ahead with changes. Don't rush. Take the necessary time to allow your people to get to the place in which they are ready to embrace change. This takes time.

Leadership Phase: Empower and Act

The second phase is about leadership development. As a change leader, you might be tempted to enact change alone. The truth is that you will need to recruit others to help you accomplish change. This second phase has two goals: empowering a team and acting to remove barriers. The first goal is to gather a team of individuals to help you. You already have a team if you've completed the deconstruction process described in previous chapters. Your deconstruction team becomes your reconstruction team. If you don't yet have a team to assist you, form one. However, I want to describe a slightly different approach to team development than the one earlier in chapter 6.

Before you gather a team, I suggest that you first prayerfully seek out a point person to champion youth discipleship in your church. You are looking for someone who is teachable and already exhibits leadership skills. It may take time to identify the right person. Be patient and continue to pray. Once you decide to approach a potential champion, begin by inviting this person to meet you for coffee or lunch and then share the vision for your ministry.

Once he or she agrees, invite your champion to meet with you weekly for prayer, Scripture study, and discussion of your youth ministry. Share with your champion what you've been praying about related to youth ministry. Talk about your concerns, hopes, and dreams in youth ministry. At the same time, study God's Word together. Read passages describing Jesus with his disciples. Study Paul's teachings on Christian growth. In essence, disciple your champion. Daniel Im states, "When it comes to developing a plan for discipleship and growth in your church, the one is as important as the many.

In fact, the only way to see your entire church grow spiritually and numerically is to start by discipling one person at a time."[8]

As you meet with your champion, discuss others who might be willing to join the youth ministry reconstruction team. This team should consist of enthusiastic supporters who believe in the vision and are willing to influence others. This "eager coalition" will serve as the backbone of your change initiative.[9] They should be influencers in your church, individuals in key positions, and supportive parents. These influencers may not serve in leadership positions in your church, but other members listen to them. You want this group to not only have your back and be supportive but also lead the charge for change.

As you prepare to gather this team, remember to move from informal to formal. For instance, don't make a broad appeal in a worship service or meeting—approach each member in an informal setting such as a coffee shop or over a meal. Share the vision and ask for feedback. Expect this process to take time as you have multiple conversations—some of these with the same person—to convey the need for change. Once you've enlisted them, it is time to gather formally to begin the change initiative in earnest.

A team approach at work may have burned your volunteers. Teams aren't promoted; individuals are. Therefore, some may not easily embrace a team approach to ministry. Others will see it as your sole responsibility to lead change in youth ministry. You must empower your team to take action by providing them with roles and responsibilities that contribute to the vision. Roles might include discipleship leader recruitment, training coordinator, and publicity. By empowering your team to take action, you are encouraging buy-in and leveraging the talents and abilities of a diverse group. Gather your team once a month to plan and share updates.

---

[8] Daniel Im, *No Silver Bullets: 5 Small Shifts That Will Transform Your Ministry* (B&H, 2017), 43.

[9] Rainer, *Who Moved My Pulpit?*, 61–62.

The second goal of this phase is to act quickly to remove barriers to change. Breaking down barriers—whether logistical, cultural, or based on perceptions—is a key component of any change initiative. Logistical barriers might include meeting space and scheduling. You might consider starting your discipleship initiative on a different evening or meeting at home rather than at the church. Cultural barriers can take time to overcome. For example, if you don't have strong discipleship culture at your church, people may not understand the need for additional discipleship. Another cultural issue you may face is a belief that all church programming should be open to everyone. You may find resistance if you begin talking about closed discipleship groups, such as invitation-only micro-groups. It will take time to help people understand these groups and why they are important. You may have to overcome perceptions about the nature of youth ministry. Some may feel things are going fine in your youth ministry because young people seem to "have fun," and parents are happy. Members of your congregation may not perceive a problem with youth discipleship and may question the need for change. Your team should help you identify anything hindering participation or progress toward change. Like the previous phase, I recommend at least three months for the Leadership Phase.

Design Phase: Plan and Train

In the Design Phase, you and your team will begin working earnestly toward launching your discipleship initiative. In this phase, you will plan your launch and train your leaders. Begin by answering the following planning questions:

- What is it that we are going to launch? (new or updated environment)
- When are we going to launch? (target date)
- Where are we going to launch? (day/time/place)
- How will we advertise it? (promotional materials)

At this point in the process, you probably have a pretty good idea about your discipleship initiative. But now you need to establish some specifics and describe your plan in detail. Suppose you intend to start youth micro-groups called D-groups. You need to define what D-groups are, how young people can join, and who will lead the groups. Start with a definition of D-groups such as:

> A D-Group is a gender-specific, closed group of three to five teenage believers who meet with a leader weekly for accelerated spiritual transformation. D-groups form through pre-existing, meaningful relationships with other believers in environments like youth small groups.[10]

I encourage you to start small when launching a new environment such as micro-groups. Plan to launch only one or two groups. Begin with your most committed teenagers. After six months, launch more groups. Establishing two start times per year enables you to train new leaders and builds anticipation for the next launch of the micro-groups.

Next, set a launch date for micro-groups to begin. You can start at any time, but people naturally think of things beginning in the fall as school begins or in January at the start of a new year. Starting in the fall or spring are both good times to launch.

Finally, choose the parameters by which groups will meet. Decide if you will require groups to meet at the church or allow them to gather in homes or other locations. Choose whether or not groups will meet on the same day and time or if you will allow groups to set their own schedule. You'll find advantages to each of these choices. Group meetings at the church building can be a good fit because teens and leaders are already accustomed to gathering in that space. It also allows you to have more

---

[10] Rob Gallaty, *Growing Up: How to Be a Disciple Who Makes Disciples*, rev. ed. (B&H, 2022), 48. I adapted this description for youth ministry.

oversight as groups meet. Group meetings at the church should also begin and end at the same time.

Allowing groups to meet outside the church on their schedule also has advantages. Group gatherings in homes or coffee shops will seem more organic and comfortable. Students and leaders may be drawn to the more casual feel. With this approach, you will give up some oversight and control, but with the right leaders, the freedom can allow groups to thrive.

Training your leaders is the next crucial step of this phase. For environments and programs that are familiar to your leaders, minimal training may suffice. However, if you launch an environment such as micro-groups that is unfamiliar to leaders and your church, more training will be required. You must decide how people will be trained to lead. Generally speaking, you have three choices: train leaders yourself, bring in guest experts to lead training, or send out your team for training at an event or church.

Training leaders yourself can have several advantages. First, you already know your leaders and have a feel for their strengths and weaknesses. You can use this knowledge to tailor the training. Second, leading the training allows for more flexibility in your training schedule. You might lead training over several weeks, at a weekend event, or a combination of the two.

You might also consider a different approach to planning and training. The Disciple/Leader Model (Figure 9) involves a youth leader forming a micro-group with three current or potential adult volunteers. The leader invites them to commit to meeting regularly for six months or a year. During this time, the leader will challenge the group to read Scripture, pray, study a book on leadership, and hold each other accountable. Throughout the time the group meets, the leader disciples the volunteers and models for them what a micro-group is like. After a year, the micro-group members form their own groups with three to five students.

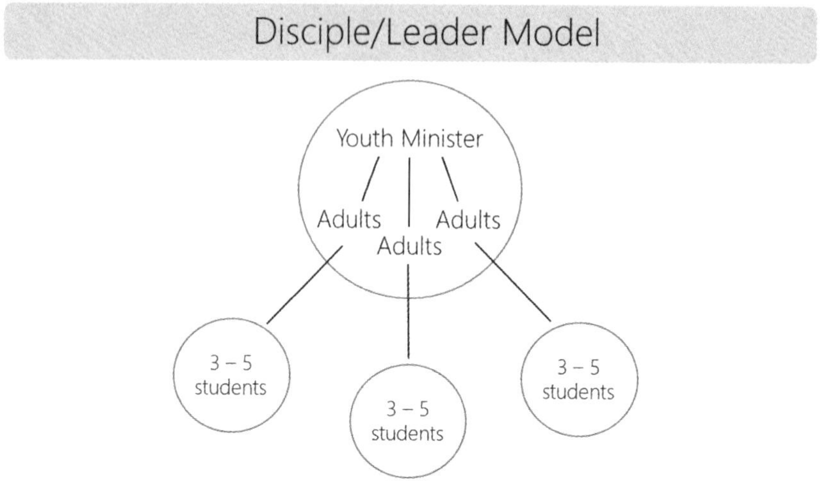

FIGURE 9: DISCIPLE/LEADER MODEL[11]

This approach has several advantages and disadvantages. A major advantage is volunteers gain the opportunity to be discipled by the leader and experience micro-groups themselves before leading their own. This "on-the-job" training prepares volunteers to confidently lead groups. One disadvantage is the delayed launch of student groups. The leader commits to at least six months of modeling the micro-group before student groups are launched. However, this approach enables you and your team to build excitement as volunteers share their experiences about the micro-group and students anticipate opportunities to join. Another option is for micro-groups to form after six months, but the leader continues to meet with and train volunteers as they lead their own groups.

Promotion of your new initiative is another component of the planning phase. Use various promotional strategies, including posters, videos, bulletin

---

[11] See Richard Dunn and Mark Senter, *Reaching a Generation for Christ: A Comprehensive Guide to Youth Ministry* (Moody, 1997), 174. My design is a slightly modified version of the model found in Dunn and Senter's foundational youth ministry book.

inserts, website announcements, social media posts, leader testimonies, and newsletters to promote your new environment or program. Consider a promotional strategy that gradually builds in intensity. For example, your first promotional materials might simply be a teaser that reads, "New Discipleship Environments for Youth Launching Soon!" No details, dates, or explanations accompany these first promotional items. Then, a month or two later, you replace the promotional materials by announcing the name of your new environment and the launch date, "D-groups for teens launch September 1." As the launch date approaches, produce additional promotional materials that further describe what D-groups are and how students can participate. Increasing awareness of your change initiative using a promotional strategy builds excitement among students and parents.

A final piece of your promotional strategy could include your pastor. Request that you or your pastor preach a sermon series on discipleship starting the weeks before launch. Plan for the final sermon of the series to coincide with your launch day. Part of the invitation at the end of service can include calls for youth to participate in the new discipleship initiative. Pastoral leadership and support of your discipleship efforts demonstrate to church members the importance of your change initiatives.

Celebrating and Sustaining Change in the Design Phase

When faced with leading change in your youth ministry, you may focus solely on the end result. While a focus on the end goal is necessary, it is not the only thing to which you need to give attention. You need to recognize the importance of acknowledging and celebrating smaller victories to keep momentum. Recognizing small successes can significantly boost morale and motivate people to continue toward additional changes.

John Kotter calls this celebrating "small wins." Small wins in youth ministry can take various forms. Celebrating small victories is crucial because it builds confidence and demonstrates the benefits of change. These small victories can motivate volunteers toward continued change. When looking for small wins, search for what Thom Rainer refers to as "low-hanging fruit."[12] I lived in Orlando, Florida, as a kid. My family had three orange trees and two grapefruit trees in our backyard. You would be amazed at how much fruit those trees produced. We could never use even a fraction of the oranges and grapefruit produced each year. But I could walk into the backyard whenever I wanted and pull off a fresh orange. The trees weren't tall, but I always picked fruit closest to the ground. Low-hanging fruit is the easiest to get.

The same is true in youth ministry. Low-hanging fruit are moments or experiences that are easy to identify and celebrate. They are examples of current ministry wins that point to the potential for more. Thom Rainer observes, "The leader seeks to find and articulate easier victories for the church that will lead to greater and potentially, more challenging victories."[13] For example, if you choose the Disciple/Leader Model, you could celebrate the fact that three volunteers are currently being discipled in anticipation of micro-groups beginning in the fall. Volunteers could share testimonies of their experiences with the micro-group. These testimonies will build excitement among students and parents.

Another example of low-hanging fruit relates to service opportunities for youth. You may anticipate that they will organize their own ministry service projects after micro-groups launch. In the meantime, whenever youth group members participate in service projects, it's a chance to highlight ministry service and the potential for more opportunities to come after the group's launch. You might make an announcement or show a video in the worship service in which you say something such as "We are thankful for the willingness of our students to serve others and we look forward to more service opportunities for our youth when D-groups launch this fall."

Consider creating a "win wall" in your youth space where you can post things like pictures of baptism, photos of students serving the community, and notes of encouragement from church members. A "win wall"

---

[12] Rainer, *Who Moved My Pulpit?*, 103.

[13] Rainer, 103.

is a visual representation that serves as a constant reminder of the group's contributions and growth. Although personal recognition and celebrations within the youth group are important, you must also celebrate wins with a wider audience. For this, you will need to publicly celebrate smaller wins by incorporating parents and the larger church congregation. I encourage you to set aside regular time for reflection and celebration. This might be a special part of a regular worship service or a dedicated celebration event. Leaders, students, and parents must connect their actions to positive outcomes to show how their contributions matter. The sum of many small wins can lead to the realization of larger goals. It fosters a growth mindset that encourages further changes.

From here, it's about maintaining the pace of change. It's all about sustaining positive momentum. A series of small victories creates momentum toward the larger change. As each small victory becomes the norm, a new culture of discipleship growth emerges. Your leaders, parents, and students will come to expect decisions for Christ and spiritual growth. This is a disciple-making culture. The famous statement, "culture eats strategy for breakfast," attributed to management expert Peter Drucker, holds significant implications for creating disciple-makers.[14] While your ministry may have well-thought-out strategies on paper, the reality often reveals a misalignment between strategy and your church culture. This misalignment can hinder your ministry's ability to make your desired changes effectively.

The timeline for the Design Phase is six months to a year. You'll use this time to plan for your launch and train your volunteers. You will celebrate small wins and build anticipation for your launch.

---

[14] See Michael J. Reidy, "Culture Eats Strategy for Breakfast . . . and what to do about it," Interaction Associates, https://www.interactionassociates.com/resources/blog/culture-strategy. The statement "culture eats strategy for breakfast" is attributed to Peter Drucker but made famous by two business executives: Mark Fields of Ford Motor Company and Richard Clark, Merck CEO.

Multiplying Phase: Launch and Evaluate

It's been a long time coming, and the day is finally here—it's time to launch your new change initiative. The final phase is the Multiplying Phase. In this phase, you will launch your strategy and evaluate its effectiveness.

Schedule a meeting with your renovation team a week before your launch date to review last-minute preparations. Ensure the preparation of meeting spaces, curriculum, and volunteer leaders. Spend time praying as a group for God to move in the hearts and lives of teenagers and volunteer leaders. On launch day, gather your renovation team and invite them to be present as the initial groups arrive. You want your team to see the fruit of their labor. Invite them to spend time in prayer as the groups gather.

You and your team will be both excited and relieved when launch day finally arrives. The tendency will be to move on to the next thing and encourage groups to continue to meet. But your job is not yet done. Remind team members they have one more task to complete—evaluation. I suggest at least two evaluation points: one week after launch and three months later. During the week after launch, you and your team should meet or have conversations with all leaders. Generally, you want to know how things went the first day. More specifically, you want to know about any problems or issues. Your team has worked hard for months or even a year, but you can't anticipate everything that might go wrong. Meet with your team the week after launch and discuss the positive and negative aspects of the first week. Formulate a plan to address the concerns and invite team members to write thank you notes of appreciation to the volunteer leaders and everyone who helped with the launch.

Sometime around the three-month mark, invite your team together one final time. Now that time has passed, you will have a clearer picture of what is working well and what needs to be addressed. Spend time in the meeting, both celebrating and evaluating. Invite your team to share stories they have heard from participants. Take time to pray and thank God for all he has done. Then spend time in the meeting reviewing problems and issues.

It may be small things such as scheduling conflicts or major issues such as inconsistent leaders. Give attention to each concern and develop a plan to address them. The crucial aspect of this evaluation is not only for the existing groups but also for the next round of groups you plan to launch. You should endeavor to learn as much as you can this first go around so that all of the issues can be worked out. It may be tempting to dismiss this final evaluation step, but if this book has taught you anything, it should be to value assessment and welcome critique to improve your ministry to teenagers.

This four-phase process can be useful when launching a variety of discipleship environments and events. Moving through this process may lead you and your team to follow a similar schedule for planning DiscipleNow, youth camp, mission trips, and retreats. Moving your planning to a year or more in advance instead of weeks before an event puts you in a better position for success.

Another benefit of this strategy relates to change itself. When you and your team can successfully launch something new, it lays the groundwork for further change. One change can lead to another. The next initiative builds on the success of the previous one. Before long, you have developed a culture of change in your youth ministry and congregation. Change is no longer avoided; it is embraced. You'll know when a culture of change has taken root when you hear members comment on change and say, "It's just the way we do things around here."[15]

Questions to Consider

1. In what ways do you convey a sense of urgency about evangelism and discipleship of teenagers and parents?
2. What is the vision God has given you for youth and parents at your church?

---

[15] See Kotter, *Leading Change*, 14.

3. In what ways are you prepared to address the challenges of being a change leader?
4. Which of the four phases for leading change did you find most challenging?
5. What are the greatest challenges in the Intentional Phase for your church?
6. What roadblocks might you face in the Leadership Phase?
7. In what ways might the Design Phase be difficult for you and your church?
8. What do you find appealing or challenging about the Disciple/Leader Model?
9. What are several small wins you could celebrate to help you with your change initiative?
10. What aspects of the Multiplying Phase did you find difficult?
11. In what ways can you incorporate evaluation into more areas of your youth ministry?

CHAPTER 8

Human Resources

Leadership Development in Youth Ministry

I served as youth minister of a normal-sized church while in seminary. It was a small youth group, and, my wife and I were the only leaders. We loved leading students together, and for the most part, being the only leaders worked just fine. However, there were a few times when, because of my wife's work schedule, I was the only adult present in a room full of teenagers. I knew then that relying on only the two of us to lead the youth ministry wasn't sustainable. We needed help.

You shouldn't do youth ministry alone. If it's just you and one other person (maybe a spouse) leading your youth ministry, recruit at least one more volunteer. According to Ken Braddy, "If you want to reach more people, you need more people."[1] This chapter will help you recruit and train adult volunteers, as well as assist with the development of student leaders.

[1] Ken Braddy, *Breakthrough: Creating a New Scorecard for Group Ministry Success* (B&H, 2022), 65.

Ministry Practice: Developing Adult Volunteers

Volunteers are vital to effective youth ministry. Therefore, developing adult volunteers is a crucial task for any youth ministry leader. Volunteers bring life experience, professional skills, and Christian maturity to your ministry context. Because discipleship is relational, you need volunteers who will develop godly relationships with students and help teens grow toward Christlike maturity. The average church employs one full-time staff person for every sixty-two attendees.[2] This means your church cannot hire enough staff to minister to every member (nor should they). Therefore, volunteers are necessary to accomplish the tasks of youth ministry.

Recruiting and training volunteers for youth ministry requires patience and discernment. Volunteers play a pivotal role in youth ministry, and you can't afford to choose leaders hastily. To build a strong leadership team of volunteers, you must pay careful attention to the selection and training of your workers.

What to Look for in a Volunteer

You don't want just anyone volunteering in your youth ministry. You want leaders who model Christlikeness and those who are a good fit within your ministry. Therefore, the first step in leadership development is identifying people who have the potential and desire to lead. You should look for individuals with specific qualities necessary to be excellent youth volunteers. At the most basic level, volunteers should enjoy spending time with teenagers. You also need to seek out volunteers that can balance out your weaknesses.

As you prayerfully consider enlisting volunteers, you want to look for specific characteristics. Use the AFTR method when looking for

[2] See the Unstuck Group, *The Unstuck Church Report* (May 2024), 4, https://theunstuckgroup.com/landing-page/ucr/#register-here.

leaders.[3] Search for volunteers who are Available, Faithful, Teachable, and Responsive.

Available

The first requirement is that he or she be available. The person might be a kid magnet and an amazing leader, but he or she must also have time to spare. Being available means a willingness to prioritize ministry. I've had volunteers who tended to view youth ministry as something they do only if they don't have something else to do. You don't want this type of leader. Being available means being present for meetings, events, and other ministry opportunities. Availability extends to being approachable and willing to build godly relational connections with youth beyond scheduled activities. When volunteers consistently offer to spend time with students, they make significant strides toward developing the trust required for deep discipling relationships.

Faithful

Your volunteers should be faithful. Faithfulness refers to both a commitment to God and your church's mission and values. Because your volunteers will serve as role models for students, they need to be faithful Christians. Their lives should be characterized by Christlike maturity. Volunteers also demonstrate faithfulness through consistent church attendance and support of your youth ministry. You are looking for people you can depend on and those you can trust to follow through on commitments.

---

[3] See Bobby Harrington and Alex Absalom, *Discipleship That Fits: The Five Kinds of Relationships God Uses to Help Us Grow* (Zondervan, 2016), 186. Harrington and Absalom cite Dann Spader for Available, Faithful, Teachable, Reliable. I changed Reliable to Responsive.

Teachable

You don't want volunteers who think they know all they need to about teenagers and discipleship. Instead, you are looking for humble individuals willing to learn. Teachable refers to someone willing to accept guidance and direction. Volunteers with a teachable spirit are more willing to embrace training opportunities and seek guidance from experienced leaders. Teachable volunteers view change as a natural part of any organization. A teachable person is a lifelong learner always looking to increase knowledge or develop a new skill.

Responsive

Volunteers who react quickly and positively to various situations are responsive. You have to expect the unexpected in youth ministry. Therefore, responsiveness is a tremendous quality in a youth ministry volunteer. Responsive volunteers are active listeners, alert leaders, and willing to help whenever needs arise. Leaders who are responsive model Christ's compassion and service. Responsiveness, along with faithfulness, builds trust between students and other leaders.

The Faith Beyond Youth Group research study by Fuller Youth Institute revealed five ways character formation fuels the discipleship of young people. The five points of the Faith Beyond Youth Group Compass are: cultivate trust, model growth, teach for transformation, practice together, and make meaning.[4] The consistency of volunteers and relational closeness cultivate trust among teenagers. Volunteers model growth as they spend time with students. Openness and appropriate vulnerability enable youth to witness what it looks like to be a believer today. Storytelling, asking questions, and providing opportunities for teenagers to lead are examples

---

[4] See Kara Powell, Jen Bradbury, and Brad M. Griffin, *Faith Beyond Youth Group: 5 Ways to Form Character and Cultivate Lifelong Discipleship* (Baker, 2023), 57.

of teaching for transformation. Young people also need a chance to practice faith together by taking action and then reflecting with leaders. When volunteers lead young people to reflect on their practices, it helps teens experience meaning-making.[5]

Recruit Volunteers Through Personal Appeals

Imagine the following scenario. The school year is about to start, and your small groups are about to begin. You have volunteers assigned to lead junior high small groups according to grade and sex. But at the last minute, one of your leaders gets a job transfer and leaves town. Now, you need an adult leader for seventh-grade boys. You are desperate, and you ask the pastor to give you two minutes at the end of the worship service on Sunday. You make your announcement, trying not to sound too concerned, and ask anyone interested to meet with you after the service.

Most leaders can relate to the feeling of desperation that a lack of volunteers creates. However, you should avoid mass appeals for help. A mass appeal is any request for help within the context of a large group—like the one described above. These include church group gatherings, Sunday bulletins or handouts, adult small group gatherings, church newsletters, and mass emails. A personal appeal is intentionally choosing one individual with whom you discuss a possible volunteer role. Having multiple conversations using this method may be necessary, but it is worth it in the end. Let me share three reasons why you should avoid making mass appeals and recruit only through personal appeals.

More Effective

Personal appeals are generally more effective than mass appeals. You are making a relational connection when you talk with someone one-on-one,

---

[5] Powell, Bradbury, and Griffin, 57.

either in person or on the phone. A personal appeal demonstrates your willingness to invest in the potential worker. When you approach an individual personally, it shows you see potential in him or her. Think about when someone approached you personally and asked you to participate or lead. Personal invitations carry enormous weight with individuals. When you speak with someone one-on-one, you can convey your passion for youth ministry and share about the difference a volunteer makes in students' lives.

Mass appeals are impersonal and can be easily ignored. What's worse, you may actually have individuals respond to a mass appeal that you do *not* want in youth ministry. Then you are faced with the awkward situation in which you have to say no to someone you don't want when they know you need help.

Deeper Dialogue

Personal appeals allow you to take the time to have a deeper conversation with individuals. In these conversations, you can talk in-depth about the roles and responsibilities of the position. A personal appeal allows the individual to ask questions and express concerns. It provides an opportunity for transparency. Don't sugarcoat a volunteer position. Avoid using terms such as "It's easy," "It won't take much of your time," or "Anyone can do it." Phrases like these lower expectations at a time in the process in which you want to raise them. Instead, convey that volunteering in youth ministry can be both rewarding and challenging. Share that it requires a great deal of time to build relational connections with teenagers and that positions like this are not for everyone. Convey that volunteering for youth ministry is a rare privilege. Modeling Christlike maturity for students will have a lasting impact. Raise the bar on your expectations and share them in your initial conversations. These deeper conversations also allow you to address any hesitations and respond to questions.

Discernment Opportunities

Personal appeals allow you to identify and cultivate potential long-term leaders. In your personal appeal, you want to be aware of an individual's characteristics that make him or her a good candidate for youth ministry. You are looking for Christlike characteristics, dependability, teachability, and margin in life to serve. Your conversations allow you to discern volunteers' strengths, passions, and potential growth. When you have several open positions, these personal conversations allow you to get a sense of which position will be the best fit for the person. Your discernment in this area can enhance their ministry experience and potentially increase retention. Leaders tend to stay in roles in which they are gifted. Your personal appeal will also foster a sense of accountability with the individual. We feel engendered to those who recruit us because we value the fact they see something in us. Skip the mass appeals for help and instead focus on personal conversations with potential leaders.

When Recruitment Isn't Recruitment

The one exception I want to note to the mass appeal approach to recruiting is the use of testimonies (either live or recorded on video). I encourage you to invite both current volunteers and students to talk at least once a year about your youth ministry. You might invite one or two people to share immediately following youth camp or mission trip. Better yet, create a two-minute video highlighting various youth events and environments that includes at least one adult sharing the joys of serving in youth ministry. This is a testimony video, but it is also a recruitment video. The goal is to make youth ministry the most exciting ministry in the church—so much so that people can't wait to volunteer!

If you want to recruit well, your ministry must have a good reputation with your congregation. This means you have to treat volunteers well. If you create a culture where volunteers are valued and they understand the long-term impact of their service to the kingdom, your recruitment efforts will be much easier. Three ways to show you value volunteers are: communicate expectations, provide time off, and celebrate your leaders.

Communicate Expectations

Whether recruiting new volunteers or leading seasoned youth ministry veterans, you need to clearly communicate your expectations. Help your leaders understand their roles and responsibilities with youth. What do you need them to do? How long do you need their help? What should they do if they have questions or need help? Answering these and other questions helps your volunteers know what is expected. Clear communication prevents misunderstandings. I encourage you to develop a job description for every volunteer role in your youth ministry. Each job description should explain the role and expectations for volunteers. Don't just write job descriptions for small group leaders; write them for everything—from parking lot attendants to youth camp sponsors. Several excellent online sources provide templates for volunteer job descriptions, including Lifeway's Ministry Grid (ministrygrid.lifeway.com) and Ministry Architects (ministryarchitects.com).

Provide Time Off

Another important way to show volunteers you value their commitment is to schedule time off from serving. When you build regular breaks from youth ministry programming into your schedule, you give volunteers time to rest and recharge. For example, I provided two seasons of time off for weekly volunteers by canceling small groups for the month of December and two months (June and July) in the summer. December is a busy month for families, and your willingness for youth ministry programming to slow down or break completely at the end of the year provides a needed break for volunteers. The same is true for the summer months. Families take vacations, and normal routines are interrupted. I would plan alternative programming for youth that replaced small groups for the summer months. These summer activities required less from volunteers, and I found that my leaders appreciated a break. The additional value of regular breaks is that they create a "semester" approach to youth ministry programming.

When I recruit new volunteers, I can explain that I'm looking for a commitment for the fall semester (August to December) and the spring semester (January to May). The summer months were also an excellent time to invite new volunteers to "try out" youth ministry by serving as a one-time event sponsor for a youth pool party or movie night. Providing time off for volunteers demonstrates a sensitivity to the well-being of your volunteers and value for their commitment to youth ministry.

Celebrate Leaders

Acknowledging and appreciating volunteers is another way to create a culture in which volunteers are valued. Recognizing your volunteers' hard work and dedication boosts morale and helps leaders feel cherished. I encourage you to celebrate volunteers both publicly and privately. Celebrations include public acknowledgments, awards for service and excellence, and special events dedicated to honoring service. Private acknowledgments include saying "thank you," writing notes, and giving gifts. Tony Bianco serves as the student pastor of the Loop campus of Houston's First Baptist Church. The youth ministry hosts a Leader Appreciation Gala each year for volunteers. The Gala has the feel of a Hollywood awards night. Volunteers and their families enjoy a formal meal and hear testimonies from students and leaders. They give out awards to volunteers and show a video highlighting ministry over the past year. Events like this provide opportunities to celebrate your leaders and acknowledge their service to Christ's kingdom.

Recruiting and keeping great leaders takes work. Creating a positive culture for your youth ministry ensures that your volunteers feel valued and makes your ministry a favored area of service in your church. Volunteers are the backbone of your youth ministry, and your leaders deserve to be recognized for their sacrifice and commitment to teenagers.

Four-Step Recruitment Process

I've served in churches in which there was so much competition between age-group ministries for good volunteers that the children's minister and I would race to talk with any new family with kids or youth that joined the church. I know the competition for great volunteers can be fierce. I encourage you to avoid inviting a person you do not know personally to volunteer in youth ministry immediately. You should develop a four-step process.

Step 1: Pray

I encourage you to pray for wisdom and discernment from God before making a personal appeal. Create a list of potential volunteers and pray over the names. Ask God to help you know who you should approach to volunteer and who you should remove from the list.

Step 2: Initial Conversation About the Open or New Position

As you share about the volunteer position, you should also seek information from the person. You need to know a few things about the person. Are they trustworthy? How well do they interact with teenagers? Have they been a member of the congregation for at least six months? Just as you are interviewing them, they are interviewing you—be prepared to answer questions and concerns they may have.

Step 3: Background Check and Sexual Abuse Awareness Training

This is part of leading youth ministry today, and you shouldn't skip this step. Your church's insurance company may require anyone who works with minors to complete sexual abuse training. But even if they don't, you should make it a policy for all youth ministry volunteers.

Step 4: Follow-Up Interview to Discuss Position Further and Invitation to Take Position

These steps could take several days or weeks to complete. Don't rush the process. Take the time to do it right.

The Long Game Approach to Recruitment

Discipling and mentoring potential volunteers is the best way to develop leaders. It requires you to start recruiting today for volunteers you will need next year. However, this approach not only trains leaders to serve in youth ministry but also models the type of leadership you want them to produce in others. For example, you might adopt the Disciple/Leader Model (Figure 9), in which you form a micro-group with three current or potential volunteers. You invite them to commit to meeting regularly for a year. During this time, you will lead the group to read Scripture, pray, study a book on leadership, and hold each other accountable. After a year, the micro-group members form their own groups with three to five students. This is the same approach I advocated when starting micro-groups (chapter 7). Although this approach takes time to see results, it offers the greatest potential for reproduction.

> Jesus' strategy illustrates a principle that church leaders witness regularly: The reach of our ministries is directly proportional to the breadth of our leadership base. Only to the extent that we have grown self-initiating, reproducing, fully devoted disciples can new

> ministries touch the brokenness of people's lives. Therefore we see unmet needs because we have not intentionally grown champions to meet those needs.[6]

Great volunteers lead to effective youth ministry. You can't be everything your group needs at all times. You are gifted, but your ability to connect with every student is limited. Volunteers fill the gaps by bringing diverse experiences and personalities to your leadership team. They also help link teenagers with older generations, which produces an interconnected congregation.

Leadership Training

Volunteers bring various skills, abilities, and talents to your youth ministry. However, your volunteers still need training to be the most effective leaders possible. For example, training your volunteers should cover interpersonal skills, conflict resolution, and behavioral guidelines. Volunteers may need help understanding today's teenagers and the developmental differences between older and younger students. Your leaders must also understand how to use the Bible study curriculum and how it fits into your discipleship process.

Consider offering a mix of formal and informal training. For example, you might require annual training at an in-person event, and online sessions for sexual abuse awareness training. You might bring in an expert from outside your church or send your volunteers to another church for training. Check out Ministry Grid (ministrygrid.lifeway.com) and Right Now Media (rightnowmedia.org) for excellent online volunteer training videos.

Another form of leadership development is mentoring. Mentoring relationships with potential and current leaders enhances leadership

---

[6] Greg Ogden, *Transforming Discipleship: Making Disciples a Few at a Time* (InterVarsity, 2003), 72.

development. Pairing leaders with experienced mentors provides ongoing training and modeling of Christlikeness.

Ministry Practice: Leadership Development of Teenagers

The goal of discipleship is Christlikeness. A component of Christlikeness is service, and I believe that all students should be called to serve the church, community, and world in some way. However, students need training to be effective leaders.

Some leaders say we should only focus on discipleship. They remind us that Jesus told us to make disciples, not leaders. Others declare that we must prioritize leadership development. According to Gary Reinecke, "One simple distinction is that discipleship focuses on *following* and leadership, on *influencing*."[7] If you were asked to choose between discipleship or leadership development—which would you choose? My answer is neither. Why? Because you don't have to choose—it's a false dichotomy. It's a logical fallacy to say you must choose one over the other. It's not an either-or decision. You can and should do both. As you disciple youth, give them opportunities to practice leadership. As you help students prepare for leadership roles, you disciple them.

Leadership is both upfront and behind the scenes. Depending on their personality and giftedness, youth may gravitate toward one or the other. You should communicate the equal value and worthiness of both roles. The problem is that we tend to only develop upfront leaders in youth ministry. You should consider ways you might affirm leaders who prefer background roles and celebrate their willingness to serve.

---

[7] Gary Reinecke, "Discipleship vs. Leadership," Gateway Leadership Initiative, August 26, 2016, https://www.glichurchplanting.com/discipleship-vs-leadership/.

Why Youth Leadership Development Is Important

Perhaps you're on the fence about prioritizing the leadership development of young people. Maybe your plate is already full, and you can't imagine adding something else. I get that, but I also know that as youth grow toward Christlike maturity, some are going to need guidance from you to be the leaders God wants them to be. Consider these three reasons for the leadership development of young people.

Making a Difference Today

Teenagers are not just the future of the church; they are the church today. Students involved in ministry service make an impact on people's lives and help them grow. Youth make a difference now, not just in the future. Teens have gifts and abilities that need to be used in the church. Youth can lead in worship services, media ministry, social media management, greeters, ushers, small group leaders, kids ministry leaders, and nursery help. In addition, teens bring fresh ideas, an openness to change, and offer a fresh perspective. Teenagers today believe they can change institutions—including the church.[8] Your willingness to develop teenage leaders encourages their commitment to your church and making a difference in Christ's kingdom.

Enhancing Spiritual Growth

As youth serve, they grow in their faith. When students serve, they realize they must rely on God. Taking youth out of their comfort zone creates opportunities for teens to further rely on God. Service can promote a sense of belonging and ownership within the church. Part of discipleship is helping young people move from consumers to contributors. This sense of

[8] See Corey Seemiller and Meghan Grace, *Generation Z Goes to College* (Jossey-Bass, 2016), 44.

belonging can enhance their spiritual growth and encourage them to remain active in the church beyond high school.

Investing in the Future

The truth is young people are also the future of the church. Leadership development impacts future leaders of our congregations. Leadership experience during middle school and high school can influence a lifetime of ministry service. Youth develop valuable life skills as they lead. Skills include communication, teamwork, problem-solving, and decision-making. When you stay in your youth ministry position long enough, you begin to see the fruit of your labor. Students who were once seventh graders in your youth group go on to serve in your youth ministry as college students and young adults. Some of the teens who would drive you crazy in junior high become deacons in the church. Still, others will follow a call to full-time vocational ministry and missions. Your commitment to developing young people as leaders can impact generations.

Developing Student Leaders

My own experience with leadership development of youth involved three steps. First, I would look for students I felt had leadership potential and ask them to serve. Second, I led students in leadership training. For example, because our local high school students could leave campus for lunch, I started a gathering called "Leadership Lunch." I invited students to join me at a fast-food restaurant near the school campus, and while they ate lunch, I'd share a few things about leadership. I would usually tell a story from a leadership book like John Maxwell's *The 21 Irrefutable Laws of Leadership.* I'd end with a few questions aimed at applying a principle to their own experiences as young leaders. Finally, I would provide weekly opportunities for young people to serve on the stage and behind the scenes in various ways. Let's look at these three in more detail.

Identify Potential Leaders

Many of your students are not ready to lead. Many of your students are also not prepared to be trained and mentored. You need to identify those ready for leadership. It might be just one student or a small group. Start with who you have. Don't wait and think, "I'll start developing student leaders when I have more students interested in leadership." Don't do this—lead the few or one today. Look for students who demonstrate a servant's heart. Potential student leaders come early and stay late, help clean up, ask to help out, and influence their peers. Student leaders are responsible, empathetic, and willing to serve. Ask your adult volunteers to help you identify potential student leaders and invite them to help you develop young people as leaders.

Provide Training and Mentors

Once you've identified potential leaders, the next step is to provide training and mentorship. Leadership training can be both formal and informal. On the formal side, you can offer classes and training meetings. Sessions can include biblical principles of leadership, communication skills, and training in specific ministry areas of the church (nursery, media, children). You may require students to complete a formal leadership application or interest form before participating. Informally, you might invite students to lunch (like my example above) or spend time with youth before or after serving in some way. You should seek to help youth understand servant leadership and how Jesus modeled it. Help teens see how they set an example for other young people to follow. Training moments like these help young people realize their potential influence.

Mentoring relationships are the most intimate discipleship environment, and they can be a tremendously effective form of student leadership development. Some of the most rewarding experiences I've had in youth ministry involved mentoring student leaders. I've mentored students called to vocational ministry and young people who wanted to be disciple-makers.

Consider inviting students to assist you as you do ministry. Invite young people to help you set up for events, visit guests, and share the gospel with students. My pastor admonished our staff to "never do ministry alone." This applies to adult volunteers and student leaders.

Pairing teenagers with experienced adult mentors can provide students with guidance and support. Mentors model Christlike maturity and provide youth with personalized training. Of course, you will want to remind mentors of your adult and student interaction policies and require mentors to complete sexual abuse awareness training. This combination of training and mentorships enables young people to be prepared for leadership now and in the years to come.

Offer Leadership Opportunities

The final step takes young people beyond the theoretical to the practical. The best training ground is experience. When you provide real-life leadership opportunities for students, you help young people learn in new ways. Youth can lead small groups, organize events, and, depending on your church policy, participate in church committees. Tim McKnight states, "When students use their spiritual gifts in the congregation, they develop multigenerational relationships while working alongside church members."[9]

Teenagers aren't perfect, and they will make mistakes. Student leaders may occasionally let you down. But don't let failures stop you from continuing to let youth lead. Debriefing students after service projects or ministry sessions allows youth to learn from mistakes and discuss alternative responses. Regular feedback and reflection take leadership development to the next level. By offering opportunities for young people to lead, the church benefits from their service and helps teens develop a sense of ownership of their faith and community.

---

[9] Tim McKnight, *Navigating Student Ministry: Charting Your Course for the Journey* (B&H Academic, 2022), 102.

Don't try to do ministry alone. Recruit godly men and women to join you in discipling teenagers and parents. Help your volunteers relationally disciple young people. Teach them how to interact with teenagers and parents. Help your young people develop as leaders in your youth group and the congregation. Your training of students today will impact the church for years to come.

Questions to Consider

1. Who were some potential adult volunteers that came to mind as you read this chapter?
2. What are some additional qualities you look for in a volunteer?
3. What are some of the most successful recruitment approaches you've used?
4. What can you do to avoid making mass appeals for volunteers?
5. Which step of the Four-Step Recruitment Process do you find most challenging?
6. What elements of the Long Game Approach to Recruitment did you find valuable?
7. Who were some potential youth leaders that came to mind as you read this chapter?
8. What's your opinion on discipleship vs. leadership development? Are they the same thing or different?

CHAPTER 9

CONSTRUCTION ZONE

REBUILDING YOUR MINISTRY

I have a friend who rebuilds antique cars. He finds old and broken-down vehicles in salvage yards and restores them. He often has to rebuild engine parts and fashion components from other cars. Steering and suspension arms are repaired, and the crankshaft is rebuilt. He adds a few modern elements, but for the most part, he wants it to look like the original. The body is repainted and the interior finishes are replaced. When completed, the car looks like it just rolled off the assembly line.

Once you've completed the deconstruction process outlined in part 1, it's time to rebuild. But unlike the restored antique car, this rebuild is meant for the modern world. You won't just put on a new coat of paint; you'll start fresh with a new foundation.

This chapter represents a change in emphasis from deconstruction to reconstruction. In the previous section, I focused each chapter on testing ministry assumptions. In this section, I emphasize ministry practices designed to help you reconstruct your ministry. Reconstructing youth ministry involves ministry practices that lead students and parents toward Christlike maturity. This chapter will help leaders reconstruct youth ministry through the practical application of the discipleship process and environments described in chapters 4 and 5. Chapter 6 led you through the steps of surveying your ministry. This chapter will help with the final steps of rebuilding your ministry. The ministry practices in this chapter are building a reconstruction team, leading teenagers in the youth group, leading teenagers in families, and leading teenagers in the congregation. If deconstruction is about eliminating ineffective programs and practices, reconstruction is about intentionally restoring them with purpose.

Ministry Practice: Building a Reconstruction Team

In this book, I talk a lot about teams and team building because you should never do ministry alone. You shouldn't attempt to deconstruct youth ministry alone, and you don't need to reconstruct your ministry alone either. Regardless of the size of your church, you need others to walk beside you on this journey.

If you enlisted people to form a deconstruction team, invite the same people to help you reconstruct it. Your deconstruction team now becomes a reconstruction team. Consider adding additional members as well. Your team should consist of enthusiastic supporters who believe in your vision. They should include key influencers within your church. Include a mix of parents, volunteers, and church staff. When you are recruiting leaders to assist with your reconstruction, look for people who are "runners." Ron Clark describes runners this way:

> They come early or they stay late. They never complain, and they provide a positive spirit. Their work ethic is strong, and their attention to detail is spot on. They are the strongest members

of the team, and they are the driving force behind the success of the organization.[1]

Your reconstruction team will help you chart a new course for your ministry. They will examine the results of your survey work and assist you with formulating a change plan. I recommend at least three meetings. The first meeting will involve reviewing the survey results and discussing initial reactions. The second meeting will focus on the reconstruction process (described below). The third meeting will challenge your group to formulate a new discipleship strategy. You can certainly accomplish this work in fewer or more steps, but I've found that people need time to process and think about your ministry in between meetings. Spreading out your reconstruction process over several weeks gives people time to pray and think about what should be done.

The first task of your reconstruction team is to review the summary of your major findings from the deconstruction process. Asking and answering questions has been at the heart of the deconstruction process. As you reconstruct, you need to continue to ask questions. John Maxwell says, "Questions allow us to build better ideas."[2] In your initial meeting with your team, ask the following questions to get your group to discuss the findings:

- What are the strengths and weaknesses of our youth ministry?
- What are the most surprising things about the findings?
- How do you feel about the results?
- What were the recommendations?
- What content and curriculum ideas do you have to address the findings?

---

[1] Ron Clark, *Move Your Bus: An Extraordinary New Approach to Accelerating Success in Work in Life* (Touchstone, 2015), 4.

[2] John Maxwell, *Good Leaders Ask Great Questions: Your Foundation for Effective Leadership* (Center Street, 2014), 10.

- What volunteer additions do you recommend?
- What are your initial ideas about how we might improve the effectiveness of our youth ministry?

Give your team ample time to process the information and discuss their thoughts and feelings. Don't rush the process. Although you've doubtless spent hours and hours thinking about the deconstruction process, most of your team members have not. They will need time. End your meeting by enlisting initial ideas from folks about how you might improve the effectiveness of your ministry. Ask team members to focus their responses on the survey results from students and parents—particularly areas with lower scores. Write all the ideas on a whiteboard or keyboard response on a computer. These initial thoughts from your team will drive the rest of the process. In my experience, the initial ideas shared in the first meeting play an essential role in the reconstruction process.

Reconstruction Framework

The Reconstruction Framework is about putting all the pieces of your youth ministry together in one cohesive strategy. It's about leading your reconstruction team to help you develop a discipleship process for each of the three arenas of youth ministry and then matching discipleship environments and entry points for each. In chapter 3, you deconstructed your youth ministry using the metric of the three arenas. In chapter 4 you defined your discipleship goals, wrote a mission/process statement, and selected your process action verbs. In chapter 5 you evaluated your discipleship environments (and considered new ones) and deconstructed your entry points. Now it's time to align your discipleship process with the arenas and connect your environments. Figure 10 illustrates the Reconstruction Framework.

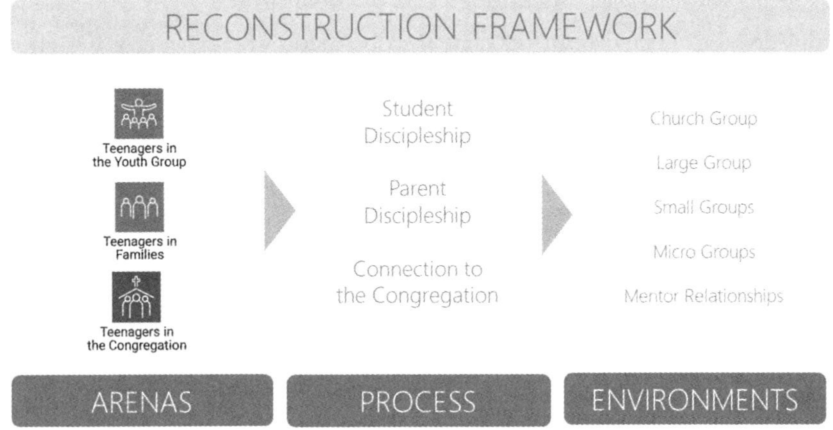

FIGURE 10: RECONSTRUCTION FRAMEWORK

Youth Ministry Arenas

The Youth Ministry Arenas are the domains in which leaders operate. The three arenas are teenagers in the youth group, teenagers in families, and teenagers in the congregation. The reconstruction framework leads you to rebuild your youth ministry in each arena.

Discipleship Process

A discipleship process provides a clear and intentional pathway that guides young people and parents from the initial stages of faith to becoming disciple-makers. I will illustrate the reconstruction process by continuing to use the sample process action verbs from chapter 4: *discover*, *connect*, *grow*, and *multiply*.

Environments

Each process step should be linked to a discipleship environment or program of your youth ministry. If your ministry does not offer an environment to help youth and parents through one or more process steps, you should consider adding environments. The Reconstruction Framework is designed to help your team rebuild your youth ministry by thinking through your discipleship process and environments in each of the three arenas. Let's look at each arena.

Ministry Practice: Leading Teenagers in the Youth Group

The Reconstruction Framework leads you to first examine the arena of teenagers in the youth group. Within this arena, you should start by reviewing the discipleship process from chapter 4. Figure 11 describes discipleship in four ways: movement, identity, Engel categories, and discipleship process action verbs.

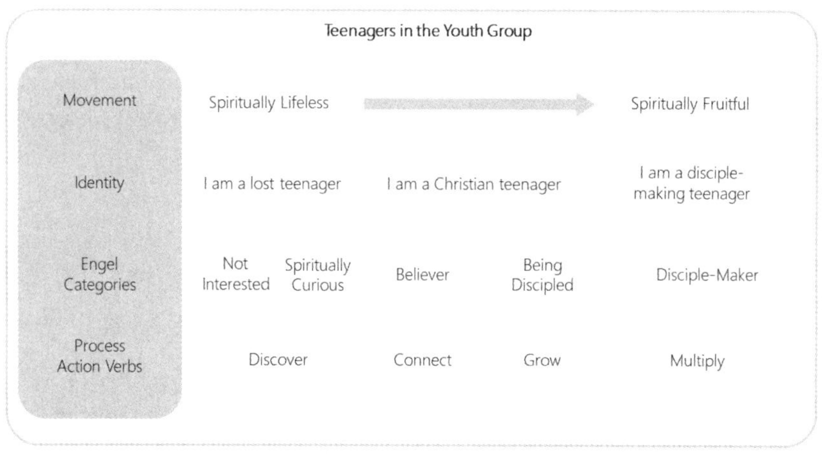

FIGURE 11: TEENAGERS IN THE YOUTH GROUP DISCIPLESHIP PROCESS

For Teenagers in the Youth Group, movement starts by leading young people who are spiritually lifeless to encounter Jesus Christ and experience salvation. Movement continues as teenagers grow in their faith and become spiritually fruitful. Spiritually fruitful youth are students who demonstrate the fruit of the Spirit, share Christ with others, and help people grow in Christlikeness.

In this arena, identity refers to how teenagers might honestly describe their spiritual condition in three phases: I am a lost teenager, I am a Christian teenager, and I am a disciple-making teenager. Each phase progresses to the next, along with the movement from spiritually lifeless to spiritually fruitful.

Each arena of youth ministry will use the same five Engel categories: (1) not interested, (2) spiritually curious, (3) believer, (4) being discipled, and (5) disciple-maker. These five categories highlight the spiritual condition of both lost students and Christian teenagers.

In addition, each arena will use the same four sample action verbs to describe a discipleship process. You and your team will likely choose other action verbs based on your understanding of the discipleship process and your church's unique culture.

Use Figure 11 (along with content in chapter 4) to discuss your mission/purpose statement and your discipleship process. If needed, take time to create (or adjust) your mission/purpose statement to align with a clear discipleship process. Select three or four key action verbs to highlight each process step. You will use these keywords as you move through each arena of the Reconstruction Framework.

The next step is to use the worksheet in Figure 12 to align environments and entry points with your discipleship process. Invite your team to place the action verbs of your discipleship process across the middle of the worksheet. Then, discuss which of your existing environments helps students take the next step in the discipleship process. Place your environments below each corresponding action verb. Finally, discuss which youth activities and events best serve as entry points into each environment listed. You may not have an equal number of process keywords, environments, or entry points. That doesn't matter. The key is to help your team see the connections between your discipleship process and your youth ministry's environments and entry points.

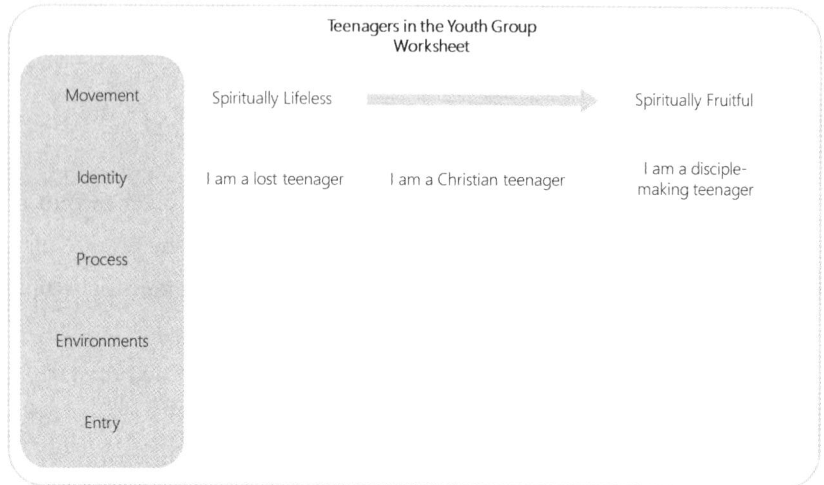

FIGURE 12: TEENAGERS IN THE YOUTH GROUP WORKSHEET

Figure 13 illustrates how your team might complete the worksheet. The sample discipleship process action verbs appear across the middle of the worksheet. The current environments appear below. Notice how the environments don't perfectly align under each process keyword. In this example, the youth group gathering serves to lead students through the steps of connection and growth. Finally, the sample worksheet lists two entry points: outreach activities and DiscipleNow (DNow) and youth camp. This example illustrates how outreach activities are designed as entry points into the youth group gathering. Major events such as DNow and Youth Camp are designed to be entry points into youth small groups.

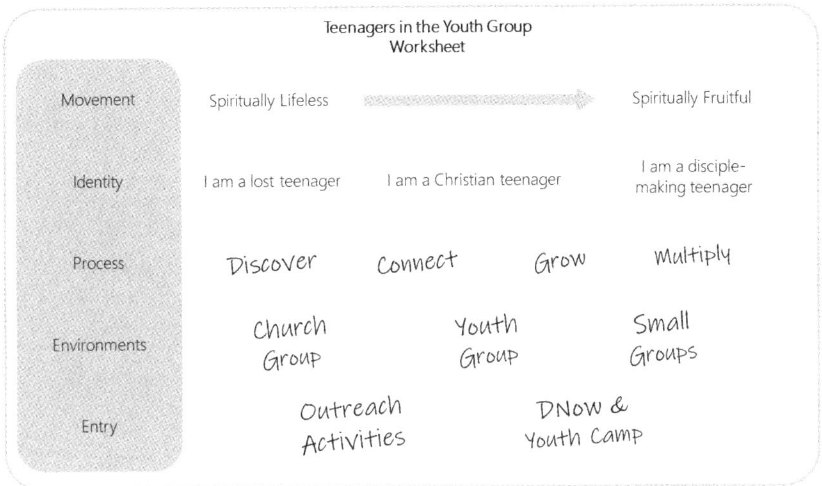

Figure 13: Sample Worksheet for Teenagers in the Youth Group

As you lead your team through the worksheet, take time to allow input from all members. Hear every argument for and against some part of the worksheet. Seek consensus on how the environments and entry points align with your discipleship process.

The arena of teenagers in the youth group might be the easiest of the three arenas for your team to discuss. The challenge will be to lead your team to have the same enthusiasm for the final two arenas. Because these two arenas may not currently be reflected in your youth ministry, you should allow ample time for your team to discuss them. The next arena, teenagers in families, provides your team with an opportunity to expand your ministry beyond the typical emphasis only on teenagers.

Ministry Practice: Leading Teenagers in Families

The Reconstruction Framework leads you to examine the arena of teenagers in families next. Just as in Teenagers in the Youth Group, Figure 14 describes discipleship in four ways: movement, identity, Engel categories, and discipleship process action verbs.

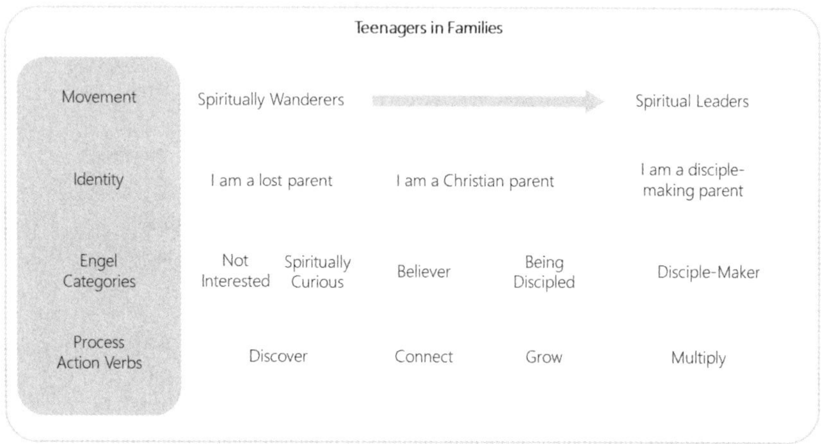

FIGURE 14: TEENAGERS IN FAMILIES DISCIPLESHIP PROCESS

For Teenagers in Families, movement starts by leading parents who are spiritual wanderers to saving faith in Jesus. Movement continues as parents grow in their faith and become spiritual leaders in the home. Parents as spiritual leaders will demonstrate the fruit of the Spirit, share Christ with others, and disciple their own teenagers.

In this arena, identity refers to how parents might honestly describe their spiritual condition in three phases: (1) I am a lost parent, (2) I am a Christian parent, and (3) I am a disciple-making parent. Each phase progresses to the next along with the movement from spiritual wanderers to spiritual leaders. The final two rows are the same as those found under teenagers in the youth group. The five Engel categories are listed along with the four sample action verbs of the discipleship process.

Invite your team to discuss Figure 14 (along with content in chapter 4) and evaluate how well your discipleship process works within the arena of teenagers in families. If needed, take time to adjust your mission/purpose statement to align with a clear discipleship process that applies to both teenagers in the youth group and teenagers in families. I caution you not to select additional keywords for a discipleship process for teenagers in families. Using different action verbs for youth and parents will be confusing. It's best to use terms that fit both arenas of youth ministry.

The next step is to use the worksheet in Figure 15 to align environments and entry points with your discipleship process. As before, invite your team to place the action verbs of your discipleship process across the middle of the worksheet. Then discuss which of your existing environments help parents take the next step in the discipleship process. Place your environments below each corresponding action verb. Finally, discuss which church activities and events best serve as entry points into each environment. Remember, you may not have an equal number of process action verbs, environments, or entry points. This process is designed for your team to understand the connections between your discipleship process and the environments and entry points for parents.

FIGURE 15: TEENAGERS IN FAMILIES WORKSHEET

The examples in Figure 16 illustrate how your team might complete the worksheet. As before, the sample discipleship process action verbs appear across the middle of the worksheet. The current environments appear below. Notice again how the environments don't perfectly align under each process keyword. In this example, adult small groups serve to lead parents through the steps of connection and growth. This sample introduces another form of small groups under multiply: men's and women's small groups. These small groups provide adults with additional opportunities for Christian growth, as well as a chance to serve together. Finally, the sample worksheet lists two entry points: family fellowship activities and men's and women's retreats for adults. This example illustrates how family fellowship activities are designed as entry points into the adult small groups. Major events such as men's and women's retreats are designed to be entry points into men's and women's small groups.

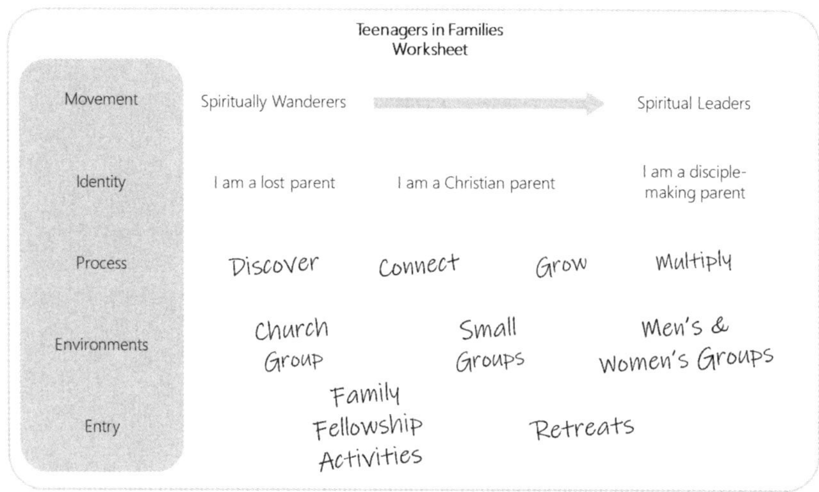

FIGURE 16: SAMPLE WORKSHEET FOR TEENAGERS IN FAMILIES

Lead your team to complete the worksheet. As before, take time to allow input from everyone. Align your environments and entry points with your discipleship process. Your team's work in the arena of teenagers in families might be among the most important tasks you complete in the reconstruction framework. Don't rush through this process. Take time, if necessary, to schedule additional meetings to complete the work in this arena. The next arena, Teenagers in the Congregation, allows your team to help teenagers make deeper connections to your church and its members.

Ministry Practice: Leading Teenagers in the Congregation

The Reconstruction Framework leads you finally to examine the arena of Teenagers in the Congregation. Figure 17 describes discipleship in four ways: movement, identity, Engel categories, and discipleship process action verbs.

Teenagers in the Congregation

Movement	Consumers	→			Contributors
Identity	I love my youth group		I love my church		I serve Christ through my church
Engel Categories	Not Interested	Spiritually Curious	Believer	Being Discipled	Disciple-Maker
Process Action Verbs	Discover		Connect	Grow	Multiply

FIGURE 17: TEENAGERS IN THE CONGREGATION DISCIPLESHIP PROCESS

For Teenagers in the Congregation, movement starts by leading students who are consumers to become contributors. Youth have a consumer mentality when they view the church as a place designed to merely feed them. Teenagers become contributors when they become spiritually mature to the point where they desire to serve others.

In this arena, identity refers to how teens might honestly describe their feelings about the church in three phases: (1) I love my youth group,

(2) I love my church, and (3) I serve Christ at my church. Each phase progresses to the next, with the movement from consumer to contributor. This arena aims to help teenagers move from a youth group-focused mentality to a church congregation and service way of thinking. You want students who don't merely refer to your church as "that church" but as "my church." But the process shouldn't end there. The chart shows that the ultimate goal is for teens to declare that their identity at your church is one of service. The final two rows are the same as those found under the previous two arenas.

Instruct your team to discuss Figure 17 (along with content in chapter 4) and evaluate how well your discipleship process works within the arena of teenagers in the congregation. As I stated earlier, do not select additional keywords for a discipleship process for teenagers in the congregation. It's best to use terms that fit all three arenas of youth ministry.

The next step is to use the worksheet in Figure 18 to align environments and entry points with your discipleship process. However, this chart introduces a new term: *connections*. Connections refer to elements of your youth ministry beyond environments or entry points. I've modified this row for both discipleship environments and connections because, for this arena, you won't necessarily need additional environments to align with your discipleship process. As before, invite your team to place the action verbs of your discipleship process across the middle of the worksheet. Then, discuss which of your existing environments, along with "connections," will help teens take the next step in the discipleship process. Place your environments and connections below each corresponding action verb. Finally, discuss which church activities and events best serve as entry points into each environment or connection point. This final process is designed to help your team understand how best to develop relational connections between youth and members of your congregation.

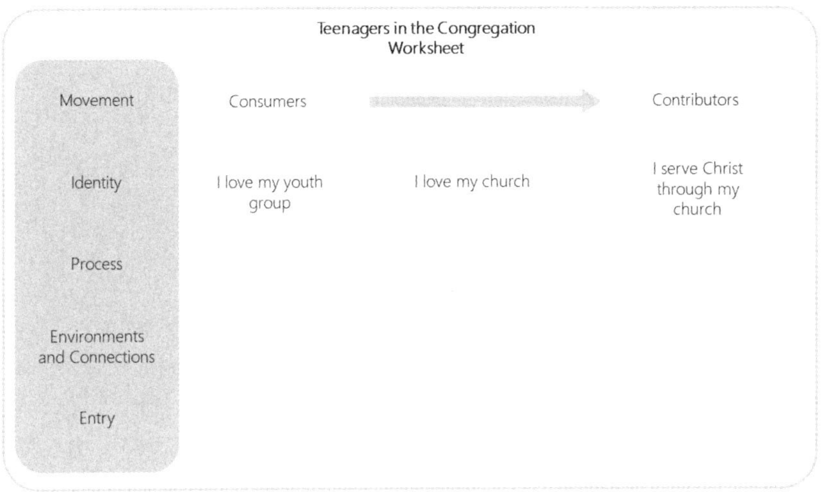

Figure 18: Teenagers in the Congregation Worksheet

The examples in Figure 19 illustrate how your team might complete the worksheet. As before, the sample discipleship process action verbs appear across the middle of the worksheet. The current environments and any connection points appear below. In this example, serving alongside church members leads youth to take the next step of connection and growth. This sample shows how student leadership development leads young people toward Christlikeness.

Finally, the sample worksheet lists two entry points: church-wide fellowships and service projects. These service projects refer to ministry service opportunities for youth to serve alongside church members. This example illustrates how church-wide fellowships are designed as entry points for youth to serve alongside church members. Service projects are designed to be entry points into student leadership development.

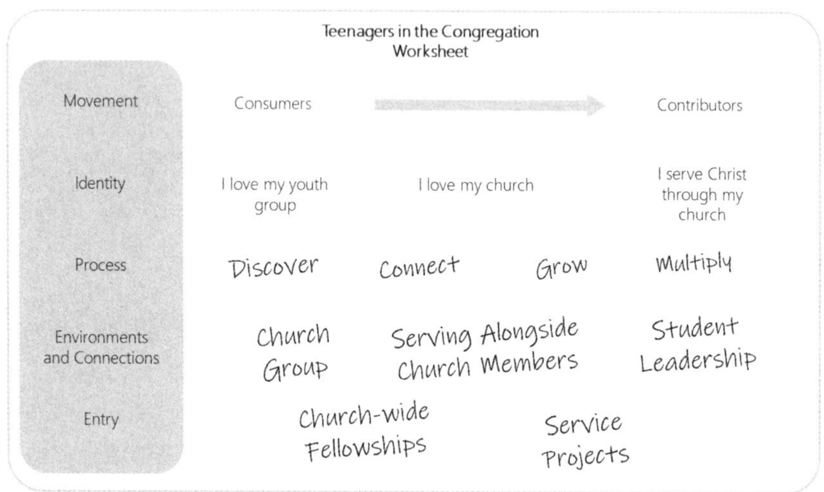

FIGURE 19: SAMPLE WORKSHEET FOR TEENAGERS IN THE CONGREGATION

As your team completes this final worksheet, allow everyone to share their thoughts on how best to connect youth with the congregation. Align your environments and connections with entry points and your discipleship process. The arena of teenagers in the congregation represents an important step toward helping students develop lasting connections to your church. Some of your team members may assume that teenagers will naturally establish connections to the church. Help them see that this is not always the case. Don't skip this process. Give extra time for discussion around teenagers in the congregation. You and your team's work on the reconstruction process has one final step: putting it all together.

Putting It All Together

The Reconstruction Framework's final step is to combine the three worksheets from each of the arenas of youth ministry into one sheet. Invite your team to use the Decision Worksheet (Figure 20) to assist with this process.

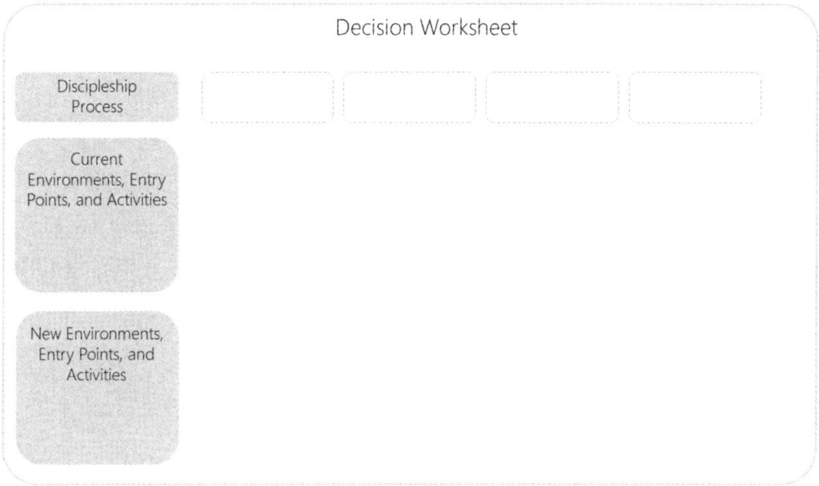

Decision Worksheet

Discipleship Process

Current Environments, Entry Points, and Activities

New Environments, Entry Points, and Activities

Figure 20: Decision Worksheet

As the name implies, rather than simply listing everything from your previous worksheets, you have some decisions to make. Start by filling in the blanks with your discipleship process. Next, list the current environments, entry points, and activities in the row below. Include environments and entry points for both teenagers and parents. Align each environment with its corresponding action verb. List any new environments that your team has discussed. Again, include environments for both teenagers and parents. Do the same thing for entry points. Include any new entry points your team may have previously discussed.

Now comes the hard part. Circle the environments (and/or connections)—both current and new—that best lead students and parents to take the next steps in your discipleship process. Draw lines connecting the circled environments to the action verb. Place a box around entry points that best connect students and parents to discipleship environments. Draw lines connecting entry points to environments.

Chances are you have some items that are not circled or boxed. These are environments or entry points that you must decide whether to keep or not. You must lead your team to prayerfully consider what is needed and what is not. These will not be easy decisions to make. As your team works through this process, it will become clear which environments and programming elements need to stay and which ones need to end.

In your final meetings with your team, you will focus on creating a new sheet that aligns the remaining environments, connections, and entry points with your discipleship process. This becomes the basis of your new discipleship strategy. Before making any changes to your existing youth ministry, read chapter 7.

Three Critical Moves

If you are overwhelmed by the content of this chapter (and the book as a whole), let me summarize all of this by helping you focus on three critical moves you can make in your youth ministry. These three changes encompass the book's recurring themes and represent the heart of what I'm trying to encourage in youth ministry today. The three critical moves are:

1. Moving from a few discipleship metrics to multiple metrics
2. Moving from one to three arenas of youth ministry
3. Moving from low relational environments to highly relational environments

Multiple Discipleship Metrics

The first move I suggest you make is toward multiple discipleship metrics. As discussed in chapter 2, most youth ministries measure success by attendance and baptism. While these measurements are vital, they represent a narrow set of metrics and provide a limited view of the youth ministry's overall health and effectiveness. High attendance numbers might indicate your church is attracting young people, but they do not necessarily reflect growth toward Christlikeness. Similarly, while baptisms are a crucial milestone in a teenager's faith journey, they represent only the beginning of a lifelong process. Incorporating additional metrics gives you a more comprehensive understanding of what is happening in your ministry. While I've discussed various metrics in part 1, if you need to focus on just a few, I suggest three: service, destination, and direction.

Service

Student and parent involvement in ministry and missions can be a vital metric to track. This metric emphasizes the importance of active participation in your church's mission. When you track ministry and mission service, you can assess how effectively your youth ministry mobilizes teenagers and parents to live out their faith through tangible acts of love and compassion. In my research, service is the number one way churches help teenagers develop lasting connections to the church. Service in the context of the three arenas means serving with parents and members of the congregation.

Your church may be like many who track worship and Bible study attendance. You may get a weekly report that shows total youth attendance each Sunday and compares attendance to last year. I suggest that you add several columns to this report—ministry service—of teenagers and parents. You should track the number of students involved in weekly service. For example, how many teenagers volunteer in the children's ministry each week? How many students serve behind the scenes in the media ministry? You should also track the number of parents serving in your church each week. How many parents are volunteering as Bible study teachers each week? How many parents serve in other areas (worship team, media team, hospitality, etc.) throughout your church?

Once you have begun to track weekly service, move on to track special ministries and mission projects. For example, how many teenagers participated in a mission trip this year? How many parents led their family to serve together in a local community ministry (homeless shelter, soup kitchen, clothes closet, etc.)? Beyond the numbers, you should also gather stories and testimonies of these efforts' impact on both the recipients and the volunteers.

Beyond tracking service participation, add another service metric related to disciple-making. How many students have engaged in gospel conversations? How many ministry service events result in people coming to faith in Christ? How many students and adults are trained to share the gospel?

Regularly celebrating student and parent involvement in service highlights how these ministries make a difference in people's lives.

Destination

The ultimate goal of every believer is to become more like Christ. Christlikeness is the destination. This metric focuses on the Christian maturity of teenagers and parents and how well your ministry is fostering deep, transformative discipleship. It is also a difficult metric to track. Unlike attendance or service involvement, destination can be a nebulous measurement. To help with this metric, you might use the Student Spiritual Growth and Influence and Parent Spiritual Growth and Leadership surveys (appendix). Add additional columns to your report to track indicators such as spiritual disciplines. For example, how many students pray daily, regularly read their Bible, or share their faith with others? Rather than weekly statistics, I suggest monthly summaries of these metrics according to age or grade. For example, one month you might survey all your seventh graders about their practice of spiritual disciplines; the next month, you survey the eighth graders. After six months, you can tally all the statistics and report on the overall practice of spiritual discipline among all youth. You might alternate between junior high and high school each month if your group is smaller. You should also train your volunteers to be on the lookout for Christlike characteristics and demonstrations of maturing faith in students.

Direction

While destination emphasizes the goals of discipleship, direction focuses on the importance of the journey toward Christlikeness. This metric recognizes that although it is important to emphasize discipleship outcomes (destination), spiritual growth is a continuous process. Daniel Im uses the term *direction* to help churches value the fact that many believers are moving toward Christian maturity but may not necessarily demonstrate the intended outcomes.[3] Directional metrics value students' and parents' progress, no matter how incremental, as they move closer to embodying Christlike maturity.

Help students and parents recognize their progress toward Christlike maturity by encouraging journaling, testimonies, and accountability partnerships. Encourage believers to keep a journal and write down prayer requests, favorite Scripture passages, and what God is teaching them. Invite students and parents to share personal testimonies about what God is doing in their lives. Accountability partners can be a catalyst for deeper discipleship. Encourage students and parents to enter into accountability relationships (micro-groups) with other believers.

You need leaders who develop relationships with students and parents to track directional metrics. Within the context of relationships, leaders observe signs that individuals are progressing on their faith journey. You should gather your volunteer leaders on at least a quarterly basis and ask questions related to the Christlike direction of students. For example, ask your volunteers, "Name some students in your small group that you would describe as making progress toward Christlike maturity."

---

[3] Daniel Im, *No Silver Bullets: 5 Small Shifts That Will Transform Your Ministry* (B&H, 2017), 23.

Three Arenas of Youth Ministry

The second move I encourage you to make is toward three arenas of youth ministry. The Reconstruction Framework leads you to rebuild your youth ministry with the three arenas in mind. As discussed in chapter 3, most youth ministries focus only on teenagers in the youth group. However, you need a strategy that not only focuses on students in a youth group but also on families and the church congregation. While I've discussed various ways to apply the three arenas to your ministry, if you need to focus on just a few, I suggest three: service, discipleship, and worship.

Service

I encouraged you in the last section to consider service as a metric for youth ministry. I'm challenging you to view service through the lens of the three arenas. Youth need opportunities to serve their church and community alongside their parents and congregation members. Engaging teenagers in service benefits the church and those they serve, but it also empowers students to develop life skills, strengthen their faith, and cultivate a sense of purpose. If ministry and mission service is not a regular part of your youth ministry, get students serving. If you already encourage service among young people, encourage more service by working with others in your church to provide increased ways for students to serve. Lead students to serve not only your church, but the community as well. Teenagers desire to make a difference in the world around them. Providing community service opportunities empowers young people to be the hands and feet of Jesus.

Service within the youth group context is good, but to make an even more significant impact on students, you must provide service in all three arenas. Students benefit from opportunities to serve alongside their parents and the church congregation. Family service projects give moms and dads a chance to demonstrate the importance of faith in a practical way. Parents and teenagers serving together should be integral to your youth ministry strategy. Consider converting one of your upcoming ministry service projects to a family service project. Invite families to serve together. Youth whose parents are unable (or unwilling) to attend can join with other families. Youth also need opportunities to serve alongside members of the congregation. Healthy intergenerational relationships are the context for teen connection to the congregation. Students who serve their church develop deeper connections to the congregation. Enlist adults in your church to assist you with training and mentoring young people for service in the church. Service within the context of the three arenas of youth ministry enables you to provide a holistic approach to Christian growth and kingdom impact.

Discipleship

You should also develop your discipleship strategy within the context of the three arenas. More than likely, you have already led students to gather for youth group and small group discipleship. Within these environments, I encourage you to focus on addressing any of the deficient areas revealed in the deconstruction process. For example, perhaps you need to provide further attention to nurturing the practice of spiritual disciplines among young people. Other possible topics include evangelism training and responding to questions and doubts.

Parent discipleship is likely not in your job description as a youth minister. However, I believe you are uniquely positioned to influence the spiritual growth of parents. Your church probably already has a Bible study or Sunday school class made up of adults who are also parents of teenagers. These existing classes could serve as an extension of your youth ministry, and you can encourage parents to get involved. Consider also facilitating a monthly gathering of parents of teenagers to discuss hot topics such as dating, smartphone use, and social media.

Discipleship within the third arena of youth ministry—the congregation—occurs anytime young people are studying God's Word or being encouraged to grow toward Christlike maturity alongside younger and older members of your church. This happens most often in the context of intergenerational worship. Your adult volunteers also provide connections to the congregation. I encourage you to include young adults and senior adults in your youth ministry. Senior adults can bring a wealth of life experience to your ministry. In addition, encouraging student involvement in men's and women's ministries at your church gives young people another opportunity to be discipled by members of your congregation. Discipleship within the context of the three arenas models faith beyond the youth group.

Worship

Today's continuing trend in youth ministry involves separate worship gatherings for only teenagers. However, teenagers need more than worship in the youth group; they need to worship alongside other members of your congregation. Intergenerational worship allows teens to actively engage with and learn from older generations of your local congregation. Through intergenerational worship, teenage believers encounter the presence of God, find spiritual renewal, and draw closer to him. Parents of teenagers also need to participate in intergenerational worship. Even if parents and youth don't sit together, the presence of parents in the worship service communicates to teenagers that worship is a priority. Intergenerational worship exemplifies the three youth ministry arenas.

Highly Relational Environments

The third move I encourage you to make is toward highly relational environments. As discussed in chapter 5, most youth ministries emphasize environments with low relational connections. I encourage you to focus your efforts on developing highly relational environments instead. While I've discussed various ways to seek highly relational environments, if you need to focus on just a few, I suggest three: small groups, micro-groups, and mentoring relationships.

Small Groups

Small groups are right in the middle on the Relational Level scale in Figure 5 (chapter 5). After the Church Group (low relational) and Youth Group (medium relational), Small Groups are the first environment to be relationally high. Discipleship is a relational process. Therefore, when you focus on relationships, your environment becomes fertile ground for spiritual growth.

Although small groups are common among churches today, they don't always have a relational emphasis. Making your small groups more highly relational requires intentionality and persistence. Small groups can be relational both within the group time and without. Leaders encourage relational connections within the group by giving time for student prayer requests and open discussions. Leaders who spend time with group members outside the class sessions encourage deeper relational connections.

Micro-Groups

Gatherings of three to five Christians in a closed-group environment are highly conducive to relational intimacy. In smaller groups, individuals are willing to share their struggles and victories. Micro-groups foster mutual accountability and transparency. Both students and parents benefit from these types of relationships. Participants in micro-groups are at a place in their Christian growth where they desire a deeper walk with Christ. Micro-group members pray, share Scripture, serve alongside one another, and discuss God's work in their lives.

If you want to start micro-groups, I suggest first leading a group yourself. Invite a few key volunteers to join you for a year. After one year, each group member will be challenged to start their own micro-groups. This approach requires a long-term commitment, but you will reap the benefits in the long run.

Mentoring Relationships

I have two questions for you as a leader: Who is mentoring you? Who are you mentoring? If the answer to both questions is no one, then I encourage you to find someone who will agree to mentor you and meet weekly with you for prayer and accountability. Likewise, I encourage you to mentor someone else. It might be an adult volunteer or a student called to vocational ministry. Make mentoring part of your ministry practice. Then, take steps to facilitate mentoring for other teenagers in your church. For example, perhaps other ministries in your church have leaders who would mentor teenagers serving in their areas. Parents of teenagers can also benefit from mentoring relationships. You can help arrange connections between parents of teenagers and older adults in the congregation. Pairing parents of teenagers with adults willing to mentor them can lead to stronger families and disciple-making parents.

Making these three moves or any of the reconstruction steps won't be easy. As you reconstruct your youth ministry, you'll face questions and opposition. When you implement these changes, you will lead your ministry toward the effective discipleship of teenagers and parents.

Questions to Consider

1. What are the strengths and weaknesses of your youth ministry?
2. What are the most surprising things about the findings?
3. How do you feel about the results?
4. What were the recommendations?
5. What content and curriculum ideas do you have to address the findings?
6. What volunteer additions do you recommend?

7. What are your initial ideas about how you might improve the effectiveness of your youth ministry?
8. In what ways do your discipleship process, environments, and entry points align with the three arenas of youth ministry?
9. What changes or additions to your ministry strategy do you need to make?
10. How can you make one or more of the three suggested moves in youth ministry?

CHAPTER 10

YOUTH MINISTRY EXAMPLES

I conducted qualitative research via interviews with youth ministry leaders in churches nationwide. Of those, I selected the following as examples. These ministry leaders told me their stories and provided meaningful reflections on their ministry to youth. The effectiveness of these churches is not because they are large and have tremendous resources (some do and others do not). They are successful because they intentionally disciple teenagers, partner with parents, and connect them to the church. I believe you will find a ministry similar to yours and be encouraged to deconstruct youth ministry in your context.

Parent Small Groups—First Baptist Church, DeSoto, Missouri

First Baptist Church, DeSoto, Missouri, has an average attendance of 350. Hayden Carter is the student pastor at FBC DeSoto and loves to disciple the next generation and help them find their identity in Christ. He is a relational leader who values connections with teenagers.

The youth ministry at FBC DeSoto is called Graceway Students. The mission of Graceway Students is to equip students with a holistic Christian worldview that cherishes the gospel, treasures the Bible, understands the faith, and desires community. Hayden also uses the phrase "Living to Know Jesus," Dying to Make Him Known to describe his student ministry. Graceway Students have two primary discipleship environments: small group Bible study on Sunday mornings and large group gathering on Sunday nights, which consist of games, worship, prayer, teaching, and small group discussion. This may sound like your typical ministry to teenagers, but Hayden also leads a component rarely seen in today's youth ministry: parent small groups.

Parent Small Group

Parents of teenagers gather in a small group on Sunday evenings when students separate into small groups for discussion and prayer. Hayden leads the small group, which is designed to hear from parents and help them disciple their teenagers. Many of the parents serve as volunteers on Sunday nights for the large group youth gathering while others come just for the parent small group. Even though Hayden does not yet have teenagers of his own, he humbly leads the group of parents to study God's Word, discuss issues related to parenting teenagers, and read Christian parenting books together. This humble attitude helps parents respect his leadership, value him as a partner, and trust him to lead their teenagers. Hayden has received overwhelmingly positive feedback since beginning the parent small group.

Hayden has a unique relationship with his pastor, Brad Delaughter. Brad was Hayden's pastor while growing up. When FBC DeSoto was looking for a youth pastor, Brad knew he wanted to have Hayden come to serve alongside him. With a strong emphasis on discipling teenagers and a desire to disciple parents of teenagers as well, the youth ministry at FBC DeSoto is uniquely positioned to impact Christ's kingdom.

Discipleship Process—First Baptist Church (First West), West Monroe, Louisiana

First West is a multi-site church in northern Louisiana with a main campus in West Monroe and another in Calhoun, Louisiana. The average church attendance is around 1,500, and First West Students average about 200 young people. Garrett Hodges serves as the high school minister. His heart is to see teenagers changed by the gospel of Jesus Christ. First West offers youth group gatherings and small groups for students. Like many youth ministries, they host DiscipleNow, youth camps, and mission trips. But unlike some ministries, First West Students, like the church as a whole, has a straightforward discipleship process: worship, reach, equip, and multiply.

Worship and Reach

Teenagers at First West gather for intergenerational worship on Sunday mornings at both campus locations. Student Worship takes place during a Wednesday night gathering called Midweek Students. Midweek Students is a weekly outreach for high school and middle school students. The goal is for students to invite their school friends to hear about Jesus. Midweek Students begins with worship and Bible study. Following the large group time, students meet in small groups.

Equip and Multiply

LIFE Groups are a vital part of bringing students into Christ-centered community. LIFE Groups for students meet on Sunday mornings. In addition to Bible study and fellowship, LIFE Groups provide students with opportunities to serve. LIFE Groups regularly volunteer together in ministry roles at the church or in community service projects. Students also serve in the church through choir, praise team, kids ministry, and VBS.

The discipleship process at First West provides a clear pathway for spiritual growth. Students gather for worship and hear the gospel, small group environments provide biblical teaching, and teens are equipped for service. Garrett and the student ministry at First West are making a difference in the lives of teenagers in northern Louisiana and beyond.

Evangelism and Relational Leadership—Thomasville Baptist Church, Thomasville, AL

Third Floor Ministries is the youth ministry of Thomasville Baptist Church in Thomasville, Alabama. The church has an average attendance of around 225. Austin Mason serves as the youth pastor. The mission of Third Floor Ministries is to See and Send. Austin invites students to see who Jesus is and then sends students out to live for Jesus. Third Floor Ministries offers small groups on Sunday mornings and a large youth group gathering on Sunday nights. Throughout the year, they engage students through DiscipleNow, choir trips, service projects, and mission trips. I've known Austin for many years, and two things stand out about him and his ministry: evangelism and relational connection.

Evangelism

Austin is an evangelist at heart. When you talk with him, you can't help but hear his heart for the Lord and desire for students to come to Christ. He shares the gospel in large group gatherings and one-on-one. Austin regularly presents the gospel in the youth group environment and invites students to respond. When you look at the social media pages for Third Floor Ministries, you'll find the usual pictures of students at camp or hanging out with friends, but what is striking are the numerous photos and videos of students being baptized. Austin has a heart for evangelism, which is evident in the number of students who come to faith in Christ.

Relational Connection

Austin is a highly relational disciple-maker. He values authenticity, transparency, and "being real with students." Austin hangs out with students, playing basketball and video games. He invites students to his home for dinner with his wife and kids. He calls his approach "unstructured discipleship." Through this unstructured approach to discipleship, Austin develops authentic relational connections with youth and parents. He has a relaxed manner and an inviting personality. He demonstrates compassion and builds trust through his personable demeanor and big smile. His discipleship approach focuses on large groups and smaller, more intimate microgroup gatherings. Austin's relational emphasis extends to every part of the youth ministry. Leaders are encouraged to develop godly relationships with students. This relational approach also extends to his intern, whom Austin currently mentors.

There are certainly larger and flashier youth groups than Third Floor Ministries, but few successfully reach young people as they do and connect with students on such a deep level. Austin's passion for students and relational emphasis should remind us what youth ministry is all about—See and Send. Third Floor Ministries is committed to reaching students with the gospel and sending them on mission for Christ's kingdom.

Discipleship Process and Parent Ministry—First Baptist Church, Houston, Texas

Houston's First Baptist Church is a multi-site church in Houston, Texas. The original campus, known as the Loop, is located at the interchange of I-10 and the 610 Loop. Three satellite campuses are located throughout the greater Houston area in Cypress, Downtown, and Sienna. The Loop campus averages about 4,000 in weekly attendance with a combined weekly average of around 7,000 on all campuses. Tony Bianco is the minister to students at the Loop campus and oversees the HUB Student Ministry, which averages between 350 and 400 young people. Students at the HUB Student Ministries have opportunities to experience youth retreats, camps, mission trips, and engaging programming. The HUB Student Ministries vision is to see students Gather, Grow, Give, and Go to see students have King Hearts and live Kingdom Lives.

Gather

The HUB Student Ministry encourages students to gather for intergenerational worship on Sundays and participate in outreach-focused student events. The Gather step is about relational connections to the community of believers.

Grow

The HUB Student Ministry desires to see students grow in discipleship through Sunday morning small groups and midweek gatherings. High school and middle school students meet in small groups according to grade on Sunday mornings. Middle school students have a midweek gathering at the church for games, videos, worship, expository preaching, and discussion groups. High school students meet in home groups for Seven7. The name comes from the fact that every zip code in the Houston area begins with the number 77. The HUB Students desire to see a gathering of high school students in every zip code. Tony describes Seven7 as the "front porch" of their ministry to students. They want Seven7 home gatherings to be a natural and normal way for teens to introduce their friends to Christ and the student ministry.

Give

The student ministry challenges young people to give of themselves in service and ministry to others. Students volunteer in various ministries at the church and serve in local and international missions. This step is about leading teenagers to live Kingdom Lives.

Go

Go Groups allow students to dive deeper into discipleship and connect with a smaller group of students and adult leaders. Students make a semester-long commitment to these closed student-led micro-groups. Teenagers meet on campus for three Go Group lunches/training sessions and then once a week for forty-five minutes online via Zoom. This allows students to connect and meet on a schedule that is best for them. Go Group members study the Bible, pray, and serve together.

Parent Ministry

Tony knows that relational connections are the key to effective ministry; therefore, he makes himself available in adult Life Group classes that parents of teenagers attend. He also keeps in contact with parents via a weekly newsletter and posts on social media. Parent discipleship takes place on Wednesday nights in the fall and spring. Parents meet for six-week training sessions on topics such as "Christ-centered parenting" led by a parent or staff member. For "Side by Side Sunday," leaders teach a relevant subject, with parents and teenagers learning together two to four times a year. Tony also takes time to listen to parents. Parent Insight Groups are a cross-section of parents who meet three or four times a year to bounce ideas around and receive feedback. Houston's First also hosts a church-wide (NextGen) Parent Conference every other year.

As much as they have going on for teenagers, the HUB Student Ministry asks students to do only four things: gather, grow, give, and go. They do this so students will have King Hearts and live Kingdom Lives. The partnership with parents encourages moms and dads to do the same.

Surveying Students—New Zion Baptist Church, Covington, Louisiana

New Zion Baptist Church is a rural church in southeast Louisiana with an average attendance of about 250. Matthew Smith serves as the youth and children's minister. The mission statement of New Zion's youth ministry is to Be One with Christ and Be One as a Community. The core values are belonging together, believing together, and becoming together.

Student Survey

Matthew created a survey using some of the questions from the Student Spiritual Growth and Influence survey (appendix) and questions gleaned from Barna and Springtide's research. Thirty-nine teenagers completed the forty-question survey. Matthew discovered a wealth of valuable information about his students. Among the findings, he found that 38 percent of students read their Bible two to four times a week, and 49 percent pray five or more times a week. Matthew also found that 46 percent do not invite other youth to church. In addition, a small percentage (13 percent) of youth said they do not feel they can ask questions and explore faith, and about a quarter (26 percent) said they don't feel free to express doubts at church. Matthew led a team of parents, adult volunteers, and youth to develop a new strategy to reach students in response to the survey results. This discipleship team recommended several changes, including teachers writing "Connect Notes" to absent students, creating deeper connections with adults in the church, increasing ministry and missions service, equipping parents for discipleship, and establishing youth micro-groups. New Zion found so much value in their initial survey of youth that Matthew made annual surveys a part of his overall youth ministry strategy.

Assessing Youth Ministry in Three Arenas—First Baptist Church, Corinth, Texas

Located north of the Dallas/Fort Worth metroplex, First Baptist Church, Corinth, Texas, has an average attendance of around 325. David Baysinger serves as the student pastor. The student ministry offers small groups on Sunday mornings and a midweek gathering with David sharing a message, followed by a discussion around tables. In addition, the student ministry encourages young people to serve in the church, on mission trips, and in the community.

However, David sensed they might more effectively reach and disciple students. He led his team of volunteers to take the Youth Ministry Arenas Assessment. It provided valuable insights and helped affirm several needs David had previously identified. The assessment led his team to address several areas, including developing a straightforward disciple-making process and creating a D-group guide.

After reviewing the assessment results, David led his team to develop a four-stage discipleship pathway based on Dann Spader's *4 Chair Discipling* and process examples from Pastor Craig Ethridge.[1] The four stages of their discipleship pathway are Seek, Believe, Grow, and Multiply. The discipleship pathway gave David and his volunteers a common language to encourage student spiritual growth. A clear discipleship pathway also allowed leaders to evaluate student progress and challenge youth to take the next steps toward Christlikeness.

The Youth Ministry Arenas Assessment also revealed a need for student micro-groups. The student ministry created a D-group Guide for youth. The guide is designed to help students "grow spiritually in small-ratio

---

[1] See Dann Spader, *4 Chair Discipling: What Jesus Calls Us to Do* (Moody, 2014). Craig Etheredge is the lead pastor at CrossCreek Church, the president and founder of DiscipleFirst Ministries, and the author of *Morning Thrive*, daily devotionals online.

discipleship groups." It leads students to gather for fellowship, Scripture memory, Bible reading, journaling, and prayer.

Using assessments to evaluate his ministry to youth enabled David and his team of volunteers to take ministry to the next level. The newly developed discipleship pathway and D-group Guide encourage Christian growth. These initiatives renewed the student ministry's passion to help youth become disciple-makers.

APPENDIX

Surveys and Assessments

The following surveys and assessments are free for personal use. You can also find free copies of the assessments at deconstructingym.com. You can use them as they are or select specific questions to create your own survey. We can assist you with administering all three as a comprehensive diagnostic of your youth ministry, and provide identifying codes and unique web links to share with leaders, students, and parents. You will receive a detailed report summarizing and analyzing the survey results. The comprehensive diagnostic is available at a reasonable cost. The fees cover the cost of analyzing your data and producing the report. For more information, visit deconstructingym.com.

Student Spiritual Growth and Influence Survey

Please share some basic information about yourself:

Sex:

- ❑ Male
- ❑ Female

Grade:

- ❑ 6th
- ❑ 7th
- ❑ 8th
- ❑ 9th
- ❑ 10th
- ❑ 11th
- ❑ 12th

Frequency of church attendance:

- ❑ I regularly attend church
- ❑ I occasionally attend church
- ❑ I rarely attend church

The main reason I attend church is:

- ❑ To make my parents happy
- ❑ To be with my friends
- ❑ To have something to do
- ❑ To gain deeper knowledge about Jesus and the Bible

Frequency of prayer:

- ❑ I regularly pray
- ❑ I occasionally pray
- ❑ I rarely pray

Frequency of Bible reading:

- ❑ I regularly read the Bible
- ❑ I occasionally read the Bible
- ❑ I rarely read the Bible

Frequency of parent church attendance

- ❑ My parent(s) regularly attends
- ❑ My parent(s) occasionally attends
- ❑ My parent(s) rarely attend

How often have you participated in a mission or ministry project with a parent?

- ❑ Five or more times
- ❑ Once or twice
- ❑ Three or four times
- ❑ Never

Respond to the following statements by indicating one of the following:

	Strongly Disagree	Disagree	Agree	Strongly Agree
1. I see myself as a follower of Jesus Christ.				
2. I am pursuing God's will for my life.				
3. I think about God outside of church or youth group.				
4. I have talked about Jesus with a non-Christian in the last few months.				
5. I would confess my faith in Jesus even if it put my life at risk.				
6. I believe that God has a purpose for my life.				
7. I have helped a non-Christian understand what it means to be a follower of Jesus.				
8. I have fasted (gone without food for a short period of time for a spiritual purpose) at least once in the last year.				
9. I set aside time for prayer and Bible reading.				
10. I regularly attend youth group gatherings.				
11. I attend a Bible study at church that is open to all teenagers whenever they want to attend.				
12. I have memorized at least three Bible verses.				
13. I attend worship that includes children and adults.				
14. I have helped another person become a Christian.				

	Strongly Disagree	Disagree	Agree	Strongly Agree
15. My church encourages teenagers to serve others.				
16. I volunteer at my church regularly.				
17. My church provides opportunities for teenagers to use their spiritual gifts.				
18. I am trained to serve in a specific area of ministry at my church.				
19. I often participate in community missions or ministry projects with adults from my church.				
20. I have participated in leadership training at my church.				
21. I have participated in a mission trip to another state or country.				
22. My youth group is a safe place to express personal doubts and questions about my faith.				
23. I am given opportunities to lead in my youth group.				
24. I feel a sense of belonging in my youth group.				
25. My youth group challenges me to think deeply about my faith.				
26. I know that my youth leaders care about me personally.				
27. I attend a small discipleship group at church that is just for those teenagers who are serious about following Jesus as disciples.				
28. My church challenges me to consider whether God might be calling me to ministry as a future career.				
29. Not counting relatives and youth leaders, more than three adults in my church are interested in me and my life.				
30. My church helps teenagers feel like they belong.				

	Strongly Disagree	Disagree	Agree	Strongly Agree
31. My senior pastor tries to make teenagers feel included.				
32. All teenagers in my community would be welcomed by adults in my church.				
33. My church has been very important for my spiritual growth.				
34. I have real friends at church.				
35. After I graduate from high school, I plan to continue attending church regularly.				
36. I have at least one parent who encourages me to grow as a Christian.				
37. I have at least one parent who encourages me to glorify God in my future career.				
38. I talk with at least one parent about spiritual issues.				
39. At least one of my parents is considered to be an active leader in my church.				
40. At least one of my parents has been very important to my spiritual growth.				
41. I have a close relationship with my father.				
42. I have a close relationship with my mother.				

Scoring the Student Spiritual Growth and Influence Survey

Convert responses using the following:

1 = Strongly Disagree
2 = Disagree
3 = Agree
4 = Strongly Agree

Directions: Transfer the numbers to this grid. Add each column and divide by the total possible points in each column to get the score.

Relationship with God	Spiritual Disciplines	Service to others
1.	8.	15.
2.	9.	16.
3.	10.	17.
4.	11.	18.
5.	12.	19.
6.	13.	20.
7.	14.	21.
Total:	Total:	Total:
Divide by 28	Divide by 28	Divide by 28
Score:	Score:	Score:

Connection to Youth Group	Connection to Church	Spiritual Influence of Parents
22.	29.	36.
23.	30.	37.
24.	31.	38.
25.	32.	39.
26.	33.	40.
27.	34.	41.
28.	35.	42.
Total:	Total:	Total:
Divide by 28	Divide by 28	Divide by 28
Score:	Score:	Score:

Sample Scoring
Total: 21
21/28=0.75
Score: 75

Composite Spiritual Growth Score:
Add the scores of Relationship with God, Spiritual Disciplines, and Service to Others, then divide the total by 3.

Composite Spiritual Influence Score:
Add the scores of Connection to the Youth Group, Connection to the Church, and Spiritual Influence of Parents, then divide the total by 3.

Parent Spiritual Growth and Leadership Survey

Please share some basic information about yourself:

Sex:

- ❑ Male
- ❑ Female

Marital Status:

- ❑ Single
- ❑ Married
- ❑ Divorced

Frequency of Attendance:

- ❑ I regularly attend
- ❑ I occasionally attend
- ❑ I rarely attend

The main reason I attend church is:

- ❑ To make my spouse happy
- ❑ To be with my friends
- ❑ To help my marriage
- ❑ To have something to do
- ❑ To gain deeper knowledge about Jesus and the Bible

Frequency of prayer:

- ❑ I regularly pray
- ❑ I occasionally pray
- ❑ I rarely pray

Frequency of Bible reading:

- ❑ I regularly read the Bible
- ❑ I occasionally read the Bible
- ❑ I rarely read the Bible

How often have you participated in a mission or ministry project with your teenager?

- ❑ Five or more times
- ❑ Three or four times
- ❑ Once or twice
- ❑ Never

Respond to the following statements by indicating one of the following:

	Strongly Disagree	Disagree	Agree	Strongly Agree
1. I see myself as a follower of Jesus Christ.				
2. I am pursuing God's will for my life.				
3. I have helped a non-Christian understand what it means to be a follower of Jesus.				
4. I have talked about Jesus with a non-Christian in the last few months.				
5. I would confess my faith in Jesus even if it put my life at risk.				
6. I believe that God has a purpose for my life.				
7. I think about God outside of church.				
8. I have fasted (gone without food for a short period of time for a spiritual purpose) at least once in the last year.				
9. I set aside time for prayer and Bible reading.				
10. I participate in an adult small group Bible study.				
11. I attend a Bible study that is open to all adults whenever they want to attend.				
12. I have memorized at least three Bible verses.				
13. I attend an intergenerational worship service at my church.				
14. I have helped another person become a Christian.				

	Strongly Disagree	Disagree	Agree	Strongly Agree
15. I attend a small discipleship group at church that is just for those adults who are serious about following Jesus as disciples.				
16. My small group challenges me to think deeply about my faith.				
17. I feel a sense of belonging in my church.				
18. I am given opportunities to lead at my church.				
19. My church is very important for my spiritual growth.				
20. My church provides opportunities for me to use my spiritual gifts.				
21. I regularly volunteer/lead at my church.				
22. I describe my relationship with my teenager as warm and affirming.				
23. I spend time with my teenager.				
24. When my teenager shares something with me I listen with empathy and compassion.				
25. I have a close relationship with my teenager.				
26. I regularly say "I love you" to my teenager.				
27. I set clear guidelines and consequences for my teenager.				
28. I am fair and loving in the discipline of my teenager.				
29. I feel that I am very important to the spiritual growth of my teenager.				
30. I talk with my teenager about spiritual issues.				
31. I encourage my teenager to grow as a Christian.				
32. I encourage my teenager to be active in the youth group.				

	Strongly Disagree	Disagree	Agree	Strongly Agree
33. I encourage my teenager to glorify God in a future career.				
34. I am open to discussing issues such as doubt and questioning faith with my teenager.				
35. I encourage my teenager to continue attending church after high school.				

Scoring the Parent Spiritual Growth and Leadership Survey

Convert responses using the following:

1 = Strongly Disagree
2 = Disagree
3 = Agree
4 = Strongly Agree

Directions: Transfer the numbers to this grid. Add each column and divide by the total possible points in each column to get the score.

Relationship with God	Spiritual Disciplines	Church Engagement
1.	8.	15.
2.	9.	16.
3.	10.	17.
4.	11.	18.
5.	12.	19.
6.	13.	20.
7.	14.	21.
Total:	Total:	Total:
Divide by 28	Divide by 28	Divide by 28
Score:	Score:	Score:

Parent-Youth Relational Health	Faith Conversations
22.	29.
23.	30.
24.	31.
25.	32.
26.	33.
27.	34.
28.	35.
Total:	Total:
Divide by 28	Divide by 28
Score:	Score:

Sample Scoring
Total: 21
21/28=0.75
Score: 75

Composite Spiritual Growth Score:
Add the scores of Relationship with God, Spiritual Disciplines, and Church Engagement, then divide the total by 3.

Composite Spiritual Leadership Score:
Add the scores of Parent-Youth Relational Health and Faith Conversations, then divide the total by 2.

Youth Ministry Arenas Assessment

The Youth Ministry Arenas Assessment tool provides vital insights about your church's effectiveness with young people.

	Strongly Disagree	Disagree	Agree	Strongly Agree
1. My church attracts teenagers.				
2. Teenagers participate in small group Bible study.				
3. Teenagers learn to develop spiritual disciplines (prayer, Bible reading, etc.).				
4. Teenagers serve in leadership roles within the youth group.				
5. Teenagers train for leadership positions in the youth group.				
6. Teenagers train to learn how to share the gospel.				
7. Teenagers in my church have the opportunity to be discipled/mentored by an adult one-on-one (or one-on-two).				
8. Adult leaders in my youth ministry are trained to disciple teenagers.				
9. My church has a clear discipleship process for teenagers.				
10. Volunteers are encouraged to contact students outside of church (phone calls, text messages, attend ball games, etc.).				
11. Families with teenagers have opportunities to serve together in missions or ministry.				
12. Parents of teenagers at my church meet together to pray for and support one another.				

	Strongly Disagree	Disagree	Agree	Strongly Agree
13. Family-focused fellowships/activities for teenagers and parents take place at my church.				
14. Older adults disciple/mentor parents of teenagers.				
15. Single parents of teenagers are welcomed and cared for.				
16. Parenting and discipleship resources are provided for parents of teenagers.				
17. My church knows how to help families and teenagers talk together about faith.				
18. I connect with parents of teenagers on a weekly basis (face-to-face, text message, phone call, email, newsletter, etc.).				
19. Adult volunteers at my church engage with parents of teenagers in their small group.				
20. Parents of teenagers know they are the primary influencers of the faith in their student.				
21. Teenagers participate in mission work in the local community alongside members of the congregation.				
22. Teenagers are encouraged to use their spiritual gifts.				
23. Teenagers have ministry opportunities to serve my local congregation.				
24. Teenagers personally know adults outside of the youth ministry.				
25. My church is welcoming to non-Christian teenagers.				
26. I help immerse teenagers in the full life and ministry of the congregation.				
27. Teenagers participate in weekly intergenerational worship.				

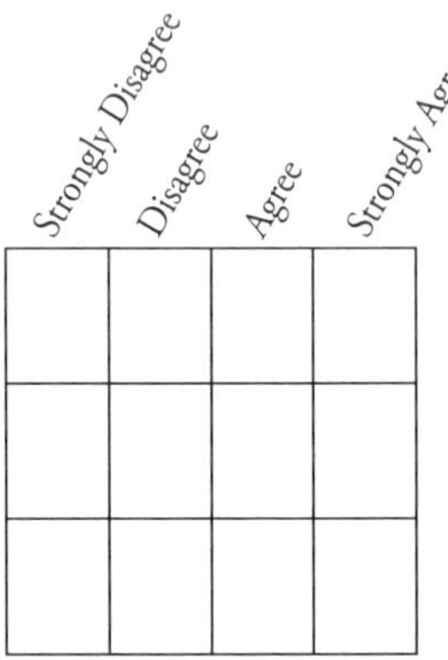

28. Adult volunteers at my church help teens feel connected to the congregation.
29. Teenagers feel the pastor, staff, and adults are approachable.
30. I help connect teenagers to older and younger members at my church.

Scoring the Youth Ministry Arenas Assessment

Convert responses using the following:

1 = Strongly Disagree
2 = Disagree
3 = Agree
4 = Strongly Agree

Directions: Transfer the numbers to this grid. Add each column and divide by the total by 40 to find your score.

Teenagers in the Youth Group	Teenagers in Families	Teenagers in the Congregation
1.	11.	21.
2.	12.	22.
3.	13.	23.
4.	14.	24.
5.	15.	25.
6.	16.	26.
7.	17.	27.
8.	18.	28.
9.	19.	29.
10.	20.	30.
Total:	Total:	Total:
Divide by 40	Divide by 40	Divide by 40
Score:	Score:	Score:

Sample Scoring
Total: 30
30/40=0.75
Score: 75

For a Total Overall Composite Score, add the individual scores together and divide by 3.

The Youth Ministry Arenas Assessment produces a total score and three sub-scores (Teenagers in the Youth Group, Teenagers in Families, Teenagers in the Congregation). Scores on the YMAA are ranked high (80–100), medium (60–79), and low (59 and below). These scores translate to exemplary (high), average (medium), and struggling youth ministries.

SWOT Analysis

STRENGTHS	WEAKNESSES
OPPORTUNITIES	THREATS

GENERAL INDEX

D

E

P

R

S

T

U

V

W

Y

Z

SCRIPTURE INDEX